The Road to
CHESS MASTERY

Also by the authors

CHESS MASTER VS. CHESS AMATEUR

The Road to
CHESS MASTERY

MAX EUWE
and
WALTER MEIDEN

DAVID McKAY COMPANY, Inc.

New York

Second Printing, April 1973

Library of Congress Catalog Card Number: 66-13502

MANUFACTURED IN THE UNITED STATES OF AMERICA

VAN REES PRESS   •   NEW YORK

Preface

Chess players often reach a certain level and subsequently seem unable to become any stronger. At certain points in their games, they attain solid and even promising positions but then have no well-formulated ideas of how to continue. They normally lose to stronger players without knowing exactly why. They are unaware of many of the finer niceties of building up a strong position, they frequently do not understand the strategic requirements of the situations in which they find themselves, and from a tactical point of view they do not analyze sufficiently accurately or imaginatively.

The study of master games—even those with excellent annotations—does not always help. The reason for each master move cannot be pointed out by the commentator, and yet the uninitiated often have no idea why many of the moves were made.

The Road to Chess Mastery is a collection of twenty-five games annotated specifically for the purpose of showing the ordinary player how to improve his chess by discussing the basic ideas behind a number of modern openings, by explaining how to handle a number of typical middle game positions, by giving frequent examples of the kind of tactical analysis a chess player must make before deciding on the next move, and by indicating the motives for all but the most obvious moves in each game. Because of the greater amount of space available to us, because of our hope of teaching the learner, and because of our frequent consultations as to the needs of the ordinary player, we have been able to include much material which would not normally appear in an annotated game. By applying what he learns in studying these games, the reader may well find himself on the road to chess mastery.

Chess mastery in its highest form is exemplified in master play. When an experienced amateur plays a master, he soon discovers that he is faced with a different style of play from that which he encounters in playing another amateur—even a very strong amateur. There is something overwhelming, often even crushing, about master play, which makes it evident that the master has specific insights and skills which the ordinary player does not possess. The master has at his disposal one extra dimension, so to speak.

Certainly the master plays a more penetrating and a more accurate tactical game, sees farther, and makes fewer errors than his amateur opponent, and in these respects the latter may find it hard although not impossible to imitate him. But the master also has a superior overall concept of chess strategy and a keen understanding of certain type posi tions of whose existence other players may not even be aware. In other words, the master knows a number of "chess secrets," which enable him to build up favorable positions which lead to a win

In the introduction of this book we describe the differences between the master and the ordinary player in the various phases and aspects of the game of chess and indicate how the latter can improve his play in each area. Then, in a series of twenty-five games between master and amateur, we show how the wins were conceived and executed.

Master-vs.-amateur games are used for several reasons. First of all, it is in this kind of game that the crushing style of the master is most evident, for ordinary players are usually not adept at neutralizing the pressure of their opponents at every point of the game; second, amateur errors tend to be more serious and more clear-cut than master errors and therefore more easily lend themselves to exploitation; third, there is probably no better way to show the learner how a player should exploit inferior play than to point out how a master actually does exploit it.

The games are arranged roughly in order of the amateurs' strength, with those of the relatively weaker player coming near the beginning of the book. But this arrangement has often been interrupted in order to group games of the same opening together. The fundamental ideas behind a number of different openings are discussed and illustrated, but the more modern openings and defenses predominate.

As the games advance, the master's opponent becomes stronger and stronger—he actually *wins* the last three games of the book. In these three games we show on the one hand in what respects the amateur has improved sufficiently to win and on the other hand why the master lost —and the master loses for different reasons than does the amateur.

We are very grateful to Mr. Norman Cotter of Wilmington, Delaware, for his careful reading of the manuscript, to Albert Klein of Columbus, Ohio, for his checking of proof with manuscript, and to Fredric Foote of Hastings, Michigan, for his very thorough study of both manuscript and proof and for the many useful suggestions he made.

M. E.
W. M.

Contents

CONTENTS

Introduction

The range of chess amateurs is great, and among the large number of casual players are those who through much practice in play against able opponents, through careful study of chess manuals, and through diligent perusal of master games have assimilated many of the principles of chess play, have learned how to make strong moves, have trained themselves to avoid serious weaknesses on the chessboard, and have reached a point where they do not make obvious tactical errors—in short, the strong players. These amateurs do not lose pieces through careless oversights. They have a finer feeling for some of the niceties of positional play than did most of the masters of the nineteenth century. They usually have no trouble in overwhelming their weaker and less informed opponents. Yet in tournament play these amateurs normally lose to today's masters.

This difference makes the ambitious chess player stop and reflect. What skills does a master possess that an amateur does not have? What line separates the master from the strong amateur? What can an amateur do to become a master—or at least to improve his chess? What is a master?

The master is thoroughly conversant with the technique of handling each phase of the game: opening, middle game, and endgame. He treats the game as a whole, each move being part of a certain strategical or tactical concept. He keenly appreciates the possibilities of all positions. He can analyze accurately and foresee rather exactly the consequences of each move. He understands the basic principles involved in the various positions. His tactical play is accurate—he makes fewer and less serious mistakes than other players. He knows a great many chess games of the past and is well informed on the lines played in the tournament games of the present.

The master and the amateur see chess positions from a different point of view. The master has a grasp and an understanding of a position and its implications that the amateur has not yet attained, and the master is aware of the interplay of various principles of chess whose existence the amateur may not even suspect.

Let us examine various aspects of chess in which the differences between master and amateur are apparent, with an eye to indicating what the amateur must do in each area to strengthen his game and to make progress toward mastership.

§ 1 The Opening

To a certain extent there is no apparent difference between master and amateur in the opening, because both may play the same theoretical lines. But there is a great difference between playing opening variations by rote and understanding them. From the very first move, the master understands why he is making each move, whether strategically or tactically. The amateur, on the other hand, often learns variations by heart and plays them mechanically. In such cases, the amateur frequently loses the thread of thought at the first deviation from "book," whereas the master, understanding the background of the moves, knows how to take advantage of the incorrect play of his opponent, if it be such.

The master generally plays the opening accurately according to theory, but he occasionally avoids the best theoretical continuations deliberately in order to escape a drawish variation or to keep from playing a line he does not like, perhaps one that is not in harmony with his temperament, or simply to confuse his opponent, as for instance was the case in Game 19, Black's 13th move. Thus, a dubious move played by a master may have quite a different meaning than the same move would have when played by an amateur.

The master also has other reasons for deviating from a theoretical line. He may and often does study special opening variations, and he may discover ways to improve them. The master, being a strong player, should be able to find slight mistakes in some of the usual lines. To find improvements is perhaps not as difficult as it may seem, for after all, what is theory? Theory is derived from two sources: the statistical compilation of the lines played in tournament games by masters and strong amateurs and the more leisurely analyses of opening variations by these same players before and after tournaments. This latter type of analysis is naturally more reliable, because there is no pressure of a time limit such as exists in a tournament game. Masters often preanalyze special lines which they then use for the first time during a tournament to surprise a relatively unprepared opponent. Experts on chess openings examine all games in which a special line of a given variation has been played, together with all available theoretical analyses of the line, and derive from their study a theoretical unit that is much more than a statistical compilation, because it interprets and reaches conclusions. The master may also be able to find improvements in these theoretical units, but this is much more difficult, because the field has already been thoroughly investigated by one or more experts who preceded him.

When the amateur deviates from theory in over-the-board play, it is usually because he is unfamiliar with it or cannot remember it. In such cases, the move he substitutes is likely to be weaker than the theoretical move, or even an outright mistake. In either case, his opponent should naturally exploit the error promptly.

In the games of this book, the amateur frequently deviates from theory. In Game 1, Black's 7th move is a theoretical mistake. In Game 5, 9 . . . N–R4 shows a lack of knowledge of the openings on the part of the amateur. In Game 9, White's 7th move is bad, because it is not according to the characteristics of the opening. In Game 10, Black's 6th move is a strategic blunder. In Game 20, it is also Black's 6th move that ruins the game. In all these cases, the consequences of the error are serious at once. In games such as 2, 4, 11, 16, and 17, the amateur does not make mistakes in the early moves of the game, but simply shows that he does not understand the opening, and this also has serious consequences in the middle game. As an improvement of theory can be considered the refutation of the move 9 . . . N–R4 in Game 5.

How the amateur can improve his opening technique

The amateur should have some acquaintance with all the main openings and an especially thorough knowledge of two or three of them. If he plans to play in tournaments, he should be well acquainted with openings and variations now in style. But it is virtually impossible for anyone who does not devote hours and hours to chess to have more than a passing acquaintance with certain variations of well-known openings. For that reason, probably the best way of improving opening play is to study the idea behind each of the principal openings and to play the opening with its basic idea in mind, at the same time giving careful attention to the tactical implications of each position. One should seek both to understand the ideas of the separate moves that constitute the individual openings and to acquire a keener appreciation of what constitutes a good chess position during and at the end of the opening phase.

The ideas behind the openings can be found in certain chess manuals, in articles in chess magazines, and often in annotated games. In the games of this book, considerable attention is given to explaining both the meaning and the aim of the openings as a whole and of the moves that make up those openings. The amateur will find it profitable to play over a number of games of a given opening. This will afford him an idea of how the opening develops, of the strengths and weaknesses inherent in it, and of some of the problems that arise in the course of it. Moreover, the advanced amateur who specializes in certain openings or variations can try to improve theory, just as the master does. Naturally, he will be more likely to discover slight errors in tournament games than in theoretical analyses.

But apart from learning the theoretical moves of any particular opening, the amateur must keep well in mind the elements of a good chess position and try, whenever confronted with an unfamiliar opening or with a strange move in a familiar opening, to reach a solid position through careful analysis.

§ 2 The Transition to the Middle Game

When most of the pieces are developed and stand ready for active battle, the opening is about over, and the middle game is about to begin. This is the phase of the game that is perhaps the most difficult of all to play, partly because it is not charted in books, partly because although the pieces stand ready to play, they have usually not yet come into contact with the opposing forces, and therefore the thinking must be largely strategical rather than tactical. It is in this part of the game that it becomes evident whether the player understood what he was doing in the opening or whether he was just making a series of moves learned by rote from a treatise on openings. In this phase, one has to make plans for the future, establish an overall strategy. The choice of the right strategy is very important, and it can also be very difficult. The strategy of the transition to the middle game has its roots in the opening.

The difference between amateur and master becomes much more apparent here than it was in the opening. Often, the amateur, completely bewildered and not knowing what to do with the position he has built up for himself, plays aimlessly, or at least falteringly, as he does in Games 8 and 14. The master, on the contrary, understanding the general type of strategy arising from the type of opening he has played and knowing the characteristics of his particular position and the objects for which he should aim, plans his strategy according to the dictates of his position and lays the basis for a successful continuation of the middle game. In the last eight games of the book, both sides know exactly what they are aiming for, and in these games we see an interesting and most vigorous clash between the aims of the opposing players in which the master usually, but not always, wins out.

How the amateur can improve his play in the transition to the middle game

There are several works on the middle game that discuss this transition phase, and very useful in attempting to improve this part of one's game is a careful examination of what the master does in this phase. Tournament games often illustrate such techniques, but they must be studied with the intention of finding out just what happens immediately after the opening. It is especially interesting to study this phase of master-vs.-amateur games in order to see how the master proceeds against the hesitating moves of the amateur, as is clearly illustrated in Games 8 and 14, for instance. Special attention is given to this phase of the game in the present work.

Meaningful play at the transition to the middle game is first of all a question of understanding the opening. In Game 9, for instance, the Black player knows that the position reached after the opening gives him chances to start an attack against the White center Pawns. By the same token, the White player knows that he has to support his center, and to this end he even brings his King into the battlefield and puts up a heroic resistance that probably would have succeeded against an opponent just a bit weaker than the master player.

§ 3 THE MIDDLE GAME

The middle game is the part of chess in which there may be pieces on every area of the board. It is characterized by the complexity of the inter-relationships between the pieces and by multiple possibilities for action.

This is the phase of chess that offers the greatest challenge to the imagination of the player. Unlike the opening, it has not been subjected to exhaustive theoretical research; unlike the endgame, it has not been compressed into a set of neat techniques. Because of the absence of clear indications of how to proceed, and because of its essential complexity, it poses many of the most difficult problems of the game. To play the middle game properly, one must on the one hand see the position as a whole in order to judge accurately what the correct line of play is, on the other see all the various details and not overlook any possibilities, whether obvious or hidden.

In the middle game, all sorts of general strategical considerations come into play: whether to build up power or exchange pieces, whether to maintain tension or exchange Pawns, whether to open files or close them permanently, whether to begin an all-out attack on the enemy King, to concentrate on winning an opponent's piece, to weaken his Pawn position, or to head for a favorable endgame by a complete liquidation of pieces. In addition to all these questions are the ever present tactical problems that must take precedence over any strategical considerations: Does the opponent have any threats that must be met? If so, how? If not, can one make threats himself? Or can one create an uncomfortable situation for the opponent that will force him to play in a way that will be detrimental to him?

In chess, as in life, not every person sees a situation from the same point of view. Confront a half-dozen players with the same complex middle-game position and you will find that these players will look at the position from different angles in their search for the best move. These elements of variety and unexpectedness enhance the charm of chess and keep it from being a purely mechanical performance that could be learned by rote or fed into a computer machine.

In the middle game proper, and in the transition to the middle game, the differences between amateur and master are especially noticeable. The amateur usually has a less all-inclusive grasp of the situation on the board and is less aware of all the possibilities of the position. If the situation is positional, the amateur often fails to find the correct strategy; if the situation is tactical, the amateur tends to see less and not to carry his analysis out as far or as correctly as would the master.

How the amateur can improve his middle-game play

There is no easy formula for becoming expert in the complex situations posed by the middle game, but an intensive study of middle games of masters with an eye to understanding each of the individual moves and their relationship to the overall strategy can make a good beginning. Both tactical and strategical play must be strengthened. Under *Tactics* we shall point out how amateurs can improve their tactical play; under *Strategy*, how they can gain a better understanding of the strategic and positional elements of chess play.

It is a good idea to look over the entire board and to develop imaginativeness in finding moves that create situations which may be favorable to oneself and annoying to one's opponent. The obvious move is not always the best move, and one must not yield too easily to the urge to play mechanically, such as putting a Rook on an open file or playing a Knight to its B3 square. These may be the proper moves, but in the position at hand there may be something much better. Quiet moves are sometimes in order, but a move that increases the pressure or makes a direct or indirect threat can be conducive to making the opponent do something that will compromise his position or at least make things more difficult for him. Moves that retain the initiative are always desirable.

Sometimes the middle game forms a complete whole based on one single theme. But often, on the contrary, it is made up of a series of strategic phases, each one of which has its own aim which, once accomplished, takes the game into a new phase with a different aim. Time and time again in the commentaries of the games that follow the reader will find: "The game is now entering a new phase . . ." Amateurs should develop an ability to recognize these phases and formulate desirable aims for them.

Although the middle game has not been categorized to the extent of the opening and the endgame, there are certain middle-game type positions that lend themselves to well-outlined procedures. Master play shows that standard Pawn formations such as the hanging Pawns of Games 10 and 12, other weaknesses in Pawn formation such as those in Games 2 and 9, the Pawn majority on the Queen side as in Game 25, etc., can be exploited by prescribed methods. Among these standard types of play are the minority attack in Game 13, open-file strategy in Games 11 and 16, wing attack on the Queen side in Game 3, wing attack on the King side in Games 17 and 19, attack against the King on the open file in Games 6 and 22, all-out attack in Games 1, 12, 20, 21, and 24, combined pressure along the diagonal and the open file in Game 23, and Pawn-chain strategy in Games 19 and 21. With a standard type of position, standard types of play can be undertaken if not with mathematical precision at least within a definitely outlined framework. By acquainting himself with the standard middle-game situations and ways of meeting them, the amateur can also improve his ability to handle the middle game.

§ 4 THE ENDGAME

The endgame is that part of chess in which so many pieces have been exchanged that the opposing Kings can take an active part in the struggle. Not all chess games reach this stage.

The endgame differs from the opening and the middle game in that it lends itself in general to a methodic and carefully outlined type of play known as technique. Due to the reduced number of pieces on the board, it is possible to foresee with much greater accuracy exactly what will happen, and research into the various types of positions has led to the charting of the proper methods of handling the various endgame situations.

The master is well versed in endgame technique. Once a given endgame situation is reached, he knows, within limits, the proper way of handling it. And since endgame situations do not normally lend themselves to innovations such as are constantly found in the opening, or to the multiple possibilities that characterize the middle game, a knowledge of endgame technique is ordinarily enough.

Not only endgame technique but also a knowledge of the outcome of endgame type positions is very useful. Such information enables one to play for a favorable endgame formation even in the middle game with the assurance that if the desired position is reached in the endgame, it will result in a win for the player.

The amateur is naturally much less well informed on endgame technique than is the master. What to the master is a matter of course in an endgame is often to the amateur hard play requiring careful analysis, with all the chances to go wrong that are inherent in any situation on the chessboard.

How the amateur can improve his endgame play

Improvement in endgame play comes from a greater knowledge of (a) the outcome of the standard types of endgames; (b) the specific way of playing the standard types of endgames.

It is of greatest importance to know the theoretical outcome of standard endgame positions, because this knowledge will serve as a guide to the direction in which to steer the game when the position is still complex enough so that a choice is possible. If, for instance, in an ending where one side has a Rook, a Knight, and a Pawn, and the other a Rook and a Knight, one knows under what circumstances a Rook and a Pawn win against a Rook, he therefore will have some idea of when to play for simplification by an exchange of Knights.

It is equally important to know how to play standard endgame positions correctly. It is not sufficient, for instance, to be left with a King and a Pawn against a King in such a position that the Pawn can queen. One must also know how to conduct the play so as to avoid stalemate, and this is a technique that can be learned; if it is not learned, a player risks missing a win whenever he finds himself in such a position. Of considerable importance in such endings is also an understanding of the meaning and the application of the concept of the opposition. The amateur should familiarize himself with such standard endgames as Rook and Pawn against Rook, King and Pawn against King, Pawn endings where the opposition is involved, with positions entailing the protected passed Pawn, the farther passed Pawn, the Queen against advanced Pawns, etc., endings consisting of a struggle between Bishop and Pawns against Knight and Pawns, where there are factors favoring the Knight, such as with Pawns on only one side of the board, as in Game 2, or blocked Pawns on the color of the hostile Bishop, or factors favoring the Bishops, such as Pawns on both sides of the board or blocked Pawns when the hostile Pawns stand on the color of one's own Bishop.

In working with the endgame, the following generalizations should be kept clearly in mind: (a) In more than 90 percent of the cases, a plus Pawn in a simple Pawn ending is decisive. (b) In formations of piece(s) and Pawn(s), the plus Pawn is decisive in perhaps 50 to 60 percent of the cases, but it becomes definitely decisive as soon as the player has some other positional advantage in addition to his plus Pawn. For instance, in Game 2, Black has greater mobility in addition to his plus Pawn. In Game 9, the opponent's King is vulnerable. In Games 7, 10, 11, 13, 16, and 23, the possessor of the plus Pawn also enjoys much greater activity of his pieces. (c) The King plays an important role in the ending. In Game 14, for instance, the Black King can go all over the board to annoy the opponent's pieces, whereas the White King is forced to confine itself to the defense of the surrounding Pawns. On the other hand, one must take into account the vulnerability of the King even in the endgame, as is exemplified in Game 9. (d) Initiative is perhaps more important in the endgame even than in other phases of the game. In Rook endings, possession of the initiative must be considered worth at least one Pawn. In Game 25, with the initiative Black is almost able to hold out against the two plus Pawns of his opponent. (e) Two connected passed Pawns are very strong, and when such Pawns reach their 6th rank, they are in general equal in power to a Rook. Curiously, if the hostile King is in the vicinity of two connected passed Pawns, two extreme possibilities can arise: (1) if the King can block the less advanced of the two connected Pawns, this Pawn formation becomes almost worthless; but (2) if the side with the two Pawns can attack the hostile King—and that possibility is usually present—the force of the two Pawns becomes even stronger, as is shown in Game 24.

In short, the endgame is a phase where knowledge counts more than insight, and one that can be learned to a great extent through study. It is not without reason that great masters such as Capablanca have advised: "Know the endgame."

§ 5 STRATEGY, TACTICS, AND TACTICAL SITUATIONS

In reading discussions of chess technique, one cannot go very far without meeting the terms *strategy* and *tactics,* sometimes very loosely applied to any sort of chess maneuver, sometimes used rather precisely to describe two different processes of chess activity. Although distinct, strategy and tactics are so closely interwoven at certain times that in working out a strategic idea, one must take into account that the whole plan might be sidetracked or changed by a tactical turn, and frequently a tactical decision depends in part on the strategic aims of a player. Over and above strategy and tactics, there is a type of position in which there exists what we shall call a *tactical situation,* because it requires calculation and yet differs from the commonly accepted definition of tactics in that it does not involve the carrying out of a preconceived strategic plan.

Whatever the exact meaning of these terms, it is of great importance for successful play to employ each of these concepts at the appropriate time. In general, all experienced players check tactical details, but many amateurs are partially or totally unaware of strategy and of the important part that it plays in successful chess and of tactics insofar as it relates to the carrying out of a strategic concept.

§ 6 STRATEGY

Strategy is the science of formulating a plan to attain given objectives in a given phase of a game. Strategy deals with overall aims rather than in specific calculations involved in the execution of those aims. Strategic thinking is most likely to be in order at times when the position is quiet and there are no immediate tactical problems to be solved. The choice of strategy to be followed grows out of the characteristics of the position.

There are a number of different types of situations that require strategic thinking:

(a) In the opening moves, there is always some basic aim. It may be controlling the center, it may be placing pieces in active attacking positions or in important defensive posts, it may be opening a file, it may be applying pressure on some areas of the board. It is important to have one's strategic aims clearly in mind in this phase, for on the one hand these aims can guide the player when the opponent departs from theory, and on the other, it will suggest to him the strategic plan for the beginning of the middle game.

(b) In any quiet position where there are no tactical problems, it is appropriate for a player to seek out an active strategy rather than to play aimlessly. Moves made with a purpose are more effective than moves made without a purpose. Applying pressure to certain points in the opponent's position, preventing an opponent from castling, and overprotecting one's own center are a few examples of types of strategic thinking. After a series of such purposeful moves, the opponent's position sometimes falls apart because of the accumulated force a player has built up.

(c) In certain quiet positions, a player can find moves which create tactical problems for his opponent, which force him to move in ways that are detrimental to him, and which consequently oblige him to accept certain weaknesses.

(d) When a weakness already exists in the opponent's position, one's strategic plan often revolves around the exploitation of the weakness. In Game 2, for instance, Black exploits White's advanced Queen-side Pawn formation; in Game 3, White exploits Black's weakened Queen-side Pawn position; in Game 4, White exploits at the same time Black's weakened squares and his uncastled-King position.

(e) Sometimes the position is ripe for the formulation of a much vaster plan of attack. For example, in Game 1, command of the center, the possession of the Two Bishops, and an accumulation of power indicate an all-out attack against the King on the King wing of the board; in Game 11, White plans an attack along the open QB file and subsequently along the 7th rank; in Game 13, the Pawn structure makes possible a minority attack; in Game 17, a combination of White's control of the center and his King-side Pawn formation and Black's slightly weakened King side call for a King-side attack.

The master is always aware of the necessity of playing with a plan, and he knows which plans are best suited to the position at hand. The amateur very often plays without any plan, as in Game 7, or chooses the wrong plan, as in Game 14, or begins a plan and then fails to carry it through, as in Game 8. Many amateur games consist of relatively unrelated moves that may not be bad tactically but lack objective and coordination.

How the amateur can improve his strategic play

Although chess annotators normally give more attention to tactical variations than to strategic concepts, there are a certain number of works on chess devoted specifically to strategy, and there are certain chess masters who emphasize strategic thinking in their annotations. The amateur can get his initiation to strategic thinking from such works, and once he has learned the importance of thinking in strategic terms, he can be on the lookout, in playing over master games, for the strategic phases of those games. In his own games, whenever he is in quiet positions, he can constantly force himself to seek moves that have an aim and follow a plan. He can also profitably study games that illustrate different types of strategy, such as the King-side attack, the center attack, the minority attack, etc., all of which are to be found in this book.

§ 7 TACTICS

Once a strategic plan has been determined, the means by which this plan is to be executed is a question of tactics. Tactics is the science of executing a strategic plan by a series of specific moves. It entails calculating the moves required to attain the objective, taking into consideration the reasonable replies of the opponent. In Game 1, for instance, where White has built up an accumulation of power, the strategy is to break through Black's Pawn wall so as to use that power, and the tactical problem is to find the moves by which the breakthrough can be made. In Game 2, where White has weakened Queen-side Pawns, Black's tactical problem is to calculate the moves by which he can exploit the weakened formation. At the end of Game 2, we encounter a typical situation in the form of the so-called eternal pin. The game shows how to exploit the pin and how to get full advantage of it in the win of a whole piece. In Game 17, where a King-side attack is indicated for White, the tactical problem is to plan the exact sequence of moves by which the attack will be carried out. The attack is crowned by the standard sacrifice of the Rook. In many other games, we see the same close relation between the combinational strategy and the ensuing tactics. Just as in Game 1, we see an accumulation of power in Games 10, 20, 21, 22, 23, and 24. In Game 13, the strategic masterpiece of Zugzwang on a full board is demonstrated by a number of variations, the majority of which are of a simple tactical nature.

One of the specific types of tactical play is the combination, which is a short part of the game, within which a certain purpose is attained by force. Its sequence of moves forms a logical chain and cannot be divided up. When looked at one by one, the moves may seem purposeless or even mistakes, yet together they form an exceedingly beautiful unit. After a series of moves incomprehensible by themselves, the solution suddenly follows, and their real purpose comes clearly to light.

In Game 15, we see how White, fearing that pure strategic means would lead only to equality, makes a sharp combination that transforms the characteristics on the board in his favor. The weakness of Black's King side means the beginning of a new and promising plan. In Game 18, Black has to carry out a difficult combination to maintain a slight advantage. In Games 3 and 4, we see how an uncastled King makes sacrificial combinations possible. In Game 11, the vulnerability of the 8th rank gives rise to combinations of several kinds. In Game 5, a vulnerable piece is the object around which combinations on the part of both sides revolve. Game 22 gives us a typical form of the sham sacrifice in a position where the King and heavy pieces are on the same diagonal.

How the amateur can improve his tactical play

Once the amateur has learned to think in terms of strategical concepts and to formulate strategical aims, he must then try to visualize the tactical steps by which the strategy can be realized. There are specific works on chess combinations that will help him develop his skill in planning and carrying out combinations. A careful study of the tactical steps by which the strategic concepts of the games in this book are carried out will also be fruitful. The study of how any strategic concept is executed tactically by the master can be very enlightening.

§ 8 THE TACTICAL SITUATION

Whenever the pieces of the opposing sides come into contact with each other in such a way as to produce a threat, or whenever they might come into contact with each other within a move so as to produce a situation that would require calculation of moves, there exists what might be termed a *tactical situation,* since the player must evaluate the results of his play if the threat or exchange is or is not carried out.

A tactical situation may arise either in the course of the execution of a strategic plan or at some point in a series of accidental or even purposeless moves, such as often occur in amateur play. When a tactical situation exists, it requires immediate attention and takes precedence over all other considerations. In such a position, a tactical error could be most serious, for it could result in some sort of positional inferiority, in material loss, or even in mate.

The importance of handling a tactical situation effectively cannot be overestimated. The minimum to be attained is to make no move that would incur a disadvantage to the player; the maximum is to find a move that would give the opponent a disadvantage of some sort. In this connection, one can often find a so-called "sharp move," that is, an aggressive move that poses a problem for the opponent and threatens him with something dire. Sharp moves make for a lively game and often get the opponent into all sorts of trouble. It should be noted that sharp moves are often—but not always—the best moves in a given position. Their exact value in each case must be determined by analysis. Every reasonable possibility must be investigated and evaluated, and the player must choose the line that offers him the greatest resources.

For many amateurs, the resolution of tactical situations through analysis *is* chess. They know of no other type of play than of examining any given position on the board carefully to discover how much they can get out of it—often without reference to positional requirements. And, indeed, the proper analysis of tactical situations *is* a most important aspect of chess, and one that players cannot afford to neglect. In fact, if any one chess skill were to be preferred above all others, it might well be that of being a skillful tactician.

How the amateur can improve his handling of tactical situations

The variations given in annotated games show how to handle given tactical situations and indicate the process of tactical analysis as carried on by masters and chess comentators. The amateur might well first make his own tactical analysis of these positions, then compare them with those of the annotator, noting carefully the types of possibilities he himself has overlooked in his analysis.

In analyzing, a certain number of general principles may be cited:

(a) Investigate every check and capture. Even when a check or capture looks obviously wrong, it might lead to some unexpected and worthwhile result.

(b) Investigate all possibilities—certain unlikely as well as all the likely moves. One of the frequent amateur failings is not to look into the suspicious but apparently wrong move; sometimes such a move is the very one that causes the most trouble for the opponent.

(c) Carry out the analysis to the end. A sequence of moves that may look bad at one point often turns out favorably if carried out a little further.

(d) Don't underrate the opponent. Don't assume that he is going to make the answer that is most favorable to you. Assume, on the contrary, that he is going to make every effort to find the very best line for himself.

(e) Investigate with special attention moves that force the opponent to answer in a certain way only, such as strong threats, double threats, attacks on the Queen, etc.

(f) Pay close attention to the order of the moves that constitute the realization of strategic or tactical ideas. Not only can a wrong order of moves give the opponent the opportunity to get out of a difficulty, but even if this is not the case, the wrong order may not be the most effective one. It may cost a player time and energy, forcing him to calculate many more variations.

§ 9 THE INITIATIVE

"The initiative" is a term used to describe a situation in chess in which one of the players is able to take command of the situation in such a way that the other player is either forced to follow the lead of the first player or has no active play himself at all. The initiative is a most valuable asset at any point in a chess game, but especially in the middle and endgame. In general, a player should always seize the initiative when he can and keep it as long as he can. The secret of gaining and retaining the initiative lies in making active rather than neutral or passive moves. The strong player presses constantly, forcing his opponent to play to his tune whenever and wherever he can. Examine positions in games between masters, and notice how of a number of moves, the master usually chooses active ones.

Every chess player has had the experience of completely dominating the play when pitted against a beginner who became so completely hemmed in after a few moves that he could undertake no effective action at all. This was because the beginner did nothing adequate to neutralize the bold thrusts of his opponent, much less to seize the initiative himself. In somewhat the same manner, but on a far more subtle scale, the master comes to dominate the game when playing the amateur. The master does not normally control the situation as overwhelmingly and in as short a time, but it frequently happens that against a master an experienced amateur may be completely tied up after a given point. Game 3 is an excellent example of this.

The initiative may be assumed in various ways, the most obvious of which is making an active move that forces the opponent to reply in a certain way and thus restricts his choice. If the opponent fails to neutralize the pressure from the opposite side, the first player's initiative becomes greater and greater and eventually overwhelming. Then, there is the device of making active moves that exert pressure on the opponent's position. Playing with tempo—that is, making a move with a threat to win something—is another way of gaining the initiative. Refusing to exchange active pieces for the opponent's passive pieces is a method of retaining the initiative. Exchanging when withdrawing would mean loss of time is still another form of keeping the initiative.

A special situation in which the initiative plays an important role is that in which one side has an accumulation of power, that is, many more pieces ready for immediate action than has his opponent. In such cases, the player with the accumulation of power must play actively, that is, he must sacrifice if necessary to bring all his pieces into action and to open a breach in the opponent's position. If he does not make the most of his accumulation of power, he may lose the advantage he has, and what is worse, he may come into a disadvantageous situation. This could have happened in Game 18, if Black had rested on his laurels after the capture of two Pawns.

One of the special forms of initiative is the attack. An attack is warranted only when the opponent has a weakness and the player has enough pieces at hand to exploit that weakness. In such a case, he has the duty to act at once, before his opponent can bring up enough pieces to resist effectively.

Once a player has the initiative, it may be difficult to wrest it from him. The amateur should always strive to keep the initiative, and when his opponent seems to be seizing it, to neutralize his pressures and parry his threats.

Normally, the master is able to play more actively because he knows how to get the initiative, and in each move he tries to find an active reply that will net him still more initiative.

How the amateur can seize the initiative

In the games of the book, the player will have a number of choices as to move. Of these choices, it will be seen that the master normally chooses the most active. The amateur must also train himself to look for such moves. In Games 3, 4, 9, 10, 13, 16, and 17, the master takes the initiative from the beginning because of his superior handling of the opening. In Game 12, we see how initiative in the form of increasing and lasting pressure finally leads to a decisive attack. In games such as 18, 21, 22, 23, 24, and 25, both sides are struggling for the initiative during a considerable period in the game. The taking of the initiative is not always apparent. In Game 7, for instance, the master takes all kinds of veiled measures, as in Black's 10th and 12th moves, and suddenly in moves 13 and 15 there become visible maneuvers that forcibly lead to the win of a Pawn in move 17.

§ 10 RESISTANCE

If your opponent has the initiative, and even if he has a strong initiative, it need not necessarily mean that you are fated to lose. In most cases—and this is one of the attractive aspects of chess—there is a way out. A position may look deplorable, but show the master the setup, and, if it is not too bad, he will point to a way to get out of the difficulty.

Resistance is one of the most important factors of chess, and one that has the greatest influence on the results. In general, it may be stated that one mistake—if not too great—does not decide a game, and if a player is able, after a bad move, to make the right move from then on, in most cases he can save the game.

Tenacity is one of the important qualities of a good chess player. In general, masters have great tenacity. This tenacity also has its psychological side. The attacker who had hoped to win the game or even to win a phase of it finds himself confronted with new problems and new difficulties that may tire him out, wear him down, and cause him to lose patience. Sometimes the stubborn defender not only saves the game, but even wins it.

The most important factor in successful resistance is finding the correct defensive moves. The amateur is, in general, not very strong in the defense. He makes two or three mistakes, and then things become much easier for his opponent. Moreover, frequently the amateur is convinced too soon that he will lose the game, and he often gets the feeling: "Why try to the very last? I'm going to lose anyway." So he plays more superficially than ever, and the game is lost rapidly. If the amateur knew that most positions are tenable, he would be inclined to think harder, and if he knew that it is worth while to put up resistance, he would do much better in many specific cases. A good example of stubborn resistance is to be found in Game 25.

True, as will be shown in Games 11, 16, 18, and 21, the mistake is sometimes too serious, and resistance is futile. But after all, this is to be expected when the winner has thrown all his energy into the game, always making the sharpest attacking move, not hesitating to sacrifice, knowing how to consolidate at the right time in order to break the opponent's resistance.

How the amateur can improve in the defense

When a player is on the defensive, he must carefully examine the position and find all the possibilities to defend a given situation, even those that on the surface are completely out of the question. He must be as imaginative and as resourceful in this area as in the attack.

When a defender is convinced that his position is lost, this should strengthen his morale rather than demoralize him, for the feeling "I have nothing to lose" should make him a more objective analyst and should lead him to consider all sorts of sacrificial possibilities that he might hesitate to look into if he thought that his position was tenable.

A few principles of effective resistance may be listed:

(a) Try to exchange as many pieces as possible, especially the attacking pieces of the opponent. Don't hesitate even to sacrifice material in order to weaken the attack. That is all the more valid if the opponent himself has sacrificed material in order to get the attack.

(b) Don't make Pawn moves on the front where the opponent is attacking unless absolutely necessary. These weakening Pawn moves should be made only when they cannot be avoided. It was the great World Champion Steinitz who pointed out this detail of the defense.

(c) Always be on the alert for possibilities of counterattack. In general, an active defense is much more effective than a passive one. In the passive defense, difficulties accumulate, whereas an active defense may throw the whole situation into a new phase, where the defender is not so hard pressed.

§ 11 Styles of Play

Not all players win chess games in the same way, and all masters have their characteristic styles of play. There are players like Morphy who prefer the open game, there are those like Steinitz who prefer the closed game. There are masters of the type of Alekhine and Tal, who win by tactical finesses and strong attacks; there are those who specialize in positional play, such as Capablanca and Petrosian.

The fact that a master plays one style predominantly does not mean that he is incapable of another, but by temperament he probably prefers one style to another, or he may let his choice of style be guided by his opponent.

In both the opening and the middle game, there are positions that can be handled in distinctly different manners. For instance, after 1 P–Q4, P–Q4; 2 P–QB4, P–K3, the sequence 3 N–QB3, N–KB3, etc., as played in Games 11, 12, and 14, leads to quite a different type of game from the sequence 3 PxP, as played in Game 13. There are numerous middle-game positions where a player has the choice between retaining a slight positional advantage and perhaps winning after a long struggle or making a snappy tactical attack that may entail some element of risk but brings a decision much sooner.

The amateur should choose the style most suited to his temperament. If he likes plenty of action, with combinations all over the board, he can study the games of Alekhine. If he prefers the quiet chess based on the accumulation of small advantages, he can greatly profit from a careful study of Capablanca's technique.

Whatever style he prefers, he must not fall into the error of adhering to that style only, when the situation calls for another type of play. When pitted against amateurs, one will constantly encounter errors of both strategy and tactics. Such errors should be exploited at once and in the manner most befitting the type of error, no matter which style one prefers. For instance, when an attacking player can win a Pawn by simplifying the position and thus reduce the struggle to an endgame, he should do so unless he is quite sure that the going attack will supply him with even more. Even if he does not handle endgames as well as the attack, and even if he does not succeed in attaining the win, still he should accept this endgame position and learn how to handle it. If he does not, his scope as a player will be too narrow even in the attack, for he will be able to play only the attack that will bring him the absolute decision, and percentagewise those attacks constitute only a small part of the whole repertory of attacks.

§ 12 THE PSYCHOLOGICAL ASPECT IN CHESS

Psychology plays a much greater part in chess than one might suspect, especially at the higher levels. It might even be stated that in world championship matches, the psychological factor is at least as important as the actual skill of the players.

On an amateur level, various types of psychological attitudes come into the picture. Some amateurs are content only when attacking, and if the opponent knows that a given player will do anything to maintain the attack, he can bait him into making unwise sacrifices. Others, on the contrary, have too much in mind the "Safety First" motto, and their lack of initiative frequently loses them the game. This is the case in Game 7, in which the amateur plays solidly but without initiative and too much with his own safety in mind. He makes a number of tame moves and thus gets into trouble. The master, without forcing anything, also builds up a solid position, but he keeps in store some aggressive weapons that he brings out at the proper time and thus wins a Pawn. There is the amateur who is impatient for action, and if his opponent waits long enough, he will often make some error in his eagerness to precipitate action.

In master play, one of the most important psychological situations is that in which one of the players is content with a draw, whereas the other wants a win. This situation can occur either when one of the players is decidedly weaker than the other and should play for no more than a draw, or when in a given match or tournament one of the players needs only a draw to attain a desired result.

Playing for a draw is quite different from playing for a win. It entails:

(a) Exchange of pieces in such a way that this does not involve the loss of tempi or a bad position of one or more of the remaining pieces.

(b) Not playing enterprising moves—first looking to the safety of one's own important squares rather than directing one's attention to the squares in the hostile position; this could almost mean "Stay on your own half of the board."

(c) Avoiding complications as soon as they threaten to arise, but in such a way as not to incur positional disadvantage. This is hard to do, since avoiding complications generally involves disadvantages.

Chess is of such a nature that winning a game can be a difficult matter, but it becomes ten times as difficult if the opponent has no aspirations whatever for a win. Then one is faced with an opponent who is unwilling to take chances, who will not play the enterprising type of game that would give one an even chance to seize the initiative.

There are such situations in some of the games in this book. In Games 23 and 24, the expert plays drawish moves. Especially in Game 23, the amateur simply consolidates his position, and the master has to expose his position in order to undertake more or less risky maneuvers.

Game 24 is a special case of the psychological in chess. There, because the master fears a draw with an inferior opponent, he asks too much of a drawish position and loses in trying to get a win out of it.

In order to win from a weaker player, or even from an equivalent player, either of whom wants only a draw, masters often use special means. Frequently at some point in the game they make a careless move in order to try to induce the opponent to put up a real fight by giving him the impression that he is entitled to play for more than a draw. Of course, the master must judge very sharply in such cases, to keep his carelessness from being too costly. Former World Champion Emanuel Lasker was a fantastic expert in such types of games. He knew exactly how much he could risk. It is he who stated that one mistake would never lose a game if the master took care not to make a second mistake. This situation occurs in Game 25, where the opponent puts up a real fight after the master's first careless move. But in Game 25 the master was too careless. He made two weaker moves (his 4th and 9th), which were, however, not outright mistakes. Often the amateur is not able to exploit such moves, but in this game, the strong amateur, already an "expert," showed that he could.

Another psychological weapon of a master is to give his opponent a choice in a difficult position. This would have been recommendable in Game 20, where the amateur should have made such a move in order to oblige his opponent to lose time, energy, and more in making up his mind, and then, after having made his choice, the opponent might fear the responsibility entailed. Everyone who has made a choice feels a certain responsibility, and this responsibility often becomes a sort of burden to him. It is quite possible that two or three moves later, the master might have the feeling, rightly or wrongly, that he had made the wrong choice. Such psychological tactics give the opponent a feeling of uncertainty. This is of the greatest importance, for as soon as one gets a feeling of uncertainty, one tends to play more weakly.

Such familiar psychological methods were considered more or less tricks in earlier times, but nowadays they are recognized as an important part of the repertory of weapons of every outstanding chess player.

In conclusion, the elements that contribute to making a chess player strong have been listed and discussed in the preceding Introduction. If you will incorporate them into your own play, you will almost certainly become stronger than you are now and thus find yourself on the road to chess mastery.

The Road to
CHESS MASTERY

Game 1

The ideal center: PQ4–PK4

Ideas behind the Nimzo-Indian Defense

Exchange of one advantage for another

The initiative vs. passive play

Inducing weaknesses in the opponent's position

Strategy vs. tactics

Center control

Use of the center in conjunction with the Two Bishops

Building up an accumulation of power

Use of an accumulation of power to break enemy resistance

Certain situations on the chessboard are more favorable than average—and these are known as advantages. There are many kinds of advantages: material (more Pawns or pieces), superior development, greater mobility, more command of space, solid Pawn formation, a secure King position, the initiative, the attack, a Knight posted on a strong square, the Two Bishops, etc. Advantages may be relatively permanent or quite temporary.

Against a good player, it is not possible to maintain all the advantages that may exist on the chessboard at a given point in a game. One often has to surrender certain of these advantages, but with best play one then gets other compensating advantages or leaves one's opponent with some sort of weakness. Whatever the compensating advantage, one must often make use of it as soon as possible; otherwise, it may disappear, leaving one with nothing but the disadvantage. Very fundamental in chess play are the ideas of surrendering one advantage for another and of using one's advantage before it disappears.

In the game that follows, Black, the amateur, gives up the advantage of the Two Bishops in return for the initiative—a very temporary advantage. Instead of making use of this initiative, he plays passively and thus permits White to exploit his compensating advantage of the Two Bishops. White is able to establish the ideal combination of two favorable chess characteristics: the center and the Two Bishops. Two Bishops usually have their maximum effect when the player holding them has a strong center, for this prevents the opponent from building up a Pawn formation that would reduce the mobility and the activity of the hostile Bishops. As a result of these two favorable factors, White is able to build up an overwhelming concentration of force in this game. Given his own accumulation of power and his opponent's lack of development, he can afford to sacrifice in order to bring his pieces to the center of the struggle rapidly. He breaks through Black's defenses, and before the amateur is able to marshal his forces, the master surrounds the Black King and mates it.

Nimzo-Indian Defense: 4 Q–B2, P–Q4 Variation

Master	Amateur
White	*Black*

1 P–Q4

The four squares in the middle of the chessboard—Q4, K4, Q5, K5 —constitute what is known as the *center*. It is a well-known fact among good chess players that the side that controls these four squares tends to have an overwhelming advantage, for it is difficult for an opponent to undertake any successful action on the board under such circumstances. This holds both in the opening and in the middle game.

The ideal center formation is PQ4–PK4, since this formation occupies two of the center squares and exerts pressure on the other two. If one player can attain this formation without the other player being able to break it up, the first player enjoys full center control with all its advantages.

In the present game, White starts at once to build up his ideal center and to establish control of the center. It is clear that by 1 P–Q4 he controls his Q4 square by occupying it. Less obvious but equally important is the second way in which 1 P–Q4 contributes to center control. It must be noted that the Pawn on Q4 exercises a measure of control over its QB5 and K5 squares, since it threatens to take any Black piece that might move there. In chess, this second type of control, the threat to take, is called *pressure*.

1 ...   N–KB3

It is highly important for Black to neutralize White's efforts to control the center and to try to establish control of it himself. This he does either by in turn occupying center squares or by bringing pressure to bear on the center. In most openings, attempts of one side to control the center are neutralized by a series of counterpressures by the opposing side. After a certain number of moves, this process tends to result in equality of control between the two sides.

In the game, instead of occupying the center by 1 ... P–Q4, Black achieves center control by 1 ... N–KB3, which exerts pressure on his Q4 and K5 squares, prevents White from establishing his ideal center with 2 P–K4, and reserves for the second player a wide range of later moves.

The reply 1 ... N–KB3 leads to a variety of openings known as the Indian Defenses. Since these Indian Defenses are more elastic than the Queen's Gambit, many players prefer to use them.

2 P–QB4

The logical move to control more center squares. It brings counterpressure on White's Q5 square.

2 ...   P–K3

This move exerts some pressure on Black's Q4 square and opens a diagonal for his KB. It often leads to the Nimzo-Indian Defense.

One of the advantages of this way of opening is that it reserves for Black the possibility of switching to the Queen's Gambit or, after White has developed his QN to B3, as he usually does, to play ... B–N5, where the Bishop assumes a very important role in the struggle for the center.

At this point may also be played 2 ... P–KN3, leading to the King's Indian Defenses (see Games 19–

22) or 2 ... P–Q3, leading to the Old Indian.

3 N–QB3

The logical move to control the center. It threatens 4 P–K4. At this point, 3 N–KB3 can lead to the Queen's Indian Defense after 3 ... P–QN3 (see Game 24).

3 ...   B–N5

This move develops the Bishop to a square where it can take an important part in the struggle for the center and continues that struggle by parrying the threat of 4 P–K4.

In the Nimzo-Indian Defense, Black usually exchanges this Bishop for the White QN, as a result of which White often gets a doubled Pawn, a disadvantage, in return for which he retains the Two Bishops, an advantage. He also gets an open QN file, an advantage.

4 Q–B2

On QB2, the Queen renews the positional threat of P–K4 and, by protecting the QN, affords White the possibility of avoiding the doubling of his Pawns if Black should play . . . BxN ch.

The question of whether or not Black should exchange his KB for White's QN is of considerable theoretical importance. A number of comparative values are involved in the question, which shows on what delicate considerations master play is sometimes based. If Black voluntarily plays . . . BxN without being forced to do so by White's P–QR3, it may not be worth while for Black to give up his advantage of the Two Bishops in order to leave White with the disadvantage of doubled Pawns. But it is certainly worth while for Black to make this exchange if White has to lose a tempo by P–QR3 in order to force this exchange. That is why 4 P–QR3, BxN ch is satisfactory for Black, whereas 4 P–K3, BxN ch is never played, because in the latter case, White does not lose a tempo.

At this point, White could also have answered 4 Q–N3, 4 P–QR3, 4 P–KN3, 4 N–B3, or 4 P–K3. After 4 P–K3, the most important continuation along with 4 Q–B2, White simply continues his development and leaves it up to Black as to whether he wishes to exchange his Bishop for a White Knight. As we have seen above, masters do not make this exchange under those circumstances.

4 . . .   P–Q4

Black again parries the threat of P–K4.

Equally good are 4 . . . P–B4, which can have some surprising possibilities, pointed out in Game 2, and 4 . . . O–O.

Since 4 . . . O–O would permit White to realize 5 P–K4, which we have been indicating as a positional threat, one might wonder why 4 . . . O–O was good. True, P–K4 is a threat in a positional sense: White occupies a broad center. But while in certain cases a broad center is an asset to the side possessing it, in other cases, a broad center can be a vulnerability. For example:

(a) After 4 . . . O–O; 5 P–K4, P–Q4!; 6 P–K5, N–K5, and Black obtains good counterchances by his advance in development.

(b) After 4 . . . P–QN3, the advance 5 P–K4 is much stronger, as the reply 5 . . . P–Q4 is not possible on account of 6 Q–R4 ch, winning a piece.

In other words, P–K4 entails advantages and disadvantages.

5 P–QR3

White forces his opponent to a decision. He must either give up the pressure on the center by removing the Bishop or exchange his Bishop for a Knight, which is, as we know, not always recommendable.

White can also play 5 PxP, which leads to a sort of exchange variation such as the one described in Game 13. It is difficult to compare the strength of this line with 5 P–QR3. It is often a question of temperament and of knowledge of a special line.

If 5 B–N5, PxP; 6 P–K3, Q–Q4, and it is difficult for White to regain his Pawn.

5 ...   BxN ch

Because he is parting with one of his Two Bishops, this exchange would be bad for Black except for the fact that he has the possibility of following it up with a sharp variation.

If Black plays instead 5 ... B–K2, the game becomes a sort of orthodox variation of the Queen's Gambit, where White has the extra move P–QR3 in hand.

6 QxB

In the Nimzo-Indian, White will usually avoid the doubling of his Pawns where he has a free choice. At this point, even 6 PxB would not lead to a doubled Pawn, as White can always undouble by PxP. However, after 6 PxB, Black has good counterplay in the center, which seems to compensate for the Two Bishops: 6 ... P–B4, and, e.g., 7 P–K3, Q–R4; 8 PxQP, KPxP; 9 B–Q2, N–K5, and Black is a little better off because he has a free game and can eliminate White's pair of Bishops (... NxB) at any time.

6 ...   N–K5!

This is the right move, not only because it wins a tempo, but because in this way Black also takes the initiative. As compensation for

having lost one of the Two Bishops, Black has the better development, and this he should use by assuming the initiative. 6 ... N–K5 is the first step toward taking the initiative.

7 Q–B2

The best square for the Queen, partly because from this point the Queen is directed toward the center, partly because it does not impede the development of other White pieces, as would be the case if the Queen had gone to Q3.

7 ...   O–O?

We have pointed out that Black's compensation for the Two Bishops is his advance in development. With his 6th move, Black tries to profit by this advance. But his 7th move does not continue in the same vein, and now the whole situation leads to nothing.

In any position, but especially in positions where the player has an advantage in time or the advantage of the initiative counterbalanced by some disadvantage in another respect, it is very important for him to discover the sharpest continuation. Often such a continuation depends on the ability of the player to find moves that embody threats.

In this position, Black should continue actively, that is, he should look for a move that forces White to defend. Here, he should play 7 ... N–QB3 and continue in combat style: 8 N–B3, P–K4; 9 PxKP, B–B4 with all sorts of threats. After

8 P–K3, things become still wilder:
8 ... P–K4 (threatening White's
QP a second time); 9 PxQP, QxP;
10 B–B4, Q–R4 ch (note how the
threats continue), 11 P–N4, NxNP;
12 QxN, N B7 dbl ch, 13 K–K2
(Black has forced White to give up
the possibility of castling), Q–K8
ch; 14 K–B3 (he now forces the
White King out into the center),
NxR (and wins the exchange). This
position has been analyzed by several strong masters, and they did
not arrive at a definite conclusion
as to the relative chances of the
two players. However, notwithstanding White's unsafe King position and his material disadvantage,
theory has established that he is
not too badly off.

Another active move, which is
preferable to the text, is 7 ... P–
QB4.

8 P–K3   N–Q2?

Another passive move. Notice
that neither of the last two Black
moves is a tactical error. Neither
loses any material. Yet, with these
two moves, Black gets positional
inferiority, and from this point on,
the game becomes a model of how
to exploit certain positional advantages, in particular the possession
of the Two Bishops and, after an
almost forced series of moves, the
majority in the center.

Black should have played an active move such as 8 ... P–QB4 or
8 ... P–QN3. The activity of the
latter move becomes apparent in
the following continuation: 8 ...

P–QN3; 9 B–Q3, B–R3!; 10 BxN
(preferable is 10 P–QN3), PxB;
11 QxP, BxP; 12 QxR, D–Q4; 13
QxP, BxP; 14 B QB, BxR, and
Black regains all the lost material
in a favorable way.

9 B–Q3

This move exerts pressure on the
center, attacks the Knight, and
forces Black either to defend or to
withdraw it, losing a move in either
case.

Up to this point, in the main lines
White's moves have all been strategic, that is, he has been concerned with building up a good
position. Tactics have not entered
into the game. Tactics is the part
of the game that requires calculation of what will happen when the
pieces come together, and whenever that possibility arises, tactical
variations must be analyzed. For
instance, 9 P–B3 is in itself a good
move with the same purposes as
the text, but it is not feasible here
because of 9 ... Q–R5 ch; 10 P–
N3, NxP; 11 Q–B2, N–KB4, and
Black emerges with a Pawn to the
good.

9 ...   P–KB4

Black attempts to retain a grip
on his K5 square.

It is clear that 9 ... KN–B3
would have meant the loss of two
full tempi for Black. In case of 9
... QN–B3, White would have
played 10 P–B3 and soon attained
P–K4.

10 P–B3

White now makes the play that would have cost him a Pawn one move ago. Why?

Positionally, it gives him the possibility of controlling the center, but at this point he again had to judge the precise tactical consequences of 10 ... Q–R5 ch. The one difference in the position is that Black now has a Pawn on his KB4, which means that he no longer has that square at his disposal for his Knight: 10 ... Q–R5 ch; 11 P–N3, NxP; 12 Q–B2. On the other hand, he can now continue 12 ... P–B5. In that case 13 PxBP, N–KB4 would be bad for White, but White can better continue with 13 N–K2, winning back the Pawn in all variations and maintaining the advantage of the Two Bishops. For instance, 13 ... N–KB4; 14 NxP, QxQ ch; 15 KxQ and White threatens both 16 NxKP and 16 PxP.

10 ...   KN–B3

White now gets the opportunity to destroy the Black center completely. 10 ... N–Q3 would have been better, in order to avoid the exchange that follows.

11 PxP   NxP

He cannot take back with the Pawn because of 12 BxP.

Note that the amateur does not make outright blunders, and to some extent he defends as well as possible. But one cannot afford to give such a positional advantage to a master player. White's preponderance is already so great that in the long run Black cannot resist, provided that White chooses the right continuations. For that reason, it is important to see how a master exploits his advantages.

Here White has an ideal combination of two advantages: (a) a majority in the center and (b) the Two Bishops. The Two Bishops require mobility, and the center supplies that mobility. It is important to note that the opponent has no center of importance that could block the White Bishops. White's own center does not reduce the mobility of his Bishops, since by pushing forward, it can activate the Bishops at the proper moment.

12 N–K2

A preparation for the key move, P–K4, in order to secure complete control of the center.

An immediate 12 P–K4 would be answered by 12 ... PxP; 13 PxP, N–B5, which would practically force White to give up one of the Two Bishops.

12 ...   P–B3

Since Black is also aiming at P–K4 in order to have some counter-

play in the center, he first has to
protect his Knight on Q4.

An immediate 12 ... P–K4 loses
a piece after 13 Q–N3, P–B3; 14
P K4, whereas it loses a Pawn
after the simple 10 DxP.

Another line of play by Black,
12 ... P–B4, looks promising, since
13 PxP would be answered by 13
... Q R1 ch, regaining the Pawn
(14 P–QN4?, NxNP), but White
can better play 13 P–K4, KBPxP;
14 PxKP, N–K2 (14 ... KN–B3;
15 P–K5); 15 PxP, and White has
a sound plus Pawn.

13 O–O

Of course, 13 P–K4 would have
been possible at this point, but
after 13 ... PxP; 14 PxP, White
would have difficulty in castling, so
he postpones P–K4 so as to play it
a move later with still greater effect.

13 ...   P–KN3

In order to weaken the threats
along the White diagonal QN1–
KR7 by the combination of the
Queen and Bishop and also to
threaten ... P–K4. If Black could
neutralize the White center, it
would do much to diminish White's
advantage. In general, Two Bishops
are of no value unless they can be
used. However, the text move has
the disadvantage of giving White's
QB a complete diagonal along
which to play, once White has
attained P–K4.

14 P–K4

The long-awaited move on which
the strategy of the last five or six
moves is based.

14 ...   KN–B3

It is not good to exchange Pawns,
since each exchange makes White's
Bishops more powerful.

Black's KN has four squares to
which he can retreat safely, and
which of the four is best is difficult
to say. Each of the four has certain
advantages, but also certain disadvantages.

In the next five moves, White
will bring his pieces into action in
such a way that he will attain a
concentration of force. Some of the
moves will be direct, that is, directed against certain definite objects; some will be indirect, simply
strengthening the position. At the
end of the five moves, the pieces
will be directed against a whole
field: center and K side. All of
these moves together build up what
we can call an accumulation of
power, the goal of which is to have
sufficient pieces at hand, whatever
may happen.

15 B–QB4

It is very important for White to bring his Bishop to this diagonal, since it plays a very important part in the course of the game, the more so because of Black's weak Pawn at K3. For that reason, it might have been better for Black to play 14 ... KN–N3 in order to prevent 15 B–QB4.

15 ...	N–N3
16 B–R2	

Black's KP is defended, but pinned; White is threatening to win a Pawn by 17 PxP, PxP; 18 QxP.

16 ...	K–N2

Parrying White's threat and also preventing White from playing B–R6.

17 B–KB4

This move places White's QB on a diagonal over which it has complete sway, since the Black KB has disappeared from the board. Although this move entails no threat, it is important in its function to control more territory and thus make its contribution toward accumulating a concentration of power.

White would never play a move such as P–K5, since this would immediately limit the action of White's QB and, after ... KN–Q4, of his KB also.

17 ...	P–KR3

This move has a positive and a negative aspect. In certain respects, it reduces the possibilities of the White QB, and if Black succeeds in playing ... P–KN4 followed by ... P–B5, the possibilities of the White QB are reduced still further. But as long as ... P–KN4 can be answered by B–K5, the text move has a less positive meaning. On the other hand, 17 ... P–KR3 weakens the Black K wing and is the cause of the rapid deterioration of the King's position.

18 QR–Q1

This is a strong preparatory move. White wants to attack, but before launching his attack, he makes certain preparations, and this is one of them. It relieves the Knight from protecting Q4 and also facilitates White's playing B–K5, because White need no longer fear the immediate ... QN–Q2 and ... NxB, since the Black Queen would then be threatened by White's QR.

18 ...	Q–K2

Black takes the Queen out of line with the White Rook.

Whenever the King or Queen stands in a straight line with a minor piece that would threaten it, were there no intervening Pawn or piece, there is always latent danger, and unless there is an imperative reason for making another move, it is wise to move the King or Queen out of line with the indirect attack of the opponent's minor piece.

19 N–N3

Mobilizing the Knight, that is, putting it where it will be available when its chance comes.

If 19 ... P–N4, White can reply 20 B–K5, followed by 21 N–R5 ch. White's moves are directed against potential threats. These moves have taken the force out of ... P–N4.

Now let us suppose 19 ... P–N4; 20 B–K5, K–N3. White cannot then reply 21 N–R5, but he can exploit the favorable position of the Knight in another way: 21 BxP! (a notable sham sacrifice), BxB; 22 PxP ch, K–B2; 23 PxB ch and not only has White won a Pawn but also his Knight is ready to threaten the Black position in new ways.

19 ...   R–Q1

This move accomplishes nothing. But Black is paralyzed and has no very good move.

20 KR–K1

Threatening 21 PxP, with Black's Queen in a bad position. White has been able to make the same in-direct threat on the K file as existed two moves earlier on the Q file.

20 ...   Q–B1

The game is now entering a new phase. In moves 15 through 20, White has built up an accumulation of power. With move 21, he starts to make use of this power. One can see how each move plays its part in the final attack (or variations) to follow.

21 PxP

In order to force a decision. Such an exchange can be made only if a forced decision exists, for by this exchange, White gives up his center, and were he not forced to reply in another manner, Black could now play ... QN–Q4. As soon as Black can post a Knight on his Q4, White does not have much advantage.

21 ...   KPxP

Forced; 21 ... NPxP is bad because 22 BxP wins a Pawn.

Neither does Black have at his disposal the in-between move 21 ... QN–Q4, for then 22 PxKP and (a) 22 ... NxB; 23 P–K7, etc., or (b) 22 ... BxP; 23 BxP ch!

(also an in-between move), KxB; 24 RxB and White is two Pawns to the good.

22 Q–B1

Attacking the Black KRP and threatening the win of the Queen.

22 . . .   P–N4

Impossible are 22 . . . Q–R1; 23 BxP ch, QxB; 24 R–K7 ch, winning the Queen, and 22 . . . N–N1; 23 BxN, followed by 24 BxP.

23 BxP

The basis of this sacrifice is an annihilation combination. It annihilates the K-wing Pawns. Such a sacrifice is possible if there are sufficient attacking pieces at the disposal of the player making the combination.

In this game, the White Queen, Knight, Bishop, and one Rook are immediately available to take part in the assault.

23 . . .   PxB
24 QxP ch

This is the logical continuation. White has made all the preceding moves in order to break Black's

resistance. At this point, he is bound to have a forced win in view of the enormous preponderance of attacking material against the naked King.

24 . . .   K–R1

After 24 . . . K–R2; 25 N–R5 wins as well. The following variations will give the student an idea of how to break the resistance in such cases. We shall see that this is not too easy, if one wishes to consider all possibilities.

(24 . . . K–R2; 25 N–R5)

(1)

25 . . . NxN; 26 QxN ch, K–N2 (26 . . . Q–R3; 27 R–K7 ch); 27 Q–N5 ch and 28 R–K7 (ch).

(2)

25 . . . QN–Q2; 26 R–K6
(2a) 26 . . . NxN; 27 QxN ch, etc.
(2b) 26 . . . N–KN1; 27 R–N6, etc.
(2c) 26 . . . N–K1; 27 R–R6 ch!, QxR; 28 Q–N8 mate.
(2d) 26 . . . N–Q4; 27 BxN, PxB; 28 R–K7 ch, K–R1; 29 R–N7, followed by mate.

(3)

25 . . . QN–Q4; 26 BxN, NxB; 27 R–K5!
(3a) 27 . . . B–Q2; 28 RxN; PxR; 29 N–B6 ch, K–R1; 30 Q–N6! wins
(3b) 27 . . . R–Q3; 28 QR–K1 (threatening 29 R–K7 ch), R–N3; 29 Q–R4 (29 R–K7 ch

would not decide in this position: 29 ... NxR; 30 RxN ch, K–R1!) and now

(3b1) 29 ... R–R3; 30 R–K8, Q–Q3 (30 ... Q–R2; 31 Kn–K7); 31 R–Q8, Q–N3; 32 R K7 ch, etc.

(3b2) 29 ... Q–R3; 30 RxN, PxR; 31 R–K7 ch, K–N1; 32 R–K8 ch, K–R2; 33 Q–K7 ch, R–N2; 34 NxR, QxN; 35 Q–R4 ch, K–N3; 36 R–K7 and wins. Now let us return to the game, in which 24 ... K–R1 was played.

25 Q–R4 ch   K–N2

If 25 ... N–R2; 26 R–K7.

26 N–R5 ch   K–N3

If 26 ... NxN; 27 Q–N5 ch!, K–R2; 28 QxN ch, K–N2; 29 Q–N5 ch, followed by 30 R–K7.

27 N–B4 ch   K–N2 (forced)
28 Q–N5 ch   K–R2

Forced, for 28 ... K–R1 loses the Queen by 29 N–N6 ch.

29 R–K7 ch!

A second sacrifice, which leads to a forced mate. Also leading to a win would be 29 N–N6, followed by 30 R K7.

29 ...,   QxR

Or 29 ... K–R1; 30 Q–R4 ch, etc.

30 Q–N6 ch   K–R1
31 Q–R6 ch   Q–R2

Or 31 ... N–R2.

32 N–N6 mate

Black, the amateur, lost because he failed to understand the underlying idea of the opening. In the Nimzo-Indian, the Black player must always be prepared to exchange his KB for White's QN. Theory has developed lines along which Black can get compensation either by forcing doubled Pawns in the hostile camp or by taking the initiative. If Black does not understand the compensations involved, he can give up his Two Bishops for nothing, with all the bad consequences thereof.

Game 2

Steinitz stated that of all chess pieces the Pawn has one peculiarity possessed by no other piece: it can only go forward, never backward. Because of this fact, warned Steinitz, be extra cautious with your Pawn moves.

Certainly, there are cases in which a Pawn is more useful on the 4th rank than on the 2nd, and perhaps still more so on the 6th rank. But this is not a general rule. There must be some clear and definite reason for advancing the Pawns at a given phase of the game and on given areas of the board. This is especially true in the opening, for Pawn moves may automatically lead to a lag in development that increases the vulnerability of advanced Pawns.

Advancing Pawns on the K side entails more risks than advancing them on any other section of the board, for K-side Pawns normally have the function of guarding the most valuable piece on the board—the King. This does not mean, however, that one can advance one's Pawns haphazardly on the Q side without disadvantageous consequences. If the opponent is able to attack the advanced Q-side Pawns with his own Pawns and force a breach in the advanced formation, many disagreeable consequences can result.

In this game, there is an unmotivated Pawn advance on the Q side which looks the more attractive because White can drive back a Black Bishop at the same time that he pushes his Pawns. But Black has counter-means at his disposal. Soon, those White Pawns are attacked and destroyed, and of White's once mighty Pawn phalanx there remains only an isolated White BP, which is soon lost. This is the first phase of the game. Next, Black has to solve the problem of how to convert his material-plus into a win. He gets the opportunity of forcing a passed Pawn. But this alone seldom solves such a problem, for in general, the opponent has just as many possibilities of stopping the Pawn as its possessor has of supporting it. But the result of the tug-of-war over the passed Pawn is often that the defending pieces are limited to certain points from which they can block the passed Pawn, which gives the pieces of the other side ample opportunity to undertake something new—a second front! This is the advantage of a clear plus!

Nimzo-Indian Defense: 4 Q–B2, P–B4 Variation

Amateur	Master
White	*Black*
1 P–Q4	N–KB3
2 P–QB4	P–K3
3 N–QB3	B–N5
4 Q–B2	

The theory and ideas behind this Nimzo-Indian Defense are explained in the notes on the opening of the previous game.

4 ...   P–B4

Black immediately attacks White's center. As was pointed out in the previous game, he could equally well reply 4 ... P–Q4 or 4 ... O–O.

5 PxP

White can also play 5 P–K3, but 5 P–QR3, BxN ch is quite satisfactory for Black both after 6 QxB, PxP; 7 QxP, N–B3; 8 Q–B3, P–Q4 and after 6 PxB, Q–R4; 7 B–Q2, O–O. Black has some pressure against the White Q wing and White's doubled BP is awkward and could become weak.

5 ...   O–O

A difficult position. White has to continue his development, always taking into account the strategical and tactical consequences of ... BxN ch; Black must find a way to win back the Pawn on his QB4 and exercise keen judgment as to the value of ... BxN ch. In one position, ... BxN ch may be bad for Black, while in a slightly different position, it may be strong. In most cases, Black does not play ... BxN ch voluntarily, but only when forced to do so by White's P–QR3.

First, let us illustrate some of the consequences of ... BxN ch. Let us say that White plays 6 P–KN3. Black could then reply 6 ... BxN ch; 7 QxB, N–K5; 8 Q–B2, Q–R4 ch; 9 B–Q2, NxB; 10 QxN, QxBP, and it is difficult to say whether Black has full equality, for after 11 R–B1, N–B3; 12 B–N2, P–Q3; 13 N–B3, White maintains a slight positional advantage, because Black's QP is backward on an open file. If, however, White tries to obtain a big advantage by 8 Q–R3, attempting to hold the Pawn, 8 . . . N–R3; 9 P–QN4?, he loses by 9 . . . Q–B3! Simultaneously, Black threatens 10 . . . QxP ch and 10 . . . QxR–tactical consequences.

Another possibility is 6 B–N5. This move enhances Black's tactical possibilities, because it could enable Black to play under certain circumstances 6 . . . BxN ch; 7 QxB, N–K5; 8 BxQ, NxQ. In this given position, it is not good, because it loses a Pawn after 9 B–K7, R–K1; 10 B–Q6. But Black can prepare the combination by 6 . . . N–B3; e.g., 7 N–B3, BxN ch; 8 QxB, N–K5; 9 BxQ, NxQ. Black still has difficulty after 10 B–B7, N–K5; 11 P–QR3, NxQBP; 12 B–Q6, N–N6.

Certainly, Black is not obliged to play . . . BxN ch; he can continue simply by . . . BxP. But in that case, White gets a fine game: good development, influence in the center, more space.

For that reason, Black answers 6 B–N5 by . . . N–R3, with the intention of controlling his K5 square after . . . NxP. If White does not do anything special against it, Black gets a good game; e.g., 7 N–B3, NxP; 8 P–K3, QN–K5,

and White cannot avoid the doubling of his BP.

White must try a sharper method to meet 6 B–N5, N–R3: 7 P–QR3 (first force the Black Bishop to declare its intentions and thus obtain the Two Bishops anyhow), BxN ch; 8 QxB, NxP (8 . . . N–K5 would not be good now: 9 BxQ, NxQ; 10 B–R4 [or even 10 B–K7] and 11 P–QN4 wins a Pawn.) Now Black threatens to annihilate the Bishops by . . . QN–K5 and in general take advantage of the fact that he has more troops in battle, e.g., 9 B–B4 (to parry . . . KN–K5), P–Q4; 10 R–Q1, KN–K5; 11 Q–B2, Q–B3, and Black has the initiative. White tries 9 P–B3, but the surprising thing is that this does not prevent the combination already mentioned several times: 9 . . . KN–K5; 10 BxQ, NxQ; 11 B–K7, apparently the refutation, but 11 . . . N–N6 also wins the exchange: 12 BxR, KxB; 13 R–Q1, NxR; 14 KxN. Black has at least an equal game.

This discussion, which is somewhat afield from the actual course of the game, is to illustrate the value of advance in development and to show how tactics enter into this opening because of the vulnerable position of the White Queen.

Thus, 5 . . . O–O is on the one hand a developing move, on the other a waiting move to see what White is going to do. It is generally considered the most active move, since the quiet continuation 5 . . . BxP; 6 N–B3, O–O; 7 B–N5 gives White a somewhat freer game.

16   GAME 2

From the above variations, we
see that sometimes the Black Knight
takes White's QBP(5), and at other
times the Bishop does. It just depends on how White plays. By
playing 6 ... BxP immediately,
Black frees White from this uncertainty.

6 P–QR3

White forces Black to declare
his intentions. As can be seen from
the preceding discussion, this is one
of the best moves, since it avoids
the complications that arise in other
lines. White can also answer 6 B–
Q2 and 6 N–B3.

6 ...   BxBP

Here the exchange 6 ... BxN
ch would have been a strategic
mistake, as Black would have no
compensation for the loss of the
Two Bishops and would even have
trouble winning back his Pawn.
For instance: 6 ... BxN ch; 7
QxB, N–K5; 8 Q–B2, NxQBP; 9
P–QN4, and White has an excellent game: 9 ... KN–R3 is forced,
and Black cannot attack White's
Pawn formation by ... P–QR4, as
he actually does in the game.

7 P–QN4(?)

Although White aggressively
pushes back Black's Bishop, the
move is doubtful, because it means
a weakening of White's Q-side
Pawns, a weakness of which Black
will soon be able to take advantage.
Of course, one cannot generalize,
but this move should always be
looked upon with suspicion. It depends on whether Black can take
advantage of it with an eventual
... P–QR4.

Or suppose that instead White
should try the plausible-looking 7
R–N5? Black could then win a
Pawn by 7 ... BxP ch; 8 KxB,
N–N5 ch, followed by ... QxB,
which illustrates how important it
is not to play by rote, but rather
to analyze at each step, especially
looking into checks and captures.

White's best move here is 7 N–
B3, maintaining that same slight
superiority we have seen in other
variations.

7 ...   B–K2
8 N–B3

The text is preferable to 8 B–N2,
because in that case White loses
the possibility of protecting his
QNP by R–QN1.

If White should play 8 P–K4,
the beginning of an entirely different line, 8 ... P–QR4; 9 P–K5,
PxP!; 10 PxN, BxP, and Black
stands best.

8 ...   P–QR4

White has an imposing Pawn
formation on the Q side. But Black,

by 8 ... P–QR4, seeks to induce the Pawns to advance in order to weaken them. This he can do the more easily, because White will not want to saddle himself with two isolated Pawns by PxP nor can he allow Black to play ... PxP without first protecting his QR. If he plays 9 P–N5, Black can occupy and hold the important QB4 square after ... P–Q3 and ... N–Q2–B4.

9 R–QN1

The alternatives do not look attractive: (a) 9 P–N5 would give Black a strong square, as explained above; (b) 9 B–N2, PxP; 10 PxP, RxR ch; 11 BxR, BxP costs a Pawn; (c) 9 N–R2, PxP; 10 PxP, BxP ch, and White cannot retake without losing his Rook.

9 ...   N–R3

Black attacks White's QNP a second time, again inviting him to advance his NP, after which Black's QB4 square would be at his direct disposal.

10 N–R2

The Knight is forced to go to the edge of the board to protect the QNP. After only a few moves, White is already obliged to limit himself to defensive measures. This is all the consequence of White's "enterprising" 7th move.

10 ...   P–Q4

Black continues his development in the regular way and at the same time enables his pieces to continue the Q-side attack. It is an attempt

to open the position in order to take maximum advantage of White's backward development, a bid to contest White's hold on the center with his QBP.

11 P–K3

If 11 PxP, Black could retake with his Queen, Knight, or Pawn and obtain a satisfactory position in each case. If he answered 11 ... PxP, he would have a slight disadvantage in his isolated QP but the advantage of allowing his QB to come out.

If 11 P–B5, Black would try to break up White's Pawn formation by 11 ... P–QN3 or first by 11 ... B–Q2, as in this game.

11 ...   B–Q2

The Bishop also wants to play its part on the Q side.

12 P–B5(?)

The die is cast, but in the wrong direction. Preferable was 12 PxQP, in order to continue after 12 ... NxP with 13 P–K4. Black can therefore do better after 12 PxQP by 12 ... PxNP, and if 13 PxNP, NxQP, attacking White's NP at the same time. However, should White try to win a Pawn by 13 PxKP, he might come into great difficulties: 13 ... BxP; 14 NxP, NxN; 15 PxN, R–R7; 16 Q–Q3, Q–B1!, etc. After the text, Black has an advance in development of no less than three moves, that is, White has four pieces developed, Black six with castling. This means that in the time that White is completing his development, Black can considerably strengthen his offensive on the Q side.

How can Black's advance in development be explained? By the fact that White had to lose time in making defensive moves such as R–N1, N–R2, etc., and by such moves as P–QN4 and later P–B5, thus continuing his questionable course instead of admitting it and playing PxP or allowing Black to exchange Pawns. White's intention was to get more room on the Q side. Now White *has* it—at the price of three tempi—and this makes the space worthless. It only creates weaknesses. True, with the text, White has established a Pawn majority on the Q side, from which may and does result a passed Pawn. The difficulty, however, is that a passed Pawn needs support, and in this case White cannot provide this support, so the passed Pawn becomes weak and eventually is lost.

12 ...   PxP

In order to open the QR file and expose White's Q-side Pawns a little more.

13 PxP

Here, as in the previous game, the master has at his disposition two clear advantages—in this game an advance in development and attacking chances against White's Q-side Pawns. The value of two advantages counts progressively. To win the game on the basis of one advantage may be a difficult job, whereas having two advantages reduces the work to much less than half. No wonder the amateur who, just as in Game 1, does not make errors, cannot withstand the logical exploitation scheme of his master opponent.

13 ...   Q–B2

The text serves to prepare an attack against White's spearhead Pawn by ... P–QN3. If Black had tried to attack White's spearhead Pawn directly by 13 ... P–QN3, then there would have followed 14 P–B6 and 15 P–N5, and Black would have had a more difficult time.

The possessor of a spearhead Pawn should handle it defensively by protecting it as much as possible, concentrating forces, and then, after a long, long consolidation, consider advancing it.

The opponent should handle a spearhead Pawn offensively by attacking it with a Pawn as soon as possible, without giving the possessor an opportunity to break through.

Black plays 13 ... Q–B2 instead of 13 ... R–B1 partly because his QR may figure in some possible later tactical turns against the White QN, partly because it may turn out that Black's KR could be mobilized to his QB1.

14 B–N2

This is a routine move, which White undoubtedly made on the theory that a Bishop is powerful when it is stationed on a long diagonal. But the move does nothing against Black's threatened ... P–QN3. The point of immediate concern in the White camp is that the White Queen is unprotected. Correct, therefore, was 14 B–Q3, in order to be able to answer 14 ... P–QN3 by 15 PxP or even by 15 Q–K2.

14 ...   P–QN3!

Taking advantage of the pin along the QB file. Black now threatens to win a Pawn. A Pawn advantage is significant in itself, but in this position, the extra QP will give Black the possibility of later converting his half-passed QP into a full-fledged passed Pawn.

It should finally be noticed that instead of the text, Black cannot play the sham sacrifice 14 ... NxBP because of the in-between moves 15 BxN or 15 B–K5 (protecting the Knight on R2).

15 B–K5

Molesting the Black Queen and driving it to a somewhat less active square (QB1), as a consequence of which Black's KR will not be able to occupy the QB file. The move also clears White's QN file for his QR.

15 ...   Q–B1

The Queen has to maintain the pin.

16 BxKN

By forcing the reply 16 ... BxB, he takes away one of the pieces attacking White's QB5.

This is the only way to save the Pawn, but on the other hand, it facilitates matters for Black by giving him more freedom.

Could White have avoided the loss of a Pawn here without the exchange 16 BxKN? Let us examine the position.

Black threatens 16 ... PxP. The exchange 16 BxQN does not help, for after 16 ... QxB, the White N(R2) is attacked: 17 N–B1, PxP; 18 PxP, Q–R4 ch.

The only possibility seems to be the sham sacrifice: 16 P–B6. What follows must be calculated exactly, as accidental combinations reign the field: 16 ... QxP; 17 QxQ, BxQ; 18 P–N5, N–B4; 19 PxB,

RxN; 20 RxP. How can this position be judged? Material is even. White has a powerful passed Pawn; his prospects seem rosy. However, Black has one strong counter trump, a better center as a result of his superior development, as appears from 20 ... KN–K5; 21 P–B7, P–B3; 22 B–Q4, P–K4!; 23 R–N8, R–R1; 24 BxN, BxB; 25 RxR ch, KxR; 26 B–R6, N–Q3, and Black wins a Pawn in the end because the White KB has to withdraw and then the White QBP is untenable.

16 ...   BxB
17 BxN

Again to reduce the number of pieces and save the Pawn on QB5. But this also means simply postponing the execution.

After 17 P–B6 (as in the former variation), QxP; 18 QxQ, BxQ; 19 P–N5, N–B4; 20 PxB, RxN; 21 RxP, R–R8 ch and Black's advantage is obvious.

17 ...   QxB

Not 17 ... RxB, because of 18 P–N5, followed by 19 P–B6.

18 N–B1

By this series of exchanges, White has actually saved his Pawn, but ...

18 ...   PxP

To isolate White's BP, which now becomes a very weak sister. White cannot retake with the Queen, since then 19 ... KR–B1 would cost a lot of material.

19 PxP

Now that a new phase of the game is beginning, let us appraise the position. White has equality of Pawns and pieces, and his isolated QBP is a passed Pawn. It is most remarkable that it was Black who by his moves has created a passed Pawn for his opponent, for the understandable reason, however, that this passed Pawn is isolated and vulnerable because Black's pieces stand more readily at his disposal —there are more attackers than defenders. The great handicap for White is that he has not castled and for the moment cannot castle. Black, on the other hand, has excellent development, controls the QR file, and has the Two Bishops.

At this point, the maximum that Black can expect is (a) to win White's QBP; (b) to prevent White from castling. The minimum would be neither to win the Pawn nor to prevent White from castling.

Black fears that he cannot attain the maximum; therefore, he tries a midway course—to win the Pawn without preventing White from castling. With this in mind, he plays 19 ... Q–R4 ch. Another try would have been 19

... KR–B1; 20 N–N3, B–QN4; 21 KR–B1. Also 19 ... KR–N1 looks very strong.

19 ...   Q–R4 ch

Attacking the uncastled White King. Black cannot prevent White's castling in the long run, because White has Knights to cover the intervening squares, but he can take advantage of the vulnerable position of the White King to make White lose time in protecting and thus himself win White's QBP. He therefore gives up trying to prevent White from castling in favor of trying to win White's isolated QBP.

20 N–Q2

White would prefer to exchange Queens, but 20 Q–Q2?, B–B6.

20 ...   B–R5

Black's pieces are free for action and harass the White Queen as much as possible.

21 N–N3

The only move. If 21 Q–R2, QxP; 22 O–O?, B–QN4, winning the exchange. So with this variant, Black would prevent castling and obtain the maximum.

21 ...   BxN

Without any hope for the maximum, Black wishes at least to win the Pawn.

22 RxB   KR–B1

The White QBP is doomed. For instance, 26 P–B6, Q–R3; 24 P–

B7, Q–R2, one of the many ways this Pawn may be eliminated.

23 O–O   RxP

Black could also have played 23 ... QxP, inviting the exchange of Queens, but since the Black Queen is more active than the White Queen, Black does not wish the Queens exchanged at this time.

White has now succeeded in castling, Black in attaining his partial aim of the win of a Pawn.

24 Q–Q3

The game is entering another new phase. Black has won a Pawn, but the win of the game will not be easy, since both sides have only K-side Pawns. This makes the short-legged White Knight relatively more powerful than the long-legged Black Bishop. For the moment, however, the Black Bishop is very strong. From its excellent post at its KB3, it exercises pressure all along the diagonal, and particularly on White's key squares QR1, QN2, QB3.

24 ...   QR–QB1

The Black strategy at this point will be (a) a routine move—doubling Rooks in order to play the Rook to B6, B7, or B8, depending on the situation; (b) safety for his King; (c) penetrating White's position, which he does with 20 ... R–B6; (d) trying to find objects of attack; (e) the push of the QP.

25 P–N3   P–N3

In a struggle between heavy pieces, it is always a good policy to create escape squares for the King.

26 R(B)–N1

White also doubles Rooks, which gives him possibilities such as R–N5 or R–N8.

26 ...   R–B6

Black can never make progress without exchanging at least one or two of the heavy pieces, first because the White Rooks control too many squares, next because White himself can play R–N8 and exchange one Rook at any time.

27 RxR   RxR

Black recaptures with his Rook rather than with his Queen because his Queen is more active than White's and he wishes to retain it.

28 Q–B1   K–N2

Sometimes such K moves are made to guard the King against sudden assaults. Here, the move is made to cut down on White's potential avenues of escape. Supposing the White Rook or the White Queen should get into trouble—if the threatened piece could escape by giving a check—this would afford it time and release.

29 N–B3

The White Knight looks for a square from which to blockade the Black half-passed QP, which will soon come into action.

29 ...   P–K4

With the clear intention of pushing the QP at the right moment.

30 K–N2

White protects his Knight in order to be able to answer the expected ... P–Q5 with PxP, which would not be possible if the Knight were unprotected. Without White's being able to play PxP, Black could probably obtain a *protected* passed Pawn, that is, a passed Pawn protected by an adjacent Pawn, and a very advanced one.

However, White defends his Knight in the wrong way, as will be seen from the continuation. Preferable was 30 Q–K2 or 30 Q–Q1. Still better would have been

30 N–K1 in order to answer 30 ... P–Q5 by 31 PxP, PxP; 32 N–Q3!, throwing up a solid barricade against the further advance of the Black QP. This barricade is the more solid because the Q3 square is of the opposite color of that of the Black Bishop.

The best way to handle a passed Pawn is to blockade it with a piece. This is especially effective if it is an isolated passed Pawn, for then it is difficult to drive the blockader away.

But if White had played 30 N–K1, Black would have postponed the advance of his QP until he could have advanced it without its becoming a blockaded passed Pawn.

| 30 ... | P–Q5 |
| 31 PxP | Q–Q4! |

A so-called "eternal pin," which decides the struggle. The White King cannot unpin, because the Knight needs protection—a well-known situation which the reader should keep in mind.

Note that although the strategic plan of Black calls for the queening of the passed Pawn, Black does not lose the opportunity offered to him gratis of making the most of a tactical situation brought about by the pin of the Knight. 31 ... Q–Q4 is an in-between move that does not cost Black any time; it is played with a threat.

32 Q–Q1

Another try to prevent the unavoidable would be: 32 Q–K2, PxP; 33 R–Q1 (33 R–N5 fails against 33 ... P–Q6; 34 RxQ, PxQ, and Black wins, since he threatens ... RxN), P–Q6; 34 Q–Q2, P–N4 and now as in the game.

However, 32 Q–K2 would have made things considerably more difficult: 32 ... PxP; 33 R–Q1, P–Q6; 34 Q–K3, P–R3 (34 ... P–Q7 fails against 35 RxP). Now (a) 35 R–Q2?, B–N4!; (b) 35 K–N1?, P–Q7; 36 RxP, QxN; (c) 35 P–R4 (White must play this), and the continuation could be: 35 ... R–N6 (a waiting move); 36 R–Q2, P–N4; 37 K–R2 (all relatively best), PxP; 38 PxP, Q–B4; 39 N–K1 (this is not forced, but if White does not eliminate Black's QP, he is bound to lose), BxP; 40 NxP (40 RxP, BxP), B–N4 and Black must win: (41 P–B4?, RxN!).

| 32 ... | PxP |
| 33 R–N2 | |

Now White loses a piece in a very instructive way, but there was nothing to be done anyway. If 33 P–R4 in order to prevent the advance of Black's NP as in the continuation of the game, 33 ... P–R3.

| 33 ... | P–N4 |

Black threatens 34 ... P–N5.

34 P–N4

If 34 P–R3, P R4.

34 ...   P–R4!

If now 35 PxP, then 35 ... P–
N5.

35 P–R3   PxP
36 PxP   Q–K5
37 Q–K2

There is no defense. The move
37 K–N3 is answered by 37 ...
B–K4 ch or 37 ... Q–B5 ch.

37 ...   QxP ch
38 K–B1   QxN

Or 38 ... RxN

39 Resigns

To a certain extent, the amateur
loses the game because he did not
realize that the advanced Pawn
on the Q side would be weak in
this very special case. The question
is very subtle, and even a master
could go wrong in such a situation.
As a matter of fact, there are even
grandmaster games along the same
line, and it is precisely on the basis
of these games that the active chess
player knows that he has to be
careful with P–QR3, P–QN4 at
such an early stage of the game.
Our amateur did not know this. He
cannot be blamed for that, and
once on the defensive, one could
even pardon him for continuing
the wrong strategy by his 12th
move P–B5. After that, he could
not escape being forced to the defense and later losing the Pawn.
He put up the best defense possible, and only toward the very end
could he have chosen a line that
would have offered more resistance.

Game 3

Chess games are not always won by a blitz attack on the King position or by drawing the King into a mating net. Sometimes the arrangement of the pieces and Pawns dictates an attack far from the King itself, and—as we have already seen in Game 2—at times the opponent's Pawn structure is the object of a winning strategy.

In principle, the strongest Pawn formation is that where all the Pawns stand in a horizontal row. At the outset of the game, the Pawns on both sides stand thus, in a position without weaknesses. As soon as a Pawn advances out of the horizontal position, it becomes a target for an enemy Pawn attack, which may result either in opening a file to the advantage of the opponent, or leaving the player who advances his Pawns with a weak Pawn position, or in both. Disadvantageous formations, such as isolated Pawns, doubled Pawns, backward Pawns, etc., all have their drawbacks, and such weaknesses can often be exploited. Another question is how to induce the opponent to create these weak Pawn positions.

One of the slight disadvantages of the fianchetto move P–N3 is that the opponent is sometimes able to advance his opposing RP to R5 in order, after exchanging this Pawn, to open the Rook file or to weaken the hostile NP on its N3.

When the opponent's King is castled short and when he has fianchettoed on the same side, the advance of the other player's KRP may result in an open KR file, which may become a powerful weapon against the hostile King, in general, more powerful than an open R file on the Q wing.

Against the uncastled fianchettoed Q wing the technique is different. There, the QBP is often advanced to hold or contest the center, leaving the fianchettoed QNP with only the QRP to defend it. In such cases, the P–QR4–QR5xQNb attack is often effective against this weakened fianchetto. It can result on the one hand in a weakened Q-side Pawn position for the player who has fianchettoed, or it could force him to protect his Q-side Pawns with pieces; once his pieces are immobilized, to protect his Pawns, the other player can take advantage of the situation in quite a different way, namely by undertaking action on some other part of the board.

English Opening

Master	Amateur
White	*Black*

1 P–QB4

Instead of occupying the center, White develops a side Pawn with the idea of avoiding contact with the opponent at the early stages of the game in order to develop rapidly.

This type of game, called the English Opening, often leads to a K-side fianchetto for both sides.

By transposition, it may also lead to any one of a number of commoner openings, such as the Queen's Gambit Declined (see Games 11–14) or to some one of the various Indian openings (see Games 9, 10, 19–22, and 24). Part of its charm lies in its flexibility.

When Black answers 1 ... P–K4, the English Opening has been called the Sicilian in Reverse, that is, the Sicilian with a move in hand. This continuation is not considered so strong for Black. White continues 2 N–QB3 and 3 P–KN3.

The Sicilian is not bad for Black—so this continuation must be good for White.

1 ...　　　　　　N–KB3

Black answers with a move that brings pressure to bear on his center squares Q4 and K5 and could lead to the Queen's Gambit, to one of the Indian openings, or to the English Opening proper, that is, all variations that do not lead to the Queen's Gambit, to Indian defenses, or to the Reti Opening.

2 N–QB3

Without coming into contact with his opponent, White brings pressure to bear on his Q5 and K4 squares, thus maintaining a balance of control in the center.

2 ...　　　　　　P–K3

This reply makes it appear as if Black wanted to play a Nimzo-Indian Defense (see Games 1 and 2).

3 P–K4

This is the so-called Franco-English Opening, an attempt by White either to attain a majority in the center or to displace the Black Knight by P–K5. Neither of these goals can be reached without compensation for Black.

White could also play 3 P–Q4, which could lead to the Queen's Gambit after 3 ... P–Q4 or to the Nimzo-Indian after 3 ... B–N5.

3 ...   P–Q4

Equally good is 3 ... P–B4, which could be followed by 4 P–K5, N–N1!, and White has no advantage from his advanced Pawn, which he will have to exchange if Black later plays ... P–Q3. For instance, 5 P–B4, N–QB3; 6 N–B3, P–Q3; 7 PxP (otherwise his KP will become weak), BxP; 8 P–Q4, N–B3; 9 PxP, BxP; 10 QxQ ch, KxQ, and Black has nothing to fear.

4 P–K5

Practically forced. After 4 BPxP or 4 KPxP, 4 ... PxP; 5 PxP, NxP, White is left with an isolated QP.

4 ...   P–Q5!

After the quiet 4 ... KN–Q2, White would obtain an advantage in space with 5 P–Q4.

5 PxN   PxN

6 NPxP

White had to choose between 6 PxNP, 6 NPxP, or 6 QPxP. The continuation 6 PxNP, PxP ch; 7 BxP, BxP would lead to equality; as for 6 NPxP and 6 QPxP, in either case, White ends up with doubled Pawns, but there are doubled Pawns and doubled Pawns. After 6 QPxP, QxQ ch; 7 KxQ, PxP, White has no flexible Pawn majority on the Q side—White's doubled Pawns cannot force a passed Pawn, whereas Black, despite his doubled Pawn, will be able to force a passed Pawn.

The rule of thumb for doubled Pawns is that if there are two united blocks of Pawns opposing each other and on the same files, but separated from other Pawn blocks, the doubled Pawn does not count. But as soon as one has a Pawn on a file where the opponent has no Pawn, then the doubled

Pawn does count when it is a question of forcing a passed Pawn.

Thus, in the example from this position (after 6 QPxP, QxQ ch; 7 KxQ, PxP), on the Q side there is no single Pawn on a file, but in the center, the Black KP is a single Pawn on a file. Therefore, the Black doubled Pawn does count, whereas the White doubled Pawn does not count. Black will be able to force a passed Pawn, White will not.

In the above example, if we should place White's KNP instead on its K2 or K3, then the Black doubled Pawn would not count either.

6 ...   QxBP
7 P–Q4

White now has a kind of center —weakened by a doubled Pawn and therefore vulnerable under certain circumstances. The doubled Pawn is useful, since it strengthens the center, protecting the Pawn on Q4, but it is also vulnerable, since after Black's ... P–B4, White cannot take under almost any circumstances, since he would thus obtain a triple Pawn. So Black can attack White's QP directly and his

QBP indirectly, that is, after proper preparation, by such moves as ... R QB1, ... N QR4, and ... D–QR3.

7 ...   P–QN3

7 ... P–B4 is more consistent, for reasons explained after White's 7th move. The game might then continue 8 N–B3, P–KR3 (otherwise White gains a couple of tempi by 9 B–N5 and 10 B–Q3); 9 B–Q3, N–B3; 10 B–K3, P–QN3.

8 B–K2

A new idea. Usually played is 8 N–B3, B–N2; 9 B–K2, N–Q2; 10 O–O, with some initiative for White. One illustration from the Flohr-Kashdan game, Folkstone 1933, which continued: 10 ... B–Q3; 11 B–N5, Q–B4; 12 Q–R4, P–QB3; 13 P–B5, a very promising Pawn sacrifice.

8 ...   B–N2
9 B–B3

This move neutralizes the Black QB and makes possible a continuation of the development by N–K2 and, moreover, prepares P–Q5 as an answer to ... P–B4.

Black should now exchange Bishops, after which both players continue their development: 9 ... BxB; 10 NxB, B–Q3 and

(a) 11 Q–R4 ch, P–B3; 12 O–O, O–O; 13 R–K1, R–B1, followed by 14 ... N–Q2. Without the check on his 11th move, White might even come into a little trouble, as will be seen under (b).

(b) 11 O-O, O-O; 12 P-QR4, N-B3, and White's doubled Pawn becomes weak after ... N-R4!

But the amateur, not understanding the decreased value of the Bishop behind a Pawn, creates a weakness in his position by playing

9 ...   P-QB3?

After this move, Black's QNP can become weak. True, it is protected by Black's QRP, but White, looking for a way to exploit the weakness, finds that he can attack this Pawn by advancing his QRP to QR4 and QR5. Black must then either defend his QNP by ... N-Q2 or take White's QRP, but in either case, Black has to take special measures on behalf of his Q-side Pawns, and in either case, Black emerges with a weakened Pawn position that will give him serious problems.

10 N-K2

Before starting the attack on Black's QNP by P-QR4, White prepares for castling, which is always a good idea, since castling might be necessary in case of an emer-

gency. Besides, the Knight can now take part in the struggle.

White could also have played 10 P-QR4 immediately, but then sooner or later he should also play N-K2, since in some variations this Knight will participate in the battle.

10 ...   B-Q3
11 P-QR4

Planning to continue the attack on Black's Q-side Pawn formation by 12 P-QR5.

To show the weakness of Black's QNP, let us suppose 11 ... O-O; 12 P-QR5,

(1)

12 ... Q-K2; 13 Q-N3 and
(1a)   13 ... N-Q2; 14 P-R6! wins at least a Pawn;
(1b)   13 ... PxP; 14 P-B5! wins a piece;
(1c)   13 ... Q-B2; 14 R-QN1, N-Q2; 15 P-B5 wins a Pawn.

(2)

12 ... PxP; 13 Q-N3
(2a)   13 ... Q-K2?; 14 P-B5 wins a piece;
(2b)   ... B-R3; 14 RxP, with a

clear superiority. How can Black develop?

(2c) 13 ... B–B1; 14 RxP, B–Q2; 15 Q–N7, winning a piece even after 15 ... Q–Q1; 16 R–R1, Q–B2; 17 QxR, N–R3; 18 QxR ch and 19 RxN

(3)

12 ... N–Q2; 13 P–R6, etc., wins a Pawn.

(4)

12 ... B–B2 (probably the best); 13 Q–N3, N–R3 (Black has managed to get out his Knight!); 14 P–B5, P–N4 (14 ... Q–Q1; 15 PxP, PxP; 16 PxP, BxP?; 17 R–QN1, or 16 ... N–B4; 17 PxN); 15 O–O, P–K4; 16 B–K3 and White has the best of it, for he threatens P–B4.

11 ...   P–QR4

To avoid one positional weakness, Black gives himself another—an unprotected and backward QNP. Variation 4 above was certainly the least evil.

12 R–QN1

White immediately seizes the initiative by attacking Black's QNP and indirectly also his QB. White's next move will show what this means.

12 ...   N–Q2
13 P–B5!   B–B2
14 PxP   NxP

White has now undoubled his Pawns, whereas Black remains not only with two isolated Pawns, but also with a cluster of vulnerable pieces that are indirectly threatened.

15 B nn

Now White prevents Black from castling, and Black's position becomes that much worse. White's play graphically illustrates a common way of gaining a positional advantage. You set out to win a Pawn, and in the process you force your opponent to give up something in order to defend it—in this case, the diagonal QR3–KB8, which White uses to prevent Black from castling.

15 ...   R–QN1

For White was threatening to win one of the loose pieces by 16 B–B5.

16 B–B5   B–R1

An unnatural move, but Black has nothing else.

17 N–N3

Preparing to bring the Knight into action via K4.

17 ...   N–Q4
18 RxR ch

White exchanges here (a) to win a tempo, since Black's KB is now vulnerable in that it is unprotected (see White's 19th move); (b) because after the exchange, he plays with proportionally more material, since Black's KR is and remains out of play.

18 ...   BxR
19 Q–N3

Thus White wins his tempo.

19 ...   Q–Q1
20 BxN!

This exchange eliminates a powerful enemy and forces the opening of the K file for direct attack.

20 ...   KPxB

If 20 ... BPxB, White wins a Bishop after 21 Q–N5 ch, Q–Q2; 22 QxB ch.

21 O–O

White has been so busy pressing his advantages that it is only now that he finds time to castle. He nows threatens Black with 22 R–K1 ch and 23 R–K7 ch.

21 ...   BxN

Black makes this exchange for two reasons: (a) to eliminate one of his own vulnerable pieces and thus free his Queen from the task of protecting it; (b) to eliminate the White Knight as an attacking piece; e.g., if 21 ... P–B3; 22 R–K1 ch,

K–B2; 23 R–K7 ch, K–N1; 24 N–B5!

22 BPxB

There is a general rule that says, "Always take toward the center," but specific circumstances often make it advisable to violate a general rule. If 22 RPxB, K–Q2 (!).

In either case, White has total control of the board. He now threatens 23 R–K1 ch, K–Q2; 24 R–K7 ch, K–B1; 25 R–R7.

22 ...   P–B3

To give the King a flight square.

23 R–K1 ch   K–B2

If 23 ... K–Q2, White carries out his threat by 24 R–K7 ch, K–B1; 25 R–R7.

24 R–K7 ch   K–N1

If 24 ... K–N3; 25 Q–B2 ch, K–R3; 26 Q–B5 and wins; e.g., 26 ... R–N1; 27 P–N4, P–N3; 28 P–N5 ch, PxP; 29 Q–R3 mate.

25 Q–B2

In order to bring the Queen to B5 and then start a mating attack.

25 ...   P–N3

Parries the threat 26 Q–B5, but now the White Queen finds another way.

If 25 ... P R3, 26 Q–N0.

26 Q–K2   Resigns

For Black has no adequate answer to 27 Q–K6 ch. If 26 ... Q–QB1; 27 R–K8 ch.

In this game, as in many others, the amateur handles the opening satisfactorily. The phase following the opening proves to be the most dangerous for the amateur. It is the phase in which the player has to stand on his own after having followed the master moves that have been given by theory.

Game 4

The right to castle is a very valuable privilege in a chess game because of the vulnerability of the King on its original square, as shown in Game 3. Correct opening strategy requires center control by both Pawns and pieces, and since this frequently implies the advancing of the KP and QP to occupy the center, the natural protection of the King by these two Pawns often disappears early in the game, and the vulnerability of the King increases. This makes it almost imperative that the King try to escape from dangerous territory by castling. Therefore, both sides have the important tactical task of seeing that the right to castle is not impaired. This castling privilege can be abrogated in several ways. A free check by a hostile Knight would force the issue—the King would be compelled to leave its original square. Check by a hostile Queen, Rook, or Bishop can often be answered by interposing a piece, but sometimes circumstances force the King to move.

How serious is the loss of the right to castle? In many positions, it means nothing at all. This is especially true in positions where the Queens have been exchanged. Even with the Queens still on the board, a King can often stand safely behind its QP and KP. But when one of the protecting center Pawns is missing, the situation can become critical, as the following game shows. There the King's position in the center is made more untenable by the judicious sacrifice of a piece to eliminate the last Black center Pawn and expose the King to the direct attack of three powerful pieces and two active Pawns. White's harmonious development is a solid basis and a guarantee of the correctness of the sacrifice.

In the course of the game, several other important chess concepts come into play, among which is that of the weakened squares that result when one of the Bishops is exchanged. In that event, the player who has made the exchange may find it much more difficult to control the squares of the color of the exchanged Bishop. The player must often take special precautions to protect the weakened squares, which gives him fewer pieces and affords him less time for other activities.

Benoni Opening

Master	Amateur
White	Black

| 1 P–Q4 | N–KB3 |
| 2 P–QB4 | P–B4 |

The Benoni Opening, so named in 1825 by A. Reinganum of Frankfurt, Germany, without his giving any special reason for the name.

The 2 ... P–B4 is a sort of a countergambit that represents an attempt on the part of Black to contest White's control of the center at once. At this point, the position is not unlike the Black attack on White's center in the Nimzo-Indian Defense as seen in Game 2, but because of White's usual reply P–Q5 in the Benoni, it soon leads to an entirely different Pawn formation and type of game.

The basic idea behind the Benoni is to entice White to advance his center by playing P–Q5, and then to attack it.

In the 1930s, the Benoni was theoretically condemned, but nowadays no refutation is known, and Black often obtains good results with it. However, this may be more because strong, enterprising players choose it than because of its intrinsic merits.

3 P–Q5

By advancing his QP, White eliminates the tension in the center and sets the Pawn formation that gives this opening its characteristics. White attains a greater mobility and more terrain, but Black in compensation, after a K-side fianchetto, gets an open diagonal for his KB. Moreover, after the moves that now follow in the game, which are usually played and considered by masters as forced for White, Black obtains the majority of Pawns on the Q side as opposed to White's Pawn majority in the center.

If instead 3 PxP, Q–R4ch; 4 N–B3, QxBP, and Black has regained his Pawn, or still better 3 ... P–K3, and White cannot maintain the extra Pawn: (a) 4 P–QN4, P–QR4!; (b) 4 B–K3, N–R3 (compare similar positions in the Queen's Gambit Accepted).

Or, if White ignores the Black attack and plays 3 P–K3, Black does not have much trouble in equalizing by 3 ... P–Q4. In the ensuing position with two opposing rows of center Pawns, the question is always: (a) Can my opponent isolate my QP by playing ... PxQP and ... PxBP? (b) Have I compensation (in this case, mobility and space)? Once the QP is isolated, an important point is: Can I push my isolated Pawn sooner, or later? In such a case, the isolated Pawn constitutes an advantage.

After 3 P–Q5, the game could branch off into one of two lines. Black can solidify his center by 3 ... P–Q3, in which case White continues by N–QB3 and P–K4, building up a strong Pawn formation. Black, in turn, by fianchettoing on the K side gets a fine diagonal for his KB, and by ... P–QN4 some chance for attack on the Q side. Or Black can try to break up White's center Pawn formation at once, which he does in the present game by playing 3 ... P–K3, after which his aims are partly the same as in the 3 ... P–Q3 line, namely: (a) to secure the long diagonal KN2–QN7; (b) chances for ... P–QN4, which will be even easier here, since White's QBP will disappear from its QB4; and consequently, (c) a Q-side majority. Nowadays 3 ... P–K3 is in vogue, and in any case, the results scored by this move are superior to those obtained in the 3 ... P–Q3 variation.

3 ...   P–K3
4 N–QB3

White supports the center.

4 PxP would give up the center. After 4 ... BPxP, Black will possibly be able to attain ... P–Q4, after which he would stand mar-

velously well. In any case, after 4 PxP, BPxP, Black would have (a) a numerical advantage in the center and (b) an open KB file.

4 ...   PxP

Black destroys part of White's center formation, which gives White a somewhat greater control of space and a majority in the center.

Instead, Black could have played 4 ... P–Q3, but he is playing for the Q-side majority.

5 PxP

White's advanced Pawn properly supported will constitute a restraining factor on Black's development.

Possible is 5 NxP, NxN; 6 QxN, which has a very special purpose of keeping the Black QP backward and leads to quite another kind of game. The compensation for Black is rapid development, because the White Queen is vulnerable at its Q5. The game might continue: 6 ... N–B3; 7 N–B3, P–Q3 (threatening 8 ... B–K3 and 9 ... P–Q4, removing the weakness); 8

P–K4, N–N5; 9 Q–Q2, P–B4, and Black has the initiative after 10 P–QR3, PxP. It is therefore doubtful that White's strategy in this variation is justified.

5 ...   P–Q3

Black consolidates his center and opens a diagonal for his QB. He will soon develop his KB to KN2, where it will exert great pressure on the long diagonal. Thus White will occupy more space in the center, but Black will exert at least equal pressure with his two favorable Bishops. It is noteworthy that neither of Black's Bishops is hemmed in by his Pawns. In this way, Black has two Good Bishops, so to speak.

6 P–K4

White plays this move (a) to strengthen his QP; (b) to make an eventual breakthrough in the center by P–K5; (c) to open a diagonal for the development of his KB.

In former times 6 P–KN3 was played here, because players "were accustomed" to this move—as in the King's Indian openings, but it is clear that after 6 P–KN3 and 7 B–N2, White's KB is very "bad," because it is blocked by its own QP and, after P–K4, by its KP.

With the text, the resultant formation, typical in the Benoni, allows Black the two advantages already mentioned: (a) the opening of an effective long diagonal by a K-side fianchetto; (b) the exploiting of his Q-side majority.

6 ...   P–KN3

When Black has completed the fianchetto by ... B–N2, he will be controlling such important squares as his K4 and Q5, would be in a position to exchange White's QN for his own KB, should this be desirable, and will be indirectly threatening White's QR behind the piece and the Pawn.

7 N–B3

The Knight brings more pressure on the center and could eventually support the advance P–K5.

7 ...   B–N5(?)

It is perhaps natural that Black should want to neutralize White's growing force, but this move is wrong on several counts:

(a) As a general principle, Black cannot afford to take the initiative so early in the game.

(b) Because Black has already played his KNP to the 3rd rank, he cannot withdraw his Bishop to its KR4 if it is attacked, but must either lose a tempo by playing it to his Q2 or QB1 or exchange it; the exchange is bad, however, partly because he will be exchanging a Bishop for a Knight, and even more so because once he exchanges his Bishop, the White squares will become weak for Black.

There is one point in favor of the text: Black exchanges White's KN and thus deprives White's K5 and Q4 squares of protection. Consequently, Black's influence in the center increases.

At this point, Black should have

continued his development with the logical 7 ... B–N2, and then White could continue 8 B–QB4 or 8 B–K2 or 8 B–KN5, leading to an interesting struggle of space against force. It would be bad for White to continue 8 P–K5 in that case, because of 8 ... PxP; 9 NxP, O–O, and Black threatens both 10 ... R–K1 and 10 ... NxP, a sham sacrifice that would win a Pawn.

8 P–KR3

White quite properly presses the Black Bishop for a decision, because he knows that Black must either exchange and lose his Good Bishop or withdraw it and lose time. Moreover, P–KR3 also restricts Black's possibilities; he cannot then play ... N–KN5 any longer.

8 ...   BxN

Black would perhaps have done better to withdraw the Bishop. By exchanging, he (a) furthers White's development; (b) deprives himself of his own Good Bishop; (c) leaves White in control of the White squares on the board; but (d) increases Black's influence in the center, because the White KN that controlled its K5 and Q4 has disappeared.

9 QxB   B–N2(?)

Although this seems to be the logical developing move here, one cannot always afford to make the apparently "logical" move. Here there is a tactical threat to take into consideration, and 9 ... P–

QR3 should be played in order to prevent the check that will now follow. Besides, 9 ... P–QR3 is not only a preventive move, but also an aggressive one, since it prepares ... P–QN4 in order to exploit the Pawn majority on the Q side.

10 B–N5 ch!

An excellent positional move that takes advantage of the weakness of Black's White squares.

10 ...   QN–Q2?

This obvious move loses. It is the decisive error of the game.

The only move is 10 ... KN–Q2!, which is remarkable. But it often happens that in case of weaknesses on the Q side, Black brings his KN to support his Q side. In this case, 10 ... KN–Q2 would have prevented the text move B–N5, by which White can force Black to give up castling, which is often very serious.

11 B–N5

This prevents Black from playing 11 ... O–O, after which 12 BxQN, QxB; 13 BxN loses a piece for Black. Notice how the absence of Black's QB has already put Black into a very compromised position.

11 ...   P–KR3

Nothing that Black can do now would keep him from losing the castling privilege. He could also have played 11 ... P–QR3 here, and with the same results: 12 BxN ch, KxB.

12 BxN ch

White makes this exchange in order to bring Black's King to a vulnerable position. Black cannot answer 12 ... QxB, because he would lose a piece after 13 BxN, BxB; 14 QxB.

12 ...   KxB

Now that Black has a pronounced weakness in his King position, White looks around for the best way to exploit the weakness.

13 B–B4

White had to do something about the attack on his Bishop, and in general it is a good idea to direct pieces against squares in the neighborhood of the hostile King. Here this is especially strong, because the King is very vulnerable in its uncastled position.

13 ...,   R–K1

Black develops a piece and brings pressure against White's PK4, thus indirectly preventing N N5, which could be answered by ... NxKP.

At this point, 13 ... N–R4 would be answered by 14 B–R2 or by 14 BxP, as later in the game.

14 O–O

With the Black Rook on the K file, White must bring his King to safety before starting his attack.

14 ...   P–R3

To prevent White's N–N5.

15 KR–K1

Since White plans to open the position by P–K5, the additional pressure of his Rook along the K file is needed.

15 ...   N–R4

This forces White to a decision. If he should now play the obvious 16 B–R2, Black would complete his development by ... Q–B3, and White would have more difficulty in making his superiority felt.

16 BxQP!!

White can make this beautiful sacrifice, because after 16 ... KxB; 17 QxP, he gets at least two Pawns for the Bishop and threatens both Black's QNP and KNP, and he has hemmed off the escape of the Black King toward its 1st rank.

16 ...   KxB
17 QxP

Among other things, White threatens to win back his piece by 18 QxP ch, and if 18 ... N–B3; 19 QxB.

17 ...   Q–B3
18 P–K5 ch!

Pressing the attack! White, who has the better development, takes optimal advantage of Black's unsafe King position. The Pawn sacrifice frees his K4 square for the Knight and forces Black to play in such a way that his QR will lose its protection.

The alternate 18 QxQNP is also good, but the text is more forcing.

18 ...   RxP
19 QxQNP   QR–K1

Forced. The plausible 19 ... RxR ch; 20 RxR favors White, because White then threatens 21 N–K4 ch, winning the Queen.

20 N–K4 ch!

White can afford this further sacrifice because Black's King is in the open and White has in hand the possibility of Q–B6 ch. The text wins two Rooks for a Knight and leads to mate.

20 ...   RxN
21 Q–B6 ch

Another powerful forcing move. Both Black Rooks must fall, and mate is in the air.

21 ...   K–K2

If 21 ... K–K4; 22 QxR ch, etc.

22 RxR ch   Resigns

For (a) 22 ... K–B1 or K–B2; 23 QxR mate; (b) 22 ... K–Q1; 23 RxR mate.

In this game, the amateur's downfall begins in the opening with the premature execution of a plan whose basic idea is not bad. Black exchanges his QB for White's KN in order to strengthen his influence in the center, but he does not realize the dangers entailed in this strategy. Had he protected his critical diagonal K1–QR5 in time by 10 ... P–QR3, or in the right way by 11 ... KN–Q2, the consequences of his dubious exchange on the 7th move would have been considerably attenuated. The storm that breaks out after his failure to protect himself is so overwhelming that the amateur never gets an opportunity to demonstrate his defensive skill

Game 5

The theory of the moves in the Ruy Lopez

The open variation (5 ... NxP) of the Ruy Lopez

Strategic planning

Two strategic lines in the open variation: 9 P–QB3 vs. 9 Q–K2

The far-reaching effects of a mistake in the opening

Danger of Knight on central outpost with no retreat

The power of tactical threats

Of all the KP openings, the Ruy Lopez (1 P–K4, P–K4; 2 N–KB3, N–QB3; 3 B–N5) offers White the greatest possibility of conserving his initial advantage of having the first move. Because of this, the Ruy Lopez has been studied more and has more columns devoted to it in works on openings than any other in the game of chess.

In the Ruy Lopez, planning is on a long-term basis. To keep his slight initial plus, White must understand wherein his advantage lies and how to choose moves that will maintain or increase it. Should he play indifferently, Black may soon obtain equality.

For the amateur, the Ruy Lopez is at the same time an easy and a difficult opening, easy in that seldom do big combinative complications arise from it in the initial stages, as is the case in openings such as the King's Gambit and in some variations of the Giuoco Piano. The Ruy Lopez moves in general along quiet lines. On the other hand, it is difficult for the amateur to have a complete understanding of the Ruy Lopez, for one cannot restrict oneself to the general lines and the standard moves, since a given move can have one meaning and value in one variation and quite another meaning and value in a different variation. Such is the case in this game, which emphasizes this special aspect of openings.

In most lines of the Ruy Lopez, the move ... N–QR4 after Black has driven the White KB to QN3 is a very good move, whether it has as its purpose to exchange the White KB or to prepare the usually effective advance of the QBP. In this game, however, both the Knight move and the advance of the QBP are incorrect for tactical reasons, as will be seen in the game.

In games between master and amateur, the latter often goes wrong not in the opening itself but in the early stages of the middle game, and at that point because opening theory is insufficient for the middle game proper.

Ruy Lopez: Open Variation (5 ... NxP)

Master	Amateur
White	*Black*
1 P–K4	P–K4
2 N–KB3	N–QB3
3 B–N5	

The Ruy Lopez, an opening that affords White more possibilities than most others.

With 3 B–N5, White exercises indirect pressure against Black's position, for by BxN he threatens eventually to win Black's KP. He cannot do so immediately, since 4 BxN, QPxB; 5 NxP(?) is answered by 5 ... Q–Q5 or 5 ... Q–N4, either of which leads to regaining the Pawn and gives Black at least an even position. But Black must continually take into account the possibility of White's playing BxN under more favorable circumstances, as we shall now show in two examples where he first protects his KP so that Black cannot regain the Pawn with his Queen after White has played NxKP: (a) 3 ... N–B3; 4 P–Q3, threatening 5 BxN, QPxB; 6 NxP, and Black cannot regain his Pawn with 6 ... Q–Q5; or (b) 3 ... P–QR3; 4 B–R4, N–B3; 5 O–O, B–K2 (see Game 6); 6 R–K1, and White again

threatens to play BxN to advantage, as for instance, 6 ... O–O; 7 BxN, QPxB; 8 NxP, and White has won a Pawn.

3 ...   P–QR3

The Morphy Variation. This is considered the strongest variation of the Ruy Lopez, since Black conserves for himself the possibility of breaking White's pressure on the Black QN at any time by ... P–QN4.

Important elements of White's strategy in this variation are: (a) direct pressure against Black's QN, and by extension against his King, which is behind the Knight; (b) indirect pressure against Black's Pawn on K4; (c) the forcing of Black to play ... P–QN4, followed by an attempt to exploit this move by playing P–QR4 at the proper time in order to weaken Black's Q side.

Black's general strategy is the opposite of White's. In general, it is directed toward preventing White from attaining the three above-mentioned goals. Moreover, Black is looking with one eye for an opportunity to exchange the

White KB eventually by means of . . . P–QN4 and . . . N–QR4.

4 B–R4   N–B3

A developing move that contributes to the centralization of Black's pieces. In some cases, Black can take White's KP, not in order to win a Pawn, for White can win it back, but to reach equality in the simplest way.

5 O–O

At this point, 5 P–Q4 is not considered as strongest, since it would relieve the pressure against the Black KP by allowing Black to exchange it.

5 . . .   NxP

This is one of the two principal standard variations in the Ruy Lopez and is called the counterattack or open variation. It is risky, because it opens the game before the Black King is safely castled. White, who has already castled, has his Rook ready to attack on the K file.

For the other main line, 5 . . . B–K2 (the closed defense), see Game 6.

How is White now going to take advantage of Black's somewhat risky position? By such a move as 6 R–K1, he can win back his Pawn immediately but without advantage, as, for instance, 6 . . . N–B4; 7 NxP, B–K2, after which White has to permit the exchange of his KB, and Black's King can go into a safe position.

It is much more important for White to find a way of taking advantage of Black's weakness along the K file than to win back his Pawn immediately. He therefore plays

6 P–Q4

White tries to open up the game still more by inviting 6 . . . PxP, which would be dangerous for Black. The move 6 P–Q4, which was not good one move earlier, is now good because Black has partially opened the K file by . . . NxP.

Notice what happens if Black plays 6 . . . PxP: 7 R–K1, P–Q4; 8 NxP, and White has already regained one of his Pawns and will regain the second as well. It is not very wise for Black to provoke complications at a time when his King is not yet in a secure position. On the other hand, Black does have some counterchances, for White's King position is not sufficiently defended. Black can start a surprising counterattack with the strong Riga variation: 8 . . . B–Q3; 9 NxN, BxP ch, only to force a draw by a perpetual check if White takes the Bishop: 10 KxB, Q–R5 ch; 11 K–N1, QxP ch, etc. But White can avoid the draw by playing 10 K–R1! Black replies 10 ... Q–R5 with all kinds of threats, which forces White to liquidate in some way or other: 11 RxN ch (the forcing liquidating move), PxR; 12 Q–Q8 ch (forcing), QxQ; 13 NxQ ch, KxN; 14 KxB, and White has the better ending, as has been shown in a number of games.

6 ...   P–QN4

Black plays this move at the right time—which is as late as possible. He must play the move now in order to be able to answer White's R–K1 by ... P–Q4. For instance, if he had played 6 ... B–K2?, then 7 R–K1, P–Q4; 8 NxP, gaining an advantage, because White gets back his Pawn and has the initiative, threatening NxN.

Black must play ... P–N4 as late as possible, because it drives the White Bishop to QN3, a more active square where it controls a more important diagonal and the Q5 square and is directed toward the Black K wing. Moreover, ... P–QN4 weakens Black's Q side, opening the possibility of White's playing P–QR4. However, this latter move is not generally as important in the open variation of the Ruy Lopez as in the closed defense.

7 B–N3

From its QN3, the KB has several threats, which can be seen from the following possible continuations:

(a) 7 ... B–K2; 8 B–Q5, N–Q3; 9 PxP, which is very favorable for White, since he has won back his Pawn and has much more freedom for an advance in development.

(b) 7 ... PxP; 8 R–K1, P–Q4, followed by (1) 9 N–B3, PxN; 10 BxP, B–Q2; 11 RxN ch, B–K2; 12 Q–K2, and Black cannot castle (12 ... O–O; 13 BxN, followed by RxB) or (2) 9 BxP, QxB; 10 N–B3, Q–Q1; 11 RxN ch, B–K2; 12 NxQP, B–Q2; 13 N–Q5, etc., with a good game.

Since 7 ... PxP does not work, Black has to return the Pawn. This he does by 7 ... P–Q4, which is very effective in building a new stand in the center and maintaining Black's KN in its powerful position.

7 ...   P–Q4
8 PxP   B–K3

Forced, since White was threatening BxP.

The game is now entering a new phase. There are strategic decisions to be made. Let us consider this position carefully, in order to determine on what basis such decisions should be made. White has four Pawns on the K wing against Black's three. Black has four Pawns on the Q wing against White's three. These are characteristics that determine the plans to be made by each side in the near future. White will try to advance his K-side Pawns, Black will try to advance his Q-side Pawns. This means that White aims at N–Q4 (or other Knight moves), followed by P–KB4, and Black aims at . . . N–QR4, followed by . . . P–QB4. However, White's KN cannot move as long as his KP is not protected. White must first drive away Black's Knight on K5 and thus protect his KP along the K file. The primary goal of White's immediate strategy is the elimination of the Black Knight. How can this goal be realized?

The most direct way is 9 QN–Q2, N–B4 (9 . . . B–K2; 10 R–K1, N–B4 results in the same position); 10 R–K1, B–K2; 11 P–B3 (necessary as a preparation for N–Q4). But now Black exchanges White's KB—in general, a success. Besides, it has been demonstrated that 11 . . . O–O; 12 B–B2, P–Q5 gives Black a very satisfactory game.

There are other ways of attacking the Black Knight. We have seen the double attack by the Rook and Knight; we also could have had attacks by Rook and Bishop, by Bishop and Knight, or by Queen and Knight, etc.

With the traditional continuation 9 P–B3, White aims to make room for his KB on B2 and to control the square Q4. At the beginning of the game, we noted that the only positive goal of Black was to exchange the White KB by . . . N–R4. Here is the very first opportunity Black gets to do it, and this explains White's move P–B3, without saying that this must be the only correct move at this point. Black answers 9 . . . B–K2, and here are two variations just to illustrate how White can manage to drive away the Black Knight, and we shall see that neither of these variations leads to a clear advantage:

(a) 10 QN–Q2, O–O; 11 B–B2, P–KB4; 12 PxP e.p., NxP(B3), a difficult position for both sides.

(b) 10 QN–Q2, O–O; 11 Q–K2, N–B4; 12 N–Q4 (after 12 B–B2, 12 . . . P–Q5 is again strong for Black), NxB; 13 QNxKN (13 NxQN, NxB!), Q–Q2; 14 NxN, QxN, and Black has the Two Bishops, but White's strategy (the advance of the K-side Pawns) is more easily realized.

As we have explained above, none of the systems introduced by 9 P–B3 leads to a clear advantage for White. On the contrary, in many cases Black gets very good counterchances, although this does not mean that he has the best of it. For that reason, for a long time the open variation was favored by many enterprising masters playing the Black pieces.

Therefore, White players began answering, as in the present game,

9 Q–K2

A new system, the Moscow system, for undermining the position of the Knight on K5 by R–Q1 and P–QB4. This move looks strange, because it gives Black the opportunity to exchange the KB either by ... N–R4 or by ... N–B4, but neither of these moves seems to be recommendable, as we shall see.

9 ...   N–R4?

The present game will show why this move is not too strong. We already know that as soon as Black relieves the pressure against White's KP, White can play N–Q4 immediately.

It is true that Black exchanges White's KB for his Knight in the simplest way and also renders impossible White's strategic plan of playing R–Q1 and P–QB4. But White can now realize his strategic goal of driving away Black's Knight on its K5 much more easily and take advantage of his superiority on the K wing.

If instead, Black simply plays 9 ... N–B4 and then exchanges his KN for the White KB, White attains his goal of playing R–Q1 and P–QB4: 10 R–Q1, NxB (better 10 ... B–K2, which leads to the line below); 11 RPxB, B–K2; 12 P–B4, NPxP; 13 PxP, O–O; 14 N–B3, N–N5 (14 ... P–Q5; 15 Q–K4); 15 PxP, NxP, and White can already win a Pawn by 16 RxP. In general, one sees how White

exerts pressure against the Black position.

Best is 9 ... B–K2; 10 R–Q1, N–B4, although the last word has not been said in this difficult situation. White has three continuations, all of which are rather complicated. We give three possibilities, just to illustrate:

(a) 11 BxP, BxB; 12 N–B3, B–B5; 13 RxQ ch, RxR; 14 Q–K3, P–N5; 15 P–QN3, B–K3; 16 N–K4, R–Q8 ch; 17 N–K1, N–Q5; 18 B–N2, NxP; 19 Q–K2, RxR; 20 BxR, NxB; 21 NxN, BxN, and the result is doubtful.

(b) 11 P–B4, P–Q5; 12 PxP, P–Q6; 13 Q–K3, NxB; 14 PxN, N–N5; 15 N–Q4, B–N5, and Black has a good game.

(c) 11 B–K3, O–O; 12 P–B4, NPxP; 13 BxP, N–R4! with equal chances.

These variations are the outcome of thorough analyses during the years. There will be many unclear points for the reader, but they do illustrate what could happen.

10 N–Q4

This move prepares both 11 P–KB3 (driving away the Black Knight) and 11 P–KB4 (promoting White's K-side Pawn majority, more consistent, it is true, from a strategical point of view) and also enables White to play NxB, as in the present game.

The move 10 N–Q4 is far superior to the older 10 R–Q1 in that 10 N–Q4 prepares the driving away of the Black Knight on K5 and allows the advance of White's KBP.

10 ...   P–QB4

For the moment, it looks as though Black has attained his aim, for he has pushed his QBP and forced the White Knight to exchange. It is, however, a curious fact that as a consequence of 9 ... N–R4?, Black's Knight on K5 is more or less displaced, especially after 10 ... P–QB4, which prevents the Knight from going to its QB4. But Black is already in difficulties. Let us consider the obvious move 10 ... B–K2: 11 P–QB3, NxB (without this exchange, White retires his Bishop to B2 and Black's 9 ... N–R4 would be quite meaningless); 12 PxN, O–O (White threatened RxP, as in the game); 13 P–QN4! and White threatens to win a piece by 14 P–B3, N–N4; 15 P–KR4. Besides, after 10 ... B–K2, White can also win a Pawn: 11 NxB, PxN; 12 Q–N4 with double attack.

What is remarkable in this game is the strategy up to the last move, with both sides playing according to a general plan, such as undermining the Knight's position, trying to take advantage of the K-side majority, etc. From here on, tactics enter because of the vulnerable position of the Knight on Black's K5 and the attempts of the Knight to escape.

The amateur is already at a great disadvantage, and it is not at all surprising that the master, who is a much stronger player, is able to realize his preponderance in a very few moves.

11 NxB   PxN

12 P–QB3

In order to make room for the KB, since Black was threatening to win a piece by 12 ... P–B5.

12 ...   NxB

Otherwise, the White Bishop goes to B2, leaving the N(R4) without any reason for being there, and at the same time harassing the Black Knight on its K5; e.g., 12 ... P–B5; 13 B–B2, followed by 13 ... N–B4; 14 Q–R5 ch or by 13 ... N–N4; 14 Q–N4, in both cases with clear superiority for White.

13 PxN

Now Black is in danger on both wings. On the Q side, White threatens to win the RP by 14 RxP, RxR; 15 QxP ch. On the K side, the threat is 14 Q–N4, Q–Q2; 15 P–B3, and the Knight has no safe place to go.

13 ...   Q–N3

This parries both threats, but only momentarily. If now 14 P–B3,

14 ... P–B5 ch forces White to take care of the check and frees Black's QB4 square for the retreat of the Knight.

If instead, 13 ... N–N4, White can win a Pawn or more in two ways: (a) 14 BxP, RxR; 15 QxP ch, etc., or (b) 14 Q–N4, N–B2; 15 QxP ch.

Note that 13 ... Q–Q2 loses because of 14 P–B3.

    14 B–K3

This renews the threat of 15 P–B3, since now Black will not be able to answer 15 ... P–B5.

    14 ...   B–K2
    15 Q–N4

Again threatening to win the Knight by 16 P–B3 and the KNP by 16 QxP.

    15 ...   O–O

A little better would have been 15 ... K–Q2, since it would not have been wise for White to take Black's NP, as this would give his opponent a fine file for a K-side attack. In that case, White also continues by 16 P–B3 and after 16 ... P–R4; 17 Q–N6, P–Q5, White wins his piece by 18 B–B1!, but not under such favorable circumstances as in the game.

    16 P–B3

Now Black must lose a piece.

    16 ...   P–Q5

If 16 ... P–KR4, White must play 17 Q–N6!, for if 17 QxRP, R–B4, and the Knight can move to N4 in safety.

    17 B–R6   Resigns

After 17 ... R–B2; 18 QxN, attacking the QR, or 18 PxN, and there is no compensation for the lost piece.

The main reason for the rapid loss of this game by the amateur is his lack of theoretical knowledge of this modern variation of the Ruy Lopez. One must be a very strong player to be able to judge from the position that 9 ... N–QR4 is dubious. After the amateur had made this bad move, he could not retrieve his position, and his game deteriorated.

Game 6

The general strategy of a K-side attack can be clearly described, but the details of the execution must be carefully checked from a tactical standpoint.

To undertake a K-side attack, a player must have control of the center, or at least have the center stabilized so that his opponent cannot start any serious action there. The opponent must have some weakness or some point of attack on his K side.

Once these two conditions exist, the general technique of the K-side attack is as follows:

(1) Get as many pieces as possible available for immediate play.

(2) Open as many lines as possible—both files and diagonals.

(3) Bring the pieces, one after the other, into increasingly favorable positions and when possible, with tempo, so that the opponent has no time to take necessary defensive measures on his K side.

(4) Sacrifice where necessary in order to bring the right pieces to the key squares.

(5) Harass the enemy King continually, strip him of all protection, making exchanges and sacrifices where feasible to accomplish this end.

(6) Make the optimum use of the threat.

The proper application of this technique gives the opponent no opportunity to bring his own pieces into the fray, the threats become overwhelming, and the enemy King is often caught in an inexorable net.

Ruy Lopez: Closed Variation (5 ... B–K2)

Master	Amateur
White	*Black*
1 P–K4	P K4
2 N–KB3	N–QB3
3 B–N5	P–QR3
4 B–R4	N–B3
5 O–O	

The Ruy López. For the basic ideas behind this opening, see Game 5.

At this point, the opening branches off into two main systems: (a) the counterattack or open variation (Game 5); and (b) the closed defense (present game).

5 ...   B–K2

The basic idea behind the closed variation is to complete the development as rapidly as possible. Black builds up a solid position and hopes to be able to maintain the center, that is, to keep his KP on its K4.

Other possibilities:

(a) 5 ... NxP, which opens the K file, loses a tempo, and affords White direct attacking chances, as shown in Game 5.

(b) 5 ... B–B4, which gives White the opportunity to make a sham sacrifice by the use of the fork trick after 6 NxP, NxN; 7 P–Q4. This does not, however, lead to any advantage after 7 ... NxP; 8 Q–K2, B–K2; 9 QxN, N–N3. Theory, therefore, prefers 6 P–B3 instead of the sham sacrifice.

6 Q–K2

The Worrall Attack. This move has two purposes: (a) White protects his KP and now threatens to win a Pawn by BxN, followed by NxP; e.g., 6 ... O–O?; 7 BxN, QPxB; 8 NxP, Q–Q5; 9 N–B3, and now 9 ... QxKP would lose a piece after 10 QxQ, NxQ; 11 R–K1 (11 ... P–KB4; 12 P–Q3); (b) he makes room for his KR at Q1, where it will take an active part in controlling the Q file.

Here, White could equally well have played the main line 6 R–K1 with the same threat. It is important to have the White KP protected. Which line one chooses is a matter of taste or temperament, but the text (Q–K2, R–Q1) requires one more move than 6 R–K1 to accomplish the same purpose. In any case, White's KB1 must be vacated in order to bring his QN there later.

Other moves, such as 6 N–B3 and 6 P–Q3, are not as sharp and enable Black to attain his goal in a simpler way; e.g., 6 P–Q3, P–QN4 (to avoid the loss of the KP); 7 B–N3, P–Q3, etc. However, the fact that the moves are less sharp does not mean that they would be inferior. It means only that Black is not already confronted with difficult problems in the very first phase of the game.

Note that 6 BxN followed by 7 NxP would not harm Black, who would then have at his disposal both 7 . . . NxP and 7 . . . Q–Q5.

6 . . .   P–QN4

As in Game 5, Black postpones . . . P–QN4 until the last possible moment, since White's KB is more directly active on its QN3 (from which point it attacks Black's KB2) than on its QR4. However, the attack of the White Bishop on Black's KB2 is no longer significant, now that Black is able to castle.

7 B–N3   O–O
8 P–B3

Prepares for the push P–Q4 and makes a place for White's KB, which might be attacked after . . . N–QR4. The White KB is the so-called "attacking Bishop." In general, it is not favorable to exchange a Bishop for a Knight, but it is still worse to permit the exchange of the "attacking Bishop" for a Knight. True, the attacking possibilities of this Bishop are not very clear here, but they generally reveal themselves in the long run.

8 . . .   P–Q3

Black, who is eager to maintain his Pawn at K4, builds up a solid Pawn phalanx. This is the obvious move to complete the development.

At this point 8 . . . P–Q4 is generally preferred. The game would then continue in gambit style as follows: 9 PxP(?),

(1) 9 . . . NxP; 10 NxP, N–B5!; 11 Q–K4, NxN;

(1a) 12 QxN (either), B–Q3! with winning attack;

(1b) 12 QxR, Q–Q6 with winning attack;

(1c) 12 P–Q4!, B–N2!; 13 QxB, N–K7 ch; 14 K–R1, NxB; 15 RxN, N–Q6; 16 R–B1, P–QB4 (even).

(2) 9 . . . B–KN5; 10 PxN, P–K5; 11 P–Q4, PxN; 12 PxP, B–R4, with excellent chances for Black.

These variations are difficult to follow, but they give an idea of the complications that may arise. In practice, White always declines the gambit by 9 P–Q3.

9 P–Q4

White takes possession of the center despite the possibility of a Black attack by . . . B–N5. Very often, White plays 9 P–KR3 in order to prevent the pin that follows.

9 . . .   B–N5

An attack on the White center—
Black pins the White Knight and
threatens to win a Pawn by 10 ...
PxP; 11 PxP, NxN.

White must meet the threat. He
has various possibilities. Let us examine the main ones:

(1)

10 B–K3,
 (1a) 10 ... PxP; 11 PxP, N–
 QR4; 12 B–B2, N–B5; 13 B–
 B1 (even);
 (1b) 10 ... NxKP; 11 B–Q5,
 Q–Q2 (a sham sacrifice); 12
 BxN(4), P–Q4; 13 B–B2, P–
 K5 (Black is a little better off).

(2)

10 R–Q1,
 (2a) 10 ... PxP; 11 PxP, P–Q4;
 12 P–K5, N–K5; 13 N–B3,
 NxN; 14 PxN, N–R4; 15 B–
 B2, Q–Q2 (even—theory);
 (2b) 10 ... Q–B1—a try to maintain the center—not bad, but
 not ordinarily applied in master
 practice.

In each of these variations, practice has shown that Black's position is sound because of his strong
B(KN5). For this reason, White
chooses a variation that locks the
center so that he no longer has to
worry about it.

10 P–Q5

In this position, Black's B(KN5)
is no longer so powerful. The point
is that White can always drive away
the Bishop by P–KR3–KN4. Such
moves weaken White's K side if

the position is open, but *not* if the
position is closed, as it is after
White's 10th move.

This move eases the tension in
the center, and under certain circumstances Black could attack the
spearhead Pawn at Q5 by ... P–
QB3, thus practically forcing the
exchange of Pawns, and should
Black later succeed in carrying
through the advance ... P–Q4, he
obtains a majority in the center.
If he does not succeed, he has a
backward Pawn on an open file.

10 ...   N–QR4

Black must move his Knight, and
by going to his QR4, he (a) makes
White waste a move to avoid ex-
changing his Bishop for Black's
Knight; (b) gives himself the pos-
sibility of playing the Knight via
N2 to better squares, such as his
QB4.

As noted in the previous game,
this Knight move is generally good
and serves two purposes: (a) to
drive back the White Bishop; (b)
to make room for the advance ...
P–QB4.

11 B–B2

The game has now entered a new phase. With a stable center, each side can begin to formulate plans.

White will aim for a K-side attack to be realized by P–KR3, P–KN4, N–Q2–B1–N3–B5 over a period of time. White's KB will play a part in this plan only if Black tries to attack the White center by P–KB4 or by P–Q4 (after having exchanged his QBP for White's QP).

Black will aim for a Q-side attack to be carried out by an advance of his Q-side Pawns. The details of Black's strategy cannot be as clearly outlined as those of White's.

11 . . .   P–B4

Perhaps better was 11 . . . P–B3, in order to more or less force White to reply 12 PxP, a reply that White has the option of playing after the text (12 PxP e.p.), after which Black is left with a backward QP, but he will always be able to push this backward QP, and he need not be in a hurry to retake with . . . NxP, but can first prepare for . . . P–Q4; e.g., 12 . . . Q–B2; 13 R–Q1, QR–Q1.

12 P–KR3

The first step in White's strategy of attacking Black's K side. This move also leads to the elimination of Black's pin on White's KN.

Black now has a choice of three moves: (a) 12 . . . BxN, which would leave White with the Two Bishops, only a small advantage in this closed position; (b) 12 . . .

B–Q2, generally preferred because in the present setup, Black's QB has little further to do on the K side and is somewhat in the way; (c) the text, 12 . . . B–R4.

12 . . .   B–R4

The disadvantage of this move is that first of all the QB can be more active on its Q2 square, second, that it may be in the way on this side of the board. On its KR4, it blocks the execution of the maneuver N–KR4–B5, and third, if it goes to its KN3 and if Black wishes to play . . . R–K1, . . . B–B1, . . . P–KN3, and . . . B–N2, as is sometimes done in this variation, the QB on KN3 would be in the way also.

13 QN–Q2

The second step in White's outlined strategy. The Knight will go to KB1 and then either to K3 or KN3, a regular procedure for the QN in the Ruy Lopez.

13 . . .   R–K1

The KR vacates KB1 in order to make room for the Bishop, which can protect Black's KN2. The Bishop is in the way, anyhow.

14 R–Q1

To make room for the Knight at KB1.

14 . . .   B–B1
15 N–B1

According to plan.

15 . . .   P–B5

The beginning of Black's attack on the Q side. He clears his QB4 square for the Knight.

16 ... P-KN4

White pushes at this point, rather than earlier, because he has to reckon with the possibility of Black's sacrifice ... NxNP. Now White has a strong defender of the K side in his N(KB1).

White delays playing N-K3 or N-N3 until he has pushed his KNP, because his attack is stronger with the KNP on KN4. If he can now bring his QN to KB5 and it is exchanged for the Black Bishop, he can retake with the KNP, thus opening the KN file for an attack against the castled King.

16 ...   B-N3
17 N-N3   N-N2

The Knight will go to its QB4, where it will occupy a strong position.

18 K-R2

To make a place for the Rook on the KN file in case that file is opened by N-B5, BxN; NPxB.

18 ...   N-B4

White's KP is now attacked three times and defended three times.

19 B-N5

One could expect 19 N-B5 here, but the text appears to be a bit stronger. White takes advantage of Black's 14 ... B-B1 to pin Black's KN.

19 ...   B-K2

It is true that the Bishop has to return to the K2 square from which it went in move 14, but this Black could not foresee at the time. Besides, 19 ... B-K2 entails the indirect-attack threat of ... NxQP, as we shall see.

20 N-B5

White's QN has finally attained the desired position in the enemy territory, where it brings pressure against the K wing and threatens to renew the pin against the Black Knight after NxB.

Steinitz, the founder of positional play, discovered during the second half of the nineteenth century the value of closing the center and then making a K-side attack by pushing the K-side pawns.

White's Knight looks very strong at its KB5, but the position loses a Pawn for White, as will soon be seen.

20 ...   BxN

Black hopes to win a Pawn by surprise. But first he must remove the Knight, for if 20 ... NxQP immediately, White replies 21 BxB, NxB; 22 NxQP, etc. But in removing the Knight, he gives White the open KN file to use for attack.

Without the prospect of winning a Pawn, Black would have perhaps chosen a later time for the exchange or not exchanged at all. The pressure of White's Knight is not yet overwhelming. Therefore Black does not yet feel the necessity of exchanging.

21 NPxB

White takes with the NP, rather than with the KP, since he wishes to open the KN file for attack.

21 ...   NxQP

A typical and well-known combination based on the indirect attack of the Black KB against the White QB. This is also possible in the form . . . N–N5 ch, which does not win a Pawn and is not advantageous to Black, either.

Now begins the struggle of the open file against the plus Pawn. The combination would have worked very well if Black had not been forced on the previous move to give his opponent the open KN file, which proves very strong for White.

22 BxB   NxB

Black now has the extra Pawn, but White has as compensation the open KN file.

White's strategy now is to occupy the KN file and concentrate all his forces against the Black King. He will bring his KR to KN1, and he has at his disposal the pos-

sible P–B6, although this is not so serious.

23 R–KN1

23 NxP looks tempting, but analysis shows that Black maintains his plus Pawn: 23 . . . NxBP!; 24 PxN, RxN or 24 NxKBP (desperado—White is trying to get the most he can for the piece he is bound to lose), KxN; 25 Q–R5 ch, P–N3; 26 QxP ch, N–N2, and White has insufficient compensation for the sacrificed piece.

23 ...   P–B3

Prevents P–B6. If 23 . . . K–R1; 24 N–N5!; R–KB1; 25 Q–R5.

24 N–R4

To open the diagonal for the Queen and strengthen the attack against Black's KRP and KNP.

24 ...   R–R2

White threatened to force a quick decision by 25 Q–N4. Now 25 Q–N4 could be answered by 25 . . . N–B1.

25 Q–R5

There is no direct threat here, but such a move must certainly cause the Black player some concern. In such positions, the indirect threat is often stronger than the direct, namely Q–N4.

     25 ...   P–(Q)4?

This is doubtful. Black hopes to get counterplay and at the same time rid himself of his backward Pawn. But Black is playing with lightning. Correct is 25 ... N–B1, after which White must play moves such as 26 R–N3, 27 QR–KN1, and perhaps at a suitable time R–N6. The fact that a forced win is not in the picture shows that the result of the struggle is still open. So we must not criticize Black's 20th and 21st moves too strongly.

     26 RxP ch

Under what circumstances can White consider such a sacrifice? (a) He has four powerful pieces, a Queen, a Knight, and two Rooks, in readiness against the hostile King position; (b) the King position, blocked by Black's own Knight, is poorly defended. Still, White must calculate accurately.

     26 ...   KxR
     27 R–N1 ch

White has fewer pieces, but all but his Bishop are mobilized for attack, whereas Black's pieces are relatively inactive. Also, Black's King is restricted and has no escape square. White must be very careful here (a) not to give Black a chance to mobilize his inactive pieces; (b) not to allow Black's King to escape.

What can Black do now? If (a) 27 ... K–B1; 28 Q R6 ch, followed by mate; (b) 27 ... N–N3; 28 PxN, P–R3 and (1) 29 N–B5 ch or (2) 29 QxP ch!!, KxQ; 30 N–B5 ch, K–R5; 31 B–Q1 mate.

So Black plays

     27 ...   K–R1
     28 Q–R6

Threatening mate on the next move by both 29 Q–N7 and 29 QxBP, and 29 ... N–N1 fails against 30 N–N6 mate.

Apparently strong, 28 Q–B7 is doubtful because of 28 ... NxP; 29 QxR, R–K2; 30 QxN, NxN.

     28 ...   NxBP

Black is compelled to offer to give back his extra piece, and his King is still in a very precarious position.

White, despite his strong attack, now finds himself in a dilemma well known to chess players. If he accepts Black's Knight, he has the attack, and he is down the exchange. But Black has now opened up enough lines so that his pieces can come to the defense of his beleaguered King, and he can almost force the exchange of some of White's attacking pieces, so that the White attack will be seriously reduced. For instance: 29 NxN, R–N1, or 29 PxN, R–N1; 30 N–N6 ch, RxN; 31 PxR, P–K5!; 32 P–N7 ch, K–N1, and White has no clear-cut continuation.

Therefore, White must find a more forceful way of exploiting his advantage, and this lies in the possibilities of giving double check. It should be noted that in some variations, White's Bishop seems to revive and exert some attacking force.

29 N–N6 ch   K–N1
30 N–K7 dbl ch

The double check prevents Black from interposing on his KN2, and the White Knight cuts off Black's defense of his KBP. Notice that after 30 NxP dis ch, Black interposes his Rook or his Knight, and White has no winning continuation.

30 ...   K–B2

The only move. If 30 ... K–R1; 31 QxBP ch.

31 QxRP ch   K–K3
32 QxN ch

32 ...   K–Q3?

If 32 ... KxN; 33 R–N7 ch wins the Black QR and gives White control of his 7th rank. Still, this would have been slightly better for Black than the text. The game might have continued 33 ... K–Q3; 34 RxR, PxP; 35 P–N4!, PxP e.p., (35 ... N–Q6; 36 RxP ch); 36 PxP, and (a) White is only one Pawn down; (b) the Black King is in a very unsafe position, cut off from its 2nd rank and standing on its 3rd rank; (c) White threatens 37 P–N4 followed by 38 RxP ch; (d) White also threatens 37 BxP, winning back the Pawn with still more threats; (e) Black has no relieving moves, such as 36 ... R–K2 or 36 ... Q–B1; 37 QxBP ch, etc. Therefore, White must win, but not without a struggle. As in so many cases, Black goes wrong because he is materially minded. His advantage of the exchange does not mean much.

33 QxBP ch   K–B2

If 33 ... N–K3; 34 N–B5 ch, followed by either (a) 34 ... K–B2; 35 QxKP ch wins but not

easily; or (b) 34 ... K–B3; 35
PxP ch, QxP; 36 R–Q1, Q–B4 (36
... Q–B6?; 37 N–K7 ch); 37 R–
Q6 ch.

34 R–N7

Closing in. The immediate 34 Q–
B6 ch leads nowhere. The move
34 NxP ch also wins, but not as
quickly.

34 ...   N–Q2

What else? White threatened to
win the Queen by 35 N–B6 dis ch.

35 NxP ch   K–N2
36 Q–Q6

Threatening among other things
37 RxN ch.

36 ...   K–R1
37 RxN

White can afford to sacrifice the
exchange, because he gets a full
Rook back.

37 ...   RxR

If 37 ... QxR; 38 N–N6 ch,
winning the Queen.

38 N–N6 ch   K–N2
39 NxR   R–R1

With some faint hope of starting
a counterattack.

40 N–B5 ch   K–B1
41 QxP ch   Resigns

For if 41 ... K–B2; 42 N–K6 ch,
winning the Queen.

Although the White Bishop
played no direct part in the attack,
it did have an indirect influence.
As soon as Black tried to attack the
White center, White's Bishop could
come into action. In this game, it
worked as a preventive, that is, it
prevented Black from taking counteraction.

Up to his 24th move, the amateur played a good enterprising
game. He treated the opening fairly
well and played a little trick on
his opponent by taking one of his
Pawns. Perhaps he was not sufficiently aware that, in compensation, White would get a very strong
attack along the open file. But more
in this game than in the previous
ones, the amateur showed initiative,
while his defense, far from being
perfect, makes a good impression
in general.

The whole game was changed
because White sacrificed a Pawn.
If Black had not permitted the
sacrifice, both players would have
continued applying pressure, White
on the K side, Black on the Q side.

In practice, a Pawn sacrifice
often gives chances and therefore
should not be judged by its absolute correctness. Chess is a game—
not a mathematical formula—and
not even a game for a computer.

Game 7

Opposed to the brilliant combinational play that features daring sacrifices and all-out attack is the quiet positional play that consists of a slow accumulation of small advantages.

In positional play there are no deep combinations, no hidden attacks. Black, as a positional player, simply first attains equality, then plays the pieces in the right places so that they are available for action when the time comes.

Positional technique is less spectacular than combinational, but more subtle and therefore perhaps harder to meet. For an amateur it is sometimes more difficult to resist the slow, insidious grip of the snake than the direct and forceful attacks of the lion. That explains why champions like Smyslov, Petrosian, and Capablanca had such very high scores against the weaker part of the tournament family.

The amateur knows that any initiative, any advance, may create weaknesses and present a welcome target to a capable opponent. In his fear to undertake something that might compromise his position, he can easily go too far in the opposite direction, and that is exactly what happens in this game. White builds up a solid position, but he fails to take the initiative. Instead, he makes waiting moves, while his opponent continually strengthens his position and is the first to make threats that cannot be parried and are so strong that the material relation is disturbed. Only

after the loss of two Pawns does the amateur realize that he has to play
his game, but then, of course, it is already too late.

Ruy Lopez: Steinitz Variation

Amateur	Master
White	Black
1 P–K4	P–K4
2 N–KB3	N–QB3
3 B–N5	N–B3

The Berlin Variation of the Ruy
Lopez.

This appears to be an excellent
reply. It develops an important
Knight to the natural square and
attacks the White KP. Emanuel
Lasker considered it the best continuation. Capablanca played the
move in connection with 4 ... P–
Q3, as illustrated in this game. Yet,
experience has shown that Black
may get a cramped game with this
system. This did not, however, prevent the older generation from playing it.

At present, the general opinion
is that 3 ... P–QR3; 4 B–R4, N–
B3, etc. (see Games 5 and 6) give
Black a freer game with more possibilities of counterattack.

Research on chess openings is
continually changing the opinions
of masters concerning the relative
strength of the various lines. The
relative strength of a variation of
a given opening depends on the
line chosen and on the point at
which theoretical research on that
line is at a given time. For instance,
in the Morphy Variation of the
Ruy Lopez, after 3 ... P–QR3;
4 B–R4, N–B3; 5 O–O, there

were times when both 5 ... NxP
(Game 5) and 5 ... B–K2 (Game
6) were considered very bad, and
certain players preferred other lines,
among them 3 ... N–B3. Today,
the moves 5 ... NxP and 5 ...
B–K2 of the Morphy line are considered strong and solid.

4 O–O

White makes a developing move
and indirectly protects his KP, for
after 4 ... NxP he can regain the
Pawn by 5 R–K1 (or by 5 Q–K2
or 5 BxN), as 5 ... P–Q4 is not
recommendable because of 6 NxP.
In practice, another variation is
preferred after 4 ... NxP, e.g., 5
P–Q4, B–K2 (5 ... PxP; 6 R–K1
is very risky for Black); 6 Q–K2,
N–Q3; 7 BxN, NPxB; 8 PxP, N–
N2 (the Rio de Janeiro Variation),
and White has won back his Pawn
with possibly a slightly better position, but the game is not simple.
The reason that the White player
rejects the simple line 5 R–K1 is
that this move may lead to simplification and drawing positions.

4 ...   P–Q3

By a transposition of moves, we
have reached the Steinitz Variation
of the Ruy Lopez, which is considered to give Black fewer chances
for counterplay than many other
lines. A general disadvantage of 4
... P–Q3 is that the Black KB is

shut in by this move. In many cases, this is unavoidable in playing the Black pieces. In general, the Black player is not in a position to seize the initiative, and in most cases he must be satisfied with a cramped but solid game. This does not mean that Black should play for a draw, but he should avoid risky variations arising from attempts to gain immediate equality or to seize the initiative prematurely, and he may well simplify as quickly as possible in order to prevent White from gaining too much initiative.

Black could also play 4 ... NxP, already discussed under White's 4th move, or 4 ... B–B4, after which the sham sacrifice 5 NxP leads to only an equal game: 5 ... NxN; 6 P–Q4, NxP; 7 Q–K2, Q–K2; 8 QxN, N–N3!

5 P–Q4

The logical continuation—a developing move combined with a threat. White threatens to win a Pawn by 6 PxP. For instance, 5 ... B–N5; 6 PxP, after which 6 ... PxP would lose a Pawn as follows: 7 BxN ch, PxB; 8 QxQ ch, RxQ; 9 NxP.

On the other hand, it should be noted that Black cannot take White's KP. If 5 ... NxP; 6 P–Q5!, P–QR3; 7 B–Q3, attacking both Knights at the same time and winning a piece.

Let us consider the effect of White's move 6 P–Q5 after another reply by Black on his 5th move, 5 ... B–N5; 6 P–Q5—in general, if you attack a pinned piece, you win

it. However, in this given situation, Black has a way out. Note that this type of position often occurs in games, be it on the Q side or on the K side. 6 ... P–QR3 (the only correct move). White now has the choice between: (a) 7 B–R4, P–QN4; 8 PxN, PxB, and White has nothing; before he tries to win the weak Black RP, he first has to protect his own KP, and besides, his own P(QB6) is just as weak as the Black double RP. (b) 7 PxN, PxB; 8 PxP, R–QN1. This looks promising, but a very simple examination of the position shows that White cannot defend his Pawn. (c) 7 BxN ch, PxB; 8 PxP, NxP, and Black's Pawns are certainly better than White's. This means that 6 P–Q5 is not a real threat; it only restricts Black's possibilities, as we have seen after 5 ... NxP.

5 ...   B–Q2

Black prefers to unpin his QN at once, thus parrying the threat 6 PxP and eliminating the sham threat 6 P–Q5.

6 N–B3

White develops an important piece and at the same time protects his KP.

6 ...   B–K2

Black need not fear 7 BxN, BxB; 8 PxP, since Black can take White's KP: 8 ... PxP; 9 NxP, BxP; 10 NxB, NxN, with an equal game.

Black could also have played 6 ... PxP, which is called "giving up the center," that is, in this case being content with a Pawn on the 3rd rank when the opponent has a Pawn on the 4th rank. As a general rule, it is best not to give up the center unless it is absolutely necessary.

7 R–K1

Now that his KP is protected by his Rook, White threatens to win a Pawn by BxN, followed by PxP; thus: 7 ... O–O? is a well-known mistake, as can be seen from the following variation: 8 BxN, BxB; 9 PxP, PxP; 10 QxQ, and

(a) 10 ... QRxQ; 11 NxP, BxP; 12 NxB, NxN; 13 N–Q3, P–KB4; 14 P–KB3, B–B4 ch; 15 NxB (now 15 K–B1? would be answered by 15 ... B–N3! and 16 PxN, PxP dis ch does not lead to anything), NxN; 16 B–N5, R–Q4; 17 B–K7, followed by 18 P–QB4, and Black stands to lose at least the exchange.

(b) 10 ... KRxQ; 11 NxP, BxP; 12 NxB, NxN (now White cannot retake on account of mate on his 1st rank); 13 N–Q3!, P–KB4; 14 P–KB3, B–B4 ch; 15 K–B1, and Black stands to lose material.

On comparing the way in which

White plays in the two variations above, we notice the remarkable fact that whether it is Black's KR or QR that is on his Q1 makes a fundamental difference in White's counterplay. That is the characteristic thing about combinations: one slight change in the position makes matters quite different.

Here is a clear example of a position in which Black is forced to give up the center.

7 ...   PxP

Black is forced to give up the center because of White's threat. White now has a slight advantage.

8 NxP

White has a free game—he occupies all four White ranks; Black occupies only his first three ranks. But White's problem is: (a) how to profit by this advantage (attack after careful preparation); (b) how to maintain the advantage, which disappears almost automatically—as in the game—as soon as Black plays ... P–Q4, after which White has nothing.

8 ...   O–O

White's strategy should now be: (a) to prevent Black from playing ... P–Q4; (b) to develop his pieces carefully; (c) much later to prepare a K-side attack.

Black's strategy must be: (a) to exchange pieces; (b) to realize ... P–Q4 and thus open his game.

White's next move is difficult to find. He plays

9 B–B1

This avoids the exchange of both White's Bishop and his Knight, for otherwise Black would have played ... NxN, etc. In general, every exchange is in favor of the player who commands less space.

Perhaps better was 9 BxN in order to double Black's Pawns. This is the most accepted line, and the continuation could be: 9 ... PxB; 10 B–N5, P–KR3; 11 B–R4, N–R2; 12 BxB, QxB. Also is played 9 NxN, PxN; 10 B–Q3. Just as in the 9 BxN variation, Black has some compensation for his weakened Pawn position in the open N file.

The move 9 P–B4, which looks aggressive, must not be undertaken without careful analysis, for it may weaken the position; e.g., 9 ... NxN; 10 QxN, BxB; 11 NxB, P–Q4! followed by (a) 12 P–K5, N–K5, threatening ... B–B4! or (b) 12 PxP, NxP, and if 13 P–B4, N–N5. It is evident that the diagonal KN1–QB5, which is opened by White's 9 P–B4, can be favorable for Black, and besides, the PKB4 hampers White's QB. A move like P–KB4 is valid only if White is sure to maintain the PK4–PKB4 front, which under some circumstances can be used as a base of a K-side attack.

9 ...   NxN

As already noted, every exchange favors Black in this position. That does not mean that Black would obtain an advantage by such an exchange. It simply enables him to move more freely. But by the same token, it cuts down the possibility of a White attack and more nearly equalizes the two positions.

10 QxN

Through this move, the amateur has treated the game as a master, but this was not too difficult, since he has simply followed the recommendations of theory. Now he is on his own, and he must know what to do with the position. But he apparently does not know. He simply waits until Black has annihilated his preponderance in the center. He fails to see that the whole struggle in this phase of the game revolves around the possibility of Black's being able to push his QP.

10 ...   R–K1

Black exerts some indirect pressure on the K file. By indirect pressure is meant pressure that will make itself felt when an intervening piece on the open line has been moved elsewhere. Indirect attacks can be very treacherous. When the masking piece moves, the indirect threat becomes a direct threat. This will be illustrated in the continuation of the game.

11 P–B3

White appears to be building up a Pawn wall in order to prevent Black from attacking. But the move lacks positive force. If Black succeeds in attaining ... P–Q4, then P–B3 will prove to be weak. Also, the diagonal KN1–QB5 now opened by White may turn out to be favorable for Black.

Possible here would have been 11 P–QN3, preparing the fianchetto of the White QB.

Also, the natural 11 B–KN5, possibly followed by 12 QR–Q1, would have been sufficient for good equality.

11 ...   B–K3

Black is very clearly preparing for ... P–Q4, which will open his game and give him full equality.

12 Q–B2

A timid move, but not too bad. White is afraid to keep his Queen on Q4, since he fears that Black, after P–Q4, will follow up with ... P–QB4 and ... P–Q5. White intends to answer 12 ... P–Q4 by 13 P–K5, N–Q2; 14 P–B4 with a powerful attack, as he has a mobile majority of Pawns on the K side.

If White had played 12 R–Q1, Black would have prepared his ... P–Q4 by 12 ... P–B3, just as in the text.

12 B–KN5 leads to full equality after 12 ... P–Q4; 13 PxP, NxP; 14 BxB, NxB.

12 ...   P–B3!

This weakens Black's QP, but it assures Black the possibility of exe-

cuting the push ... P–Q4 whenever he desires. We have seen that an immediate advance does not mean much (12 ... P–Q4; 13 P–K5.) However, after the exchange of Queens (... Q–N3!), the push could become rather strong. All this is shown in the continuation of the game.

13 B–Q2

To discourage Black from playing ... Q–R4, but Black is not interested in playing ... Q–R4. The normal reply would have been 13 B–K3, in order to prevent the exchange of Queens.

13 ...   Q–N3!

Black's ultimate aim is to play ... P–Q4 and gain equality in the center. If Black pushes his QP at this point, White can either take or advance his own KP. It is important to examine both possibilities with care. As long as the Queens are on the board, the advance is better for White, because it means the realization of the majority of Pawns on the K side, and as such, is a powerful weapon in the attack against the hostile King. With the Queens off the board, such a K-side attack is generally out of the question, and an advance of Pawns leads in most cases only to weaknesses that can be exploited by the defending player.

By 13 ... Q–N3, Black makes possible an exchange of Queens in order to render ineffective the White attack by P–K5 after Black's ... P–Q4. The Queen, as the most important piece, takes the greatest part in the mating attack. Without Queens, it is almost impossible to attack successfully against a King defended by a Pawn wall, and that is why exchanging Queens means so much, under the circumstances.

14 N–R4?

This move protects White's QNP, which is being attacked, and threatens the Black Queen, but it removes the Knight from the center of the board and takes away the pressure that the Knight was exerting on White's Q5 square.

White was afraid to play 14 QxQ, because after 14 . . . RPxQ, Black has a half-open file that compensates for his doubled Pawn but not more than that. But if White then answers now or later P–QR3, he has no particular difficulty because of Black's half-open file.

14 . . .   QxQ ch

According to plan, Black exchanges and then pushes his QP.

15 KxQ

By a series of very simple moves, Black has made possible his own strategy (. . . P–Q4) and has left White with two significant weaknesses: (a) White's Knight is temporarily out of play; (b) his King is on an open diagonal that will soon be available to Black and is somewhat hemmed in by his own Pawns.

15 . . .   P–Q4!

Black has finally attained . . . P–Q4, which now gives him more than equality because of White's two weaknesses.

16 P–K5?

This looks strong because it stations a Pawn in enemy territory and mobilizes the K-side majority, but we have already learned that without Queens such a push loses in importance, because no mating attack is involved. In addition, the Pawn is weak as long as it is not supported by the KBP, and we shall see from the game that it is not easy to add the needed protection by P–KB4.

If White had realized that he had missed his chance to take advantage of his preponderance in space, he would have played for simplification at once by exchanging Pawns. Instead, White still thinks that on the basis of his opening he has the right and perhaps the duty to undertake something. But there is no basis for that at all. White has already destroyed that possibility by allowing the advance of the Black QP.

After 16 PxP, NxP; 17 P–QB4, N–N5, Black is only a little better off than White—his minor pieces are more centralized and more co-operative. After a series of color-less moves, it could not be ex-pected that White would be able to attain complete equality.

16 ...   N–Q2

Now White's KP is indirectly at-tacked, that is, once the two Black Bishops leave the K file with tempo, White's KP will be threatened. Also, the White King is in a rather uncomfortable and restricted posi-tion. So White is faced with two problems: (a) how to avoid the loss of a Pawn after ... P–QN4, ... B–QB4 ch, and ... B–KB4 (see the game); and (b) how to avoid the displacement of his King after ... P–QN4 and ... B–QB4 ch.

17 P–KN3

White sees the distant danger of the restricted King position, but not the immediate danger to his KP. He does not realize that both Bishops, which mask the threat ... RxP, can move away with tempo.

The reply 17 P–KB4 also en-tails difficulties: 17 ... P–QN4; 18 N–B3, B–B4 ch; 19 K–B3 (19 B–K3?, P–Q5!), P–N4! and if 20 PxP, B–B4! and the King is in a bad position and exposed to attack by minor pieces, since the King is no longer protected by Pawns.

Note that 17 P–KN4, preventing ... B–KB4 and making room for the King, would be a blunder on account of 17 ... B–R5 ch.

17 ...   B–KB4

Winning a tempo with the attack against the QBP.

18 QR–B1

White is obliged to relegate the QR to the duty of protecting the QBP because of 18 P–B3, P–QN4, and the White Knight is lost.

After 18 B–Q3, BxB; 19 PxB, P–QN4; 20 N–B3, B–B4 ch, Black wins the KP just as in the game. After 18 P–QB4, PxP; 19 BxP?, P–QN4, he wins a piece.

18 ...   P–QN4

To secure his QB4 square for his KB.

19 N–B3   B–B4 ch

In a marvelously simple and clear manner Black has increased his positional advantage to the point where he wins a Pawn. Both Bishops were played with tempo, and thus Black's indirect attack on White's KP was converted into a direct attack that White could not parry because of the necessity of taking care of the threats made by the Black Bishops.

20 K–N2   NxP

It was the indirect threat initiated against the White KP in move 10 that has led to the winning of this Pawn. But Black has not only won a Pawn; he has also maintained the initiative.

Compare this position with that of eight or ten moves earlier. Black has extended his forces enormously. Now Black occupies four ranks, White only three.

21 P–KN4

White, who has been ultracautious so far, now throws caution to the winds and makes a brutal attempt to regain the lost terrain. The text is neither good nor bad, since White is lost anyway. It has the advantage of giving White the initiative for just a few moves.

21 ...   B–N3
22 K–N3

Affords added protection to the KNP, so that now White threatens 23 P–B4 followed by 24 P–B5. An immediate 22 P–B4 is refuted by 22 ... NxP.

22 ...   P–KR4

To parry the threat.

23 B–KB4

To drive back the strong Knight.

23 ...   P–B3

Protects the Knight and opens a second square of retreat for the Bishop.

24 BxN

To get rid of a troublesome piece that might make moves such as ... N–B5, and to be able to play B–Q3.

24 ...   PxB

The exchange gives Black a strong Pawn center.

25 B–Q3

Despite the fact that he would be left with an isolated Pawn should Black exchange, White offers the Bishop exchange in order to eliminate the Two Bishops and to free the QR from defending the QBP. If Black should exchange, White's QR is on just the right file (25 ... BxB; 26 PxB threatens 27 NxNP or NxQP).

25 ...   B–B2

Naturally Black does not wish to activate White's QR.

26 P–N5

Threatening 27 P–N6 and after 27 ... B–K3, 28 RxP.

26 ...   P–N3

To meet the threat.

27 R–K2

Preparing to double his Rooks.

27 ...   B–Q3

Protects the center and at the same time threatens to win a piece by 28 ... P–K5 dis ch.

28 K–N2   K–N2
29 QR–K1

At last all White's pieces are working!

White has finally freed his game, but at the cost of a weak KBP and certain other disadvantages, namely, that Black has the Two Bishops and full occupation of the center. This means that his Bishops are not permanently blocked by Pawns as long as the center remains mobile. On the other hand, the mobility of White's minor pieces is limited.

29 ...   R–K2
30 N–Q1

In order to bring the Knight to better squares and to render ... B–N5 meaningless. Preferable was N–N1–Q2 to protect the KBP, which will soon become a serious weakness.

In accordance with the idea that one's strategy of attack should be focused on the weaknesses of one's opponent, Black now plays

30 ...   R–KB1

The beginning of an attack against White's backward KBP, which soon leads to the win of a second Pawn.

31 N–B2

White is looking for better squares for his Knight.

31 ...   B–K1

Making a place for the other Rook.

32 P–N3

Despair again. Perhaps White foresees 32 N–R3, R(2)–KB2; 33 N–N1, P–B4 (threatening to win a piece by 34 ... P–B5); 34 P–B3, B–B3. White is now in a hopeless position. Black has all kinds of threats: P–B5, P–Q5, P–K5, the last being the most vigorous: 35 ... P–K5; 36 PxP, PxP; 37 BxP, BxB ch; 38 RxB, R–B7 ch followed by mate. The sad thing is that White cannot strengthen his position in any way. Both 35 R–KB2 and R–KB1 are refuted by 35 ... P–K5. White now decides to give up a second Pawn in the hope of obtaining counterplay in some direction or other.

32 ...   R(K2)–KB2

Again the master's clear style—no deep combination, only playing the pieces in the right place—will lead to the win of another Pawn.

33 P–QB4

There was nothing better.

33 ...   RxP
34 PxQP   PxP
35 B–N1   B–B3

Again putting the pieces in the right place. Two Bishops and two Rooks are now directed against the White King—a tremendous concentration of force.

36 R–Q1   R(6)–B5
37 B–K4

White's last hope: 37 ... PxB; 38 RxB.

37 ...   B–B4!

Wins by force.

38 N–Q3

Other moves lose a piece.

38 ...   PxB
39 NxB   P–K6 dis ch
40 Resigns

For if 40 K–N1, R–N5 ch, etc., and if 40 K–N3, R–N5 ch; 41 K–R3, R–B6 mate.

The entire game is characterized by sound and simple play on the part of Black and hopeless efforts on the part of White to escape from his opponent's iron grip.

Game 8

The theory of the Dutch Defense

Attaining equality in the center

Placing Bishops and Knights on their most effective squares

Preventive strategy

Maintaining center tension

The consequences of aimless play

Conceiving and carrying out a long-term strategic plan

Creating and taking possession of a strong square

One of the most striking differences between master and amateur can be found in their conception and execution of strategy. The amateur gropes falteringly for a plan, often uncertain of what the correct strategy is, frequently failing to carry it out once it is conceived. The master comprehends the position as a whole and derives his strategy from the requirements of that position. He conceives a solid plan and then proceeds to execute it, making necessary allowances for and changes because of the tactical situations that arise. He plays each move with a purpose. It is not surprising, therefore, that his pieces are usually in just the right place to cooperate in a concerted assault against the opponent's weaknesses.

Not only does the amateur fall short in lacking a clearly outlined strategy of his own; by trying to avoid complications, he also tends to make it easier for his opponent to formulate his strategy. For instance, in general the amateur does not like unsolved tension on the board, because such a situation forces a player to take a host of possibilities into consideration in choosing a move and makes it much more difficult and sometimes even impossible to settle on a definite strategy. The amateur prefers to know what he is about. He therefore tends to dissipate the tension through Pawn exchanges, but in so doing he facilitates not only his own task but also that of his opponent. As long as tension exists and multiple possibilities remain, it is difficult to formulate a definite plan, but by eliminating the tension and establishing a stable position, the amateur gives his opponent the welcome opportunity to formulate a well-founded strategy.

Dutch Defense

Amateur	Master
White	*Black*

1 P–QB4

This move, which we have already seen in Game 3, is in accordance with the general principle of control of the center. It does not weaken the Q side in any way, and it exercises a measure of control over White's Q5 square. But it has the additional characteristic of being very flexible and leading to any number of openings.

1 ...   P–KB4

This move is also in accordance with the general principle of control of the center, since the Black KBP now exercises some control over its K5 square. Likewise, it may later become a spearhead of a Black attack against the White K side. But it may also constitute a weakness on the Black K side.

2 P–Q4

By a transposition of moves, we get the Dutch Defense.

The normal sequence for the Dutch Defense is 1 P–Q4, P–KB4, but many players hesitate to answer 1 P–Q4 directly by 1 ... P–KB4 because of 2 P–K4, the Staunton Gambit, which leads to very violent play. White gives up a Pawn for a strong attack. Both

Marshall and Denker have played the Staunton Gambit with great success.

2 ...   N–KB3

Black now exercises control over his K5 square with both his KN and his KBP.

3 N–QB3

White also makes a bid to secure some measure of control over his center squares K4 and Q5.

3 ...   P–KN3

The Leningrad Variation of the Dutch Defense, which develops the Black Bishop to KN2. The normal variation, 3 ... P–K3, is not inferior to the text.

4 N–B3   B–N2

This position is different from that in the King's Indian only in that Black has already played P–KB4, which has the advantage of exerting pressure on his K5 but the disadvantage that the Black center is weakened to some extent as long as Black has not succeeded in pushing his KP to its K4.

5 P–K3

White has the choice of developing his KB via K2 or KN2. Since the Black KBP is already on B4, the fianchetto P–KN3 followed by

6 B–N2 entails the disadvantage that Black might later launch an attack against it by pushing his KBP.

5 ...   ...

6 B–K2

In this type of opening, the KB is more useful at K2, where it might subsequently go to B3, than at Q3, where it would be directed against a chain of Pawns and might come into trouble if Black should eventually play ... P–K4 and thus threaten to fork by P–K5. On the other hand, 6 B–Q3 would eventually enable White himself to play P–K4 with advantages and disadvantages.

6 ...   P–K3

Black is planning ... P–K4 after due preparation, that is, after ... P–Q3 and ... QN–Q2.

Why he does not play 6 ... P–Q3 is instructive from a positional point of view. After 6 ... P–Q3; 7 P–Q5, P–K4; 8 PxP e.p., BxP, and White has the possibility of posting his Knight on Q5 after careful preparation and at some future time. The subsequent ex-

change on Q5 (... BxN; PxB) would leave Black with a backward Pawn on the QB file, and this Pawn could easily become the object of attack, since the file would then be open for White. If Black played ... P–B3 in order to drive the Knight away, Black's QP would then become weak. If after 6 ... P–Q3; 7 P–Q5, Black played 7 ... QN–Q2 with the intention of posting his Knight on his QB4, White would continue 8 N–Q4, and Black's K3 square would remain a constant nuisance to him.

7 O–O   P–Q3

8 B–Q2(?)

White's QB has to be developed either to Q2 or, in the other direction, to QN2 or QR3. On Q2 it strengthens the White position from a defensive point of view but not from an offensive point of view. Moreover, on Q2 the Bishop is in the way of other pieces such as the Queen and the KN. Therefore, it would be better to develop the Bishop in the other direction despite the fact that in that case Black can push his KP without further preparation: e.g., 8 P–QN3, P–K4; 9 PxP, PxP and if 10 NxP?, N–K5; 11 NxN, BxN. But instead of playing 10 NxP?, White should continue 10 B–R3 with a fine game: e.g., 10 ... R–K1; 11 QxQ, RxQ; 12 KR–Q1, R–K1; 13 N–Q5!, NxN; 14 PxN, and Black is in trouble because his QBP can easily become weak on the open file. This means that 8 ... P–K4 is premature. It is always risky to open the game as long as you are behind in development.

8 ...   QN–Q2

Preparing for ... P–K4.

9 R–B1   P–K4

In two moves Black has finally attained ... P–K4, thus achieving equality in the center. But because of the fact that his KBP stands on B4 next to the KP, he already has the initiative in the center.

10 Q–B2

With this move, White clears the first rank for the free movement of his Rooks and exerts pressure on the as yet closed QB file. This would be important if the QB file were open or half-open, but since it is still closed, White's move only keeps Black from wanting to open it by moves such as ... P–QB3 followed by ... P–Q4, but does not absolutely prevent him from doing so. Nonetheless, the text is not a bad move.

10 ...   P–B3

To prevent White from playing N–Q5, which is not worth much

under present circumstances, but might become strong in case of moves like ... Q–K2 or ... Q–K1, since ... NxN, PxN is then favorable to White in that it gives him an attack on the QB file.

The text move will not be followed by ... P–Q4 at present, since Black is not trying to open the file.

The opening is now completed, and there are no pressing tactical problems. At this point White therefore determines the general line along which his game is to be played—in other words, his strategy.

White considers two possible lines:

(a) 11 PxP, PxP; 12 KR–Q1. It should be noted that after this exchange in the center, the force of the Black ... P–K5 would be weakened a bit, since after the push the White Knight could be posted at White's Q4 square.

(b) 11 P–QN4, hoping to get a Q-side attack. He could follow it up with P–N5, and then Black could scarcely exchange Pawns, because the QB file, where White is so strong, would be opened.

One cannot say which system is best. Each has its advantages and disadvantages. But at this point White must look into the situation and get some idea of what he is planning and why. He chooses (b) and plays

11 P–QN4   P–K5

Black also makes an important strategic decision. He decides to play on the K side. By the advance of his KP, the center of gravitation is transferred to the K side, where he momentarily has an overwhelming amount of space.

12 N-K1

The Knight would be better situated on its Q2, where it might have gone had the QB been developed to N2.

12 ...   P-QR3

Black, not wishing to have his own strategy on the K side interrupted by the necessity of defending against White's strategy on the Q side, makes this move so as to be able to meet the White P-N5 more adequately. If White now plays P-N5, the QR file can be opened for Black.

13 P-QR4(?)

An unnecessary preparation. White was doubtless intimidated by Black's PQR3-PQN2-PQB3 formation, and he probably played 13 P-QR4 mechanically without even analyzing the results of 13 P-N5 and appraising the resultant position.

White could well have played an immediate 13 P-N5!, RPxP; 14 PxP. In that case, Black should have tried ... N-N3, followed by ... B-K3, in order to control the Black Q4 square. But in any case, White's battery along the QB file would have gained force. The game might have developed: 14 ... N-N3; 15 P-QR4, B-K3; 16 PxP, PxP; 17 P-R5, RxP (17 ... N-B5; 18 NxP wins a Pawn); 18

NxP, R-R7; 19 NxN ch, BxN; 20 Q-Q3, with chances for both sides.

13 ...   K-R1

To get the King out of the line of check by the Queen or KB in case White continues his advance P-N5, etc.

14 P-B3

Apparently White has forgotten about his plan to strike on the Q side with P-N5. Yet, the text is a good move. White strikes at the center, at the spearhead of Black's chain of Pawns. If Black answers 14 ... PxP, then 15 BxP and 16 P-K4 cannot be prevented. This gives reason to the strategy of attacking the spearhead instead of the base of Black's chain of Pawns. After all, the White pieces come into action rapidly.

If White does follow his original plan and plays 14 P-N5, Black is faced with some problems. Black should not open the QB file with 14 ... BPxP; 15 BPxP, for then the White doubling on the QB file has its justification. Even 14 ... RPxP; 15 BPxP is not trustworthy, for White has pressure against

Black's QB3 square and can take advantage of the half-open QB file. Best would be 14 ... P–B4, but in that case White would have succeeded in taking from Black his Q4 square and prevented him from playing ... P–Q4 to support his PK5.

14 ...   R–K1

To defend the Pawn on K5 and to make room for the Knight on KB1.

15 P–B4?

But White does not understand the strategic requirements of the position and by 15 P–B4 relieves the pressure in the center and therefore makes it easier for Black to formulate an overall plan, because he no longer has to take into account the vulnerability of his KP. Tension in the center should never be alleviated except when absolutely necessary.

White could have played 15 PxP, NxP; 16 NxN, PxN, and he would have had prospects on both sides. But White could also first have made the waiting move 15 K–R1 in order to exchange Pawns after Black had played 15 ... N–B1, which he would probably play in order to clear the diagonal for the Bishop, etc. After the exchange on White's K4, the best place for Black's QN is on his KB3. Note that White does not make this exchange as long as the Black QN can reach its KB3 in one move. But he does exchange after that Knight has gone to its KB1.

15 ...   N–B1

White's last move has made Black's center secure. Black now conceives a new strategy, a K-side attack, which will be to play ... P–KN4 after suitable preparation. This will be a kind of Pawn-chain strategy, where White's KB4, the spearhead of the Pawn chain, will be attacked, since the base of the chain, White's K3, is unattainable. Pawn-chain strategy will be discussed in detail in Game 19.

16 P–N3

To make a place for the Knight. Again, if White's QB had been developed to QN2, the KN could have gone to Q2 on the 12th move, and that would have been a much better square for it.

It should be noted that White has no really effective plan. In fact, he has no real plan at all. The amateur is groping, playing from move to move.

16 ...   B–K3

The QB must be developed. It now vacates the QB square for the QR, and from K3 it exercises pressure on White's QB4 square. As soon as Black can bring his Queen to KB2, White may be induced to advance his BP, thus securing Black's Q4 square for his QB.

Note that White's attacking plan on the Q side, once so promising, is already far less so: 17 P–N5, RPxP and (a) 18 BPxP, N–Q4, and Black has managed to occupy the strong center square; (b) 18

RPxP, Q–QB2, followed by 19 ...
Q–B2, and Black exerts pressure
against White's Pawn formation.

17 N–Q1

Planning N–B2–R3 and perhaps
N5.

17 ...   Q–K2

Connecting Rooks and affording
Black the possibility of playing ...
Q–KB2.

18 N–B2   P–R3

In order to be able to play ...
P–KN4 safely. It is remarkable how
slowly plans are carried out in a
closed position—a move on one
wing, then on another wing, just
waiting for the optimal opportunity.

19 P–R3

Since 19 N–R3 does not achieve
anything after 19 ... QN–R2,
White himself plans to push his
KNP, attacking the base of Black's
Pawn chain.

19 ...   P–KN4

Black hopes that White will exchange Pawns, after which Black
will have the open KR file.

20 PxP?

Much better would have been 20
N–N2, after which Black can never
play PxP without having the
White Knight take over a powerful position on his KB4. Black
would then be compelled to change
his strategy and, after very careful
preparation, play to push his KNP.
Again the same type of error as
in his 15th move—the amateur
makes things easier for his opponent.

20 ...   PxP

The important thing is that the
KR file is now open for attack.
Much later, since it will be a slow
process, Black will bring his Rook
and/or Queen to this file.

21 P–N4

The best under the circumstances, soon isolating Black's KP,
but this does not appear to do
much harm.

21 ...   N–N3

To bring the Knight into the
game and to clear the first rank for
the free movement of the Rooks.

There is no clear line in this
phase of the game. Black will try
to develop his pieces to better
places, to attain a concentration of
power. Possibly N(N3) will go to
R5.

22 PxP

In this and the following move,
White is impatient, does not like
to wait, tries to get a little more
freedom.

Perhaps he should have resumed the attack on the Q side by 22 P–N5, even if this attack does not accomplish as much as it would have a few moves earlier, when it might have given White some counterchances.

22 ...	BxP
23 N–N4	BxN

Black exchanges with the Bishop here in order to fix White's Pawn on a square from which he can attack it. The alternate 23 ... NxN; 24 PxN loses a tempo for Black and gives White the opportunity to strengthen his weaknesses.

24 PxN

White should consider 24 BxB, which exchanges one piece more.

24 ...	Q–Q2
25 Q–Q1	

Forced, since 25 R–B5, N–R5; 26 RxP, B–R3 loses. The Rook has no retreat.

25 ...   P–Q4

To open the Black QN1–KR7 diagonal for the Queen, and in the event that White does not push his QBP to try to secure the Black Q4 square for the Knight. Note that Black plays this move only after White's possibility of opening the QB file has disappeared.

26 N–N2(?)

White should have done something to prevent Black from getting a strong square on his Q4.

Bad is 26 PxP?, because it gives Black's Q4 square to the Black Knight.

But 26 P–B5! is good, in that it prevents the Black Knight from occupying that square. But in that case Black achieves his other goal —the attack along the KR file. He continues ... K–R2, ... R–R1, ... K–N1. His attack will be difficult to stop.

Also deserving of consideration is 26 P–N5, although after this move Black occupies the strong center square at Q4 as well: 26 ... QPxP; 27 PxBP, PxP; 28 RxP, N–Q4.

26 ...   PxP

Now Black secures his Q4 square for the Knight itself. This square is much more important to him than the resultant isolated KP, which cannot be attacked anyway.

27 RxP

Forced, for 27 BxP loses the KNP.

27 ...   N–Q4

The Knight takes a dominating post from which it cannot be dislodged. At this center square it paralyzes the entire Q side. It does not attack anything at the moment, but it might soon.

Such a post is known as a strong square, that is, a square that cannot be controlled by hostile Pawns and is in or near enemy territory. A strong square is one in which the following three conditions are fulfilled: (a) no hostile Pawn can control the square; (b) the square is in or near enemy territory; (c) sooner or later, you must be able to have more pieces than the opponent on the square. This leads to occupation of the square, preferably by a Knight.

28 Q–K1

Since Black's KN has occupied his strong Q4 square, the Black pressure against White's KN4 square has diminished. This permits the White Queen to move, but the text does not accomplish much. White was planning 29 Q–N3, 30 KR–QB1, 31 K–B2.

Perhaps 28 B–K1 would have been better. Then, if 28 ... Q–Q3; 29 B–B2, followed by 30 Q–K1 and 31 B–N3. Or perhaps it would have been preferable to try to escape with the King by 28 K–B2. But if the White King succeeds in going toward the center, the Black Knight on its Q4 will exercise an important restraining influence.

28 ...   Q–Q3

This not only prevents the White Queen from coming to N3 but also, after ... B–B3 and ... K–N2, pre-

pares the attack ... R–KR1 and ... Q–R7 ch.

29 R–B1(?)

A terrible loss of time. White's King is in a horrible position. Something must be done, possibly 29 R–KB5 followed by 30 Q–B2, after which the White King can escape via the 1st rank, if necessary.

29 ...   B–B3
30 P–QN5

Far too late. The best try is still 30 R–KB5.

30 ...   RPxP
31 PxP   K–N2

All according to plan. Black is now ready for 32 ... R–R1, etc.

32 PxP   PxP
33 K–B2

Losing a tempo, but it is too late to find the right way: 33 B–B4, R–R1; 34 K–B2, R–R7, threatening 35 ... N–R5. Black has a clear superiority. All his pieces are available for action—an example of concentration of power.

In other words, the idea, 33 B–B4 and 34 BxN, is good in general, since when one is under attack, it is a good idea to exchange pieces where possible in order to cut down attack. But here, that is not sufficient.

Or 33 R–KB5, R–R1; 34 B–B1, Q–R7 ch; 35 K–B2, N–R5 always wins, for Black simply plays ... NxR and ... R–R6.

| 33 ... | R–KB1 |

To force back the White King.

34	K–N1	R–R1
35	R–R1	Q–R7 ch
36	K–B2	QR–KB1
37	Resigns	

The threat of 37 ... BxP dis ch or any other discovered check promises the loss of big material, but in any case the White King is so bottled up that there seems no way out.

The game might have continued: 37 Q–N1 (37 R–R7 ch?, B–K2 dis ch!), N–R5 (Black can wait) and

(a) 38 R–R7 ch, B–K2 dis ch; 39 K–K1, NxN ch

(b) 38 R–N1, B–K2 dis ch; 39 B–B3 (after 39 K–K1, 39 ... QxR ch leads to mate), RxB ch; 40 K–K2, RxP ch!! 41 BxR, N–QB6 ch

(c) 38 K–K1, NxN ch; 39 K–Q1, N(N7)xP ch; 40 K–B1, QxB, etc.

Game 9

The theory of the Grünfeld: attack on the broad Pawn center

The weakness of a broad Pawn center

Motives for Queen exchange

Exploitation of two weaknesses

Attack against the King in the open

The mating net

In previous games we have seen players control the center either by occupying it with Pawns and pieces or by bringing pressure to bear on it with pieces from afar.

In the Grünfeld-Indian, Black deliberately allows White to occupy the center with Pawns and then attacks it. In the present game, Black weakens

The typical Grünfeld Pawn formation

Position after 6 PxN

the broad Pawn center by exchanges, forcing White to defend what is left of it with his King. Finally, Black breaks up the center entirely, and the White King, denuded of its protectors, becomes a target for the Black Rook and Two Bishops, which dart about harassing the White King wherever possible, giving it no respite.

The effectiveness of the technique described depends on the type of Pawn center White gets. Small differences can make the building up of a Pawn center sound or unsound. In the Grünfeld-Indian, the presence of White's QN on his QB3 makes the line 3 ... P–Q4; 4 PxP, NxP; 5 P–K4 much more attractive for Black than analogous positions in similar openings.

Because small differences in the type of Pawn center are so subtle, it is difficult for an amateur to find his way in these openings. Good-

80

looking moves may turn out to be disadvantageous mistakes. A considerable knowledge of the Grünfeld is necessary in order to follow the right line.

In this game the amateur makes an obvious move that turns out to be a strategic error. The amateur defends well, and against another amateur he might have gotten a draw or even more, but the master exploits the amateur's error to the maximum, giving his opponent no chance to escape.

Grünfeld-Indian Defense

Amateur	Master
White	*Black*
1 P–Q4	N–KB3
2 P–QB4	P–KN3

The characteristic move of the King's Indian openings, which will be taken up in detail in Games 19–22.

Classical strategy was to occupy the center with Pawns. This strategy is illustrated in the Ruy Lopez and to some extent in the Nimzo-Indian Defense (Games 1, 2, 5, 6, 7). The text is an illustration of modern strategy, which does not occupy the center with Pawns but rather directs pieces toward the center with the intention of waiting to see what the opponent is going to do in the center and then act accordingly.

Depending on how White continues, Black can have different Pawn formations in the King's Indian. For instance:

(a) PQ3–PK4 (the King's Indian: Game 19, with White KB on K2; Game 22, with White KB on KN2)

(b) PQ3–PQB4: 3 P–KN3, B–N2; 4 B–N2, P–Q3; 5 N–QB3, O–O;

6 N–B3, followed by (1) 6 . . . P–B4; 7 O–O (Yugoslav) or (2) 6 . . . N–B3; 7 P–Q5, N–QR4 (Panno Variation)

(c) PQ4:

3 P–KN3, P–Q4 or 3 P–KN3, B–N2; 4 B–N2, P–Q4 (Grünfeld Variation of the King's Indian, (Game 21);

3 N–QB3, P–Q4 (Grünfeld—present game)

3 N–QB3, B–N2; 4 N–B3, O–O; 5 P–KN3, P–Q4. This variation is perhaps still a little stronger for Black than the Grünfeld.

(d) PB3: 3 P–KN3, P–QB3; 4 P–Q5 (Game 20).

It is important to know under what circumstances these different Black Pawn formations should be employed. This cannot be sharply defined. We shall see something of them in this game and in Games 19, 20, 21, and 22.

3 N–QB3

White contests Black's control of the White K4 square.

3 . . .   P–Q4

(See diagram opposite)

The thematic move of the Grün feld Indian. This is a most peculiar way of becoming active in the center, because it offers the center QP in exchange for the non-central QBP, thus indicating a willingness to continue with a clear minority in the center but with the possibility of attacking the broad White center in an effective manner, which does not exist in the Marshall variation of the Queen's Gambit Declined (1 P–Q4, P–Q4; 2 P–QB4, N–KB3; 3 PxP, NxP). This possibility of attacking the broad White center in an effective manner is due to (a) the exchange . . . NxN to follow, and (b) the position of Black's fianchettoed KB.

This same move can be made in other similar openings, but often with different consequences. Compare 3 . . . P–Q4 in this opening with the same move in the above-cited Marshall line, where it is weak because neither (a) nor (b) obtains, and in Game 21, where it is neither weak nor strong, for only (b) obtains.

White can meet Black's demonstration in the center in a number of ways: (a) 4 N–B3; (b) 4 Q–N3; (c) 4 B–B4; (d) 4 P–K3. The best is probably 4 N–B3, followed by 5 Q–N3; e.g., 4 N–B3, B–N2; 5 Q–N3, PxP (5 . . . P–B3; 6 P–K3, P–K3; 7 B–Q3, O–O; 8 O–O, QN–Q2; 9 B–Q2 is another line); 6 QxBP, O–O; 7 P–K4, B–N5; 8 B–K3, KN–Q2, etc.—Smyslov's idea—attack against the White Q side

with two Black Knights on the Q wing.

4 PxP

White decides to take the Pawn and destroy Black's center. That is exactly what he does in the above-cited Marshall line and in Game 21, but there is an important difference, namely that in the Marshall line, White has not already developed his QN to QB3. This gives Black's KN considerably fewer possibilities in the Marshall line than it does in the Grünfeld-Indian.

4 . . .   NxP

Black has allowed his QP to be exchanged for White's QBP. In general, it is not wise to give up a center Pawn for a side Pawn. But here there are special considerations.

5 P–K4

To take complete possession of the center.

If White, not wishing to give Black a broad center as a target, should reply 5 P–K3, then Black would have an easy game in that he could develop his pieces and undermine the center; e.g., 5 . . . B–N2; 6 N–B3, P–QB4, etc.

Or 5 NxN, QxN would win Black a tempo by promoting his development and also give him a powerful position.

5 . . .   NxN

In this line, Black can take White's QN, but not in the above-cited Marshall line. This resource of being able to take White's QN makes all the difference in the world between the two lines.

6 PxN

The White center now seems very strong. Actually it is very vulnerable.

The vulnerability of White's center stems from the fact that Black can attack White's QP many, many times and that White's QBP is not a very substantial protection, because Black can play ... P–QB4 without having to fear the reply PxP, since this would leave White with such a poor Pawn position that his extra Pawn would be a liability rather than an asset.

How can Black play so as to counteract White's center?

6 ...   P–QB4

Black will play both ... P–QB4 and ... B–N2. Possibly either move could be made first. As a matter of fact, without ... P–QB4, the move ... B–N2 does not have much force. So White must know that if Black plays 6 ... B–N2, the move ... P–QB4 will follow in any case. Were this not true,

then Black should consider playing 6 ... B–N2 immediately, since White would not then know where the next blow would come from.

The move ... P–QB4 is found in a number of openings, such as the Queen's Gambit Accepted, with the purpose of exchanging the QBP for the QP, thus neutralizing the center. Here, this is not the case. In the Grünfeld, Black exchanges his QBP for White's QP in order to weaken White's center.

In Pawn positions like this, White will never be able to reply PxP, because he would end up with two isolated Pawns, e.g., 7 PxP, Q–R4; 8 Q–B2, B–N2; 9 B–Q2, QxP(4), and White has two isolated Pawns with no compensation whatever. It is a great handicap to White not to be able to take the Black Pawn without incurring the disadvantage mentioned.

White could play 7 P–Q5, but a center Pawn that advances too soon will be forced to exchange, and this means loss of time and, in this case, also isolated Pawns, e.g., 7 ... B–N2; 8 B–Q2, P–K3; 9 B–QB4, Q–R4; 10 Q–B2, P–QN4, and after 11 B–K2, PxP; 12 PxP, O–O, White's QP may become very weak. Besides, Black already has the initiative. After 13 N–B3, R–K1, White cannot castle.

7 N–B3(?)

White attempts to defend his QP a third time. But at any time Black can nullify this defense by pinning the Knight with ... B–

KN5. Therefore, 7 N–B3 is not adequate.

White should have played 7 B–QB4 followed by 8 N–K2. In that case, Black's attack against White's QP is less effective. The Pawn is adequately protected. If Black then tries to pin White's KN by ... B–KN5, White replies P–B3, which shows the big difference between the two types of development by the Knight.

Theory claims that the following continuation leads to an equal position: 7 B–QB4, B–N2; 8 N–K2, N–B3; 9 B–K3, and White's QP is attacked four times, defended four times, so that White has maintained his center. Although he has maintained the center, White does not have an advantage, since having the center constitutes an advantage only if the side having it can make use of it by advancing, driving away pieces, and/or creating room for attacking purposes. White can do nothing of this sort here. Theory continues: 9 ... O–O; 10 O–O, PxP; 11 PxP, B–N5; 12 P–B3, N–R4; 13 B–Q3, a very difficult position that has occurred in several grandmaster games and has been won alternately by White and Black.

Old-fashioned is 7 B–N5 ch: (a) 7 ... B–Q2; 8 BxB ch, QxB (to maintain the possibility of ... N–B3); 9 N–B3, B–N2; 10 O–O, PxP; 11 PxP, N–B3 (Kashdan-Alekhine, London 1932); (b) Dubious is 7 ... N–B3; 8 BxN ch, PxB; 9 B–K3, B–KN2; 10 N–K2, PxP; 11 PxP, P–QB4, and White

can make a sacrifice: 12 PxP, BxR; 13 QxB, which gives good chances (13 ... O–O; 14 B–R6); or White can perhaps postpone the exchange B–R1 ch, e.g., 7 ... N–B3; 8 N–K2, B–N2; 9 O–O, PxP (otherwise 10 P–Q5); 10 PxP, O–O; 11 BxN, PxB; 12 B–R3, preventing ... P–QB4.

7 ...   B–N2
8 B–QB4

If there is no threat, just continue development.

8 ...   PxP

One might think that this exchange would relieve the pressure against White's QP. On the contrary, it exposes the QP to a direct attack, as will become evident in the continuation.

Black might have played 8 ... N–QB3 or 8 ... B–N5, increasing the pressure against White's QP, but Black already has a forced continuation in mind at this point, and to avoid the work of calculating what would happen if White should not retake on his Q4 with his BP, he puts the problem immediately.

If Black should play 8 ... Q–B2, indirectly threatening White's KB, the answer 9 B–Q3 would be bad because of 9 ... PxP; 10 PxP, Q–B6 ch, winning the piece. White can answer either 9 B–N3, in which case, 9 ... PxP; 10 PxP, Q–B6 ch; 11 B–Q2 does not mean anything, or 9 Q–N3, attacking the KBP.

9 PxP

White would be left with a very weak QBP after 9 NxP.

9 ...   N–B3

White's QP is now attacked three times, defended only twice.

10 B–K3

White could also defend with 10 B–N2, but Black's continuation would be the same, perhaps still stronger.

Notice that White cannot play 10 P–Q5, since Black's KB could take White's QR.

Let us now consider 10 P–K5, which looks playable because it lessens the influence of Black's KB on the diagonal.

In certain positions of this type, P–K5 is very strong. (See Game 21, where this advance helps take advantage of the hole at KB3 in Black's position. This is not the case in the present game.) Positionally, P–K5 creates two definite and permanent weaknesses: the QP and the hole on Black's Q4; but it is not easy for Black to exploit these weaknesses. In this position,

10 P–K5, B–N5; 11 B–K3, O–O; 12 O–O, BxN, and White must retake with the Pawn, which leaves him with a weakened K-side position. Black could continue by ... P–K3, ... N–K2, and ... N–Q4, taking advantage of the hole in White's position.

10 ...   Q–R4 ch

This attack forces White either to give up the castling privilege (11 K–B1 or K–K2) or to weaken his QP still more by 11 Q–Q2 or 11 B–Q2.

11 Q–Q2

Since this leads to a weakening of White's QP, 11 K–K2 might have been preferable.

11 B–Q2 would have been answered by 11 ... Q–R6! Now White's QP is attacked twice, and 12 B–K3 fails because of 12 ... Q–B6 ch.

11 ...   QxQ ch

In general, the attacking player will not exchange Queens. However, he will exchange if (a) the opponent's Queen is stronger than his, or if (b) it suits his plans strategically or tactically. In this position, Black exchanges because he has a definite plan to attack White's QP, and as part of this plan it is important for him that the White King be in an exposed position.

12 KxQ

Other moves cost a Pawn by depriving the White QP of one of its supporters.

White and Black are still equal in pieces. The Queens have disappeared from the board, and the game is entering a new phase. White has several weaknesses: his center Pawns are vulnerable and are being attacked; his King, deprived of its right to castle, is located on a center file; his QR is on a diagonal in direct line with Black's fianchettoed Bishop.

How can Black take advantage of the White weaknesses? If he can find a move that will at the same time threaten one of the defenders of the vulnerable Pawn at White's Q4 and open the way for further attack on that Pawn and by extension on the White King, he will have attained his end. So he plays

12 ...   B–N5!

Black threatens to win the QP by removing one of its defenders.

13 K–B3

The only good move, but it shows that the amateur has no fear

of putting his King into an exposed position on the board. Probably he is well aware that as soon as the Black threats come to an end, the King will stand very active here. In general, in the endgame the King should go to the "front."

Naturally, there are some bad moves: (a) 13 P–Q5 would lose the exchange; (b) 13 K–Q3 loses a Pawn after 13 ... BxN; 14 PxB, O–O–O; 15 B–Q5 (15 BxP?, N–K4 ch), N–N5 ch; 16 K–B4, NxB; 17 PxN, R–Q2, etc.; (c) 13 P–K5 does not lose material, but White has difficulties in the continuation; e.g., 13 ... BxN; 14 PxB, O–O, followed by moving the Black Rooks to QB1 and Q1.

13 ...   R–QB1

Black now threatens to win a piece by ... N–R4.

White has two weaknesses: (a) his QP; (b) his King's position. Black has the option of exploiting the new weaknesses by 13 ... R–QB1 or of increasing pressure on the one weakness by 13 ... R–Q1. To defend against pushes from two directions is more difficult than to defend against the double push; that is, weaknesses of quite different kinds are the hardest to defend against. They become a progressive evil. For that reason, Black exploits the new weakness by 13 ... R–QB1 instead of playing 13 ... R–Q1, which would increase the pressure on the one weakness, but would not be optimal. Black should reserve his Q1 square for his KR, so that the QR can come into the game on the QB1 square.

At this point, Black could have exchanged by 13 ... BxN, in order to strengthen the pressure against White's QP and to give him a doubled Pawn, which would have been fairly good, but by so doing he would have left White with the Two Bishops, which in the long run might have compensated for the eventual loss of a Pawn (compare the comment on Black's 18th move). Black has shown a great deal of self-control in not exchanging. Ninety-nine out of a hundred players would have done so from sheer laziness, for from now on, Black always has to consider whether the White Knight could leave its present position, thus improving White's chances without incurring any liability.

14 QR–QB1   O–O

Black mobilizes his KR also. Notice that he does not immediately try to exploit the weakness. As a general rule, first strengthen your position, that is, concentrate your forces. Black could have tried to exploit the weaknesses immediately by 14 ... N–R4, but this leads to nothing after 15 K–N4.

15 KR–Q1

Again, a very strong move. White is determined to stay and survive the storm.

In deciding on this move, White examined the position after Black's 14 ... O–O and asked himself how

Black could take advantage of the presence of his White King on the same file as the Black Rook. How about 15 ... P–QN4? He went through the plausible continuation 16 BxP, NxP dis ch; 17 K–N4! How would Black have to continue? By 17 ... N–B7 ch; 18 K–R4, R–B6 (threatening mate on QR6); 19 R–Q3. White concluded that in the resultant position, he would be somewhat better off than now. Conclusion: 15 ... P–QN4 does not win immediately. That is why White chose the text move.

However, what else could White do? (a) 15 K–N3?, BxN; 16 PxB, BxQP, losing a Pawn; (b) 15 K–Q3, BxN; 16 PxB is also very strong for Black: 16 ... KR–Q1; 17 B–Q5, N–N5 ch; 18 K–Q2, NxB; 19 PxN, P–B4, and White's position is badly compromised; (c) 15 P–K5, P–QN4! is stronger for Black than in the game, because White's KP is weaker on K5 than on K4; (d) 15 P–QR4, P–QR3, and White finds himself confronted by the same problem and has to choose between the same moves: K–N3, K–Q3, P–K5, KR–Q1.

15 ...   P–QN4!

Black takes advantage of the indirect pin (were Black's Knight not on the QD file, the pin would be direct). The combination leads to the win of a Pawn in a few moves, as we shall see.

Black could have continued 15 ... KR–Q1, in order to follow his original principle, "First concentrate your forces," and this would have been all right. But it is a question of comparing the advantage one can attain by bringing the blow immediately or later. In this special case, it would not make too much difference. White could continue 16 P–K5 (he has practically nothing else), and 16 ... P–QN4 leads to developments similar to those in the game.

16 BxNP

Forced, since after any other Bishop move, Black gets his discovered check without losing the NP.

16 ...　　　　　　NxP dis ch
17 K–N4

Forced in order to protect the Bishop.

17 ...　　　　　　NxN

Also very strong is 17 ... N–B7 ch, but it is not decisive. The text is preferable, because it wins a Pawn in an excellent position.

18 PxN　　　　　　BxP

It now becomes evident why Black did not exchange on his 13th move. Now a Black Bishop, rather than a Black Knight, is on White's KB6. This makes an enormous difference. Were a Black Knight now on White's KB3, White could continue 19 BxP, and although Black could then maintain his material advantage by 19 ... NxP, the White passed QRP supported by the King and the Two Bishops would give him great power, which would more than compensate for the loss of a Pawn. Here one sees what Two Bishops can mean under special circumstances. After all, it is unfortunate for White that Black did not make the obvious exchange on his 13th move. In that case, White's courageous counterplay and exact calculation would have been rewarded.

19 RxR

White does not have much choice. After 19 R–Q7, RxR; 20 BxR, R–B1; 21 B–K3, we come to the same position as in the game.

19 ...　　　　　　RxR
20 R–Q7

The only counterchance.

20 ...   B–B6 ch

Also good would have been 20 ... BxP, but Black tries to get the maximum force of his Two Bishops against an unprotected King.

21 K–R3

If 21 K–N3, P–QR4, and now 22 RxKP fails against 22 ... B–Q8 ch; 23 K–R3, B–N5 ch, etc.

21 ...   P–QR4!

Indirectly protecting Black's KP, for if 22 RxP?, B–N5 ch.

22 B–Q3

Black threatened to win White's KP.

22 ...   R–N1

With threats such as 23 ... B–Q8 and 24 ... B–N7 mate, or 23 ... R–N5 and 24 ... B–N7 mate.

23 B–B2

To meet the threats as best he can. Another possibility is 23 R–B7, B–K4! and

(a) 24 R–R7, B–Q8 and White cannot stop mate either on his QN2 or Q6;

(b) 24 R–B4, B–Q8!; 25 B–B2, B–K7 and the White Rook is lost:

(1) 26 R–R4, B–N7 mate;

(2) 26 R–B5, B–Q3, winning the Rook;

(3) 26 R–B6, B–N7 ch; 27 K–R4, B–N4 ch, winning the Rook.

One sees the force of the Rook and Bishops against the King in the open—dangers of double attacks and of mate.

23 ...   B–K7

Black threatens to win the White Rook by 24 ... B–N7 ch; 25 K–R4, B–N4 ch.

If Black had played 23 ... R–N5, White would have met the threats by 24 B–N3 or 24 B–B1.

24 R–B7

If 24 B–Q3, B–Q8; 25 B–B1 (the only move), B–N5 ch; 26 K–N2, B–Q7 dis ch, followed by an early mate.

If 24 R–R7, B–N7 ch; 25 K–R4, B–N4 ch and (a) 26 K–N3, B–Q6 dis ch or (b) 26 KxP, B–B6 mate.

24 ...   B–K4!
25 Resigns

The Rook has no moves:

(a) If the Rook leaves the QB file, e.g., 25 R–R7, 25 R–Q7, or 25 RxP, the win is forced as follows: 25 ... B–N7 ch; 26 K–R4, B–N4 ch and (1) 27 K–N3, B–Q6 dis ch, etc.; (2) 27 KxP, B–B6 mate.

(b) 25 R–B6, B–N7 ch; 26 K–
R4, B–N4 ch; 27 King moves,
BxR, winning the Rook.

(c) 25 R–B5, R–Q3;

(1) 20 K–R4, BxR; 27 BxB, R–
QB1, winning a Bishop and remaining with a full Rook to the
good;

(2) 26 B–N3, R–QB1, winning
a full Rook.

In comparison with previous
games, we note here a big improvement on the part of the ama
teur. His stronger play consists in
(a) a series of enterprising moves
with his King; (b) a readiness to
take the initiative if Black should
miss the right continuation; (c)
exact defense against the many
subtle threats of his opponent.

Game 10

The 1 N–KB3 opening

How to take advantage of hanging Pawns

How to take advantage of double isolated Pawns

Motives for Queen exchange

Over a number of games a chess player is likely to meet various type-formations which have special characteristics and require a particular type of play by either side. Even a rather strong player is often unable to handle such formations properly if he has never heard of them and has no inkling of the pitfalls to which they may lead. Knowledge of the existence of a given formation warns the player that it might be well to consider it more closely and to learn its strengths and weaknesses and the standard technique of treating it.

This game illustrates how a player who is ignorant of the dangers inherent in hanging Pawns innocently gets himself into a position that already before the tenth move is practically untenable.

Black's QBP and QP are hanging Pawns

Position after 8 ... PxP

Through exchanges of center Pawns, one is sometimes left with a pair of Pawns on adjacent files that are separated from all other Pawns by at least one file on either side. These are known as *hanging Pawns*. Under some circumstances, hanging Pawns can be strong, under others they can constitute a greater liability than the isolated Pawn, for they form, so to speak, a duo of two isolated Pawns.

When there are many pieces on the board —in particular, minor pieces—the squares controlled by the hanging Pawns can become strong outposts. In this game, however, the hanging Pawns are weak, mainly as a consequence of poor development.

91

There are several types of technique for exploiting the vulnerability of hanging Pawns:

(a) Attack them with pieces, forcing the opponent to protect them with his pieces. Then attack the defending pieces, exchanging them at the propitious moment. This technique often results either in the win of a Pawn or in giving the opponent still other Pawn weaknesses.

(b) Force one of the hanging Pawns to advance, and then place a piece on the square in front of the backward Pawn.

(c) Attack one of the hanging Pawns by your own Pawn, forcing an exchange that gives the opponent an isolated Pawn.

Grünfeld Reversed

Master	Amateur
White	*Black*

1 N–KB3

The classical way to control the center squares is to occupy them with Pawns (1 P–K4 or 1 P–Q4). The text move, 1 N–KB3, undertakes the control of the center by pieces. From its post at KB3, the Knight exercises a measure of control over the center squares Q4 and K5. It prevents Black from playing 1 ... P–K4. Instead of committing White to a definite line, this move reserves for him a maximum number of possibilities, just as does a similar move for Black in the Indian openings (see the comments under Black's first move in Game 1).

1 ...   P–Q4

We now have a sort of Indian opening in reverse, that is, White has developed his KN, and Black has played ... P–Q4.

2 P–KN3

With this move, the opening becomes a King's Indian in reverse. See Games 19–22 for a discussion of the basic ideas of the King's Indian.

The reply 2 P–B4 leads to the pure Reti opening creating positions similar to that in Game 25, the basic idea of which is to postpone the occupation of the center by Pawns. In case Black does not follow that strategy and does occupy the center by one or more Pawns, White will attack these center Pawns by his own BP's, usually by the QBP. When the center is cleared in that way, White will later occupy the center with his own Pawns. One typical example: 2 ... P–K3; 3 P–KN3, N–KB3; 4 B–N2, PxP; 5 Q–R4 ch, B–Q2; 6 QxBP, B–B3; 7 O–O, QN–Q2; 8 Q–B2, B–K2; 9 N–B3, O–O; 10 R–Q1, N–N3; 11 P–K4, Q–B1; 12 P–Q4. The White strategy has been a complete success. White now occupies the center by both his Pawns, and Black has a cramped game.

2 ...	P–QB4
3 B–N2	N–QB3

This reply gives White the opportunity to play a Grünfeld in reverse, which he would not have had if Black had answered 3 ... N–KB3 or 3 ... P–KN3.

4 P–Q4

This *is* the Grünfeld in reverse. For the basic lines of the Grünfeld, see Game 9.

We must note that in the Grünfeld Reversed, White has the Grünfeld position plus one extra move, namely, his KB is already developed, which would not be the case at the corresponding point in the Grünfeld.

4 ...   P–K3

The quietest and most solid continuation. Other moves, such as 4 ... N–B3, are also possible.

Not recommendable is 4 ... PxP, leading to the exchange variation of the Grünfeld: 5 NxP, P–K4; 6 NxN, PxN; 7 P–QB4, after which Black is in great difficulties. This is exactly the position of the previous game, with colors reversed, except that White has one extra move. It is clear that a move more in this wild position must mean more than it would in a quiet position, and for that reason the text is probably best.

5 O–O   N–B3

Developing moves.

6 P–B4

The first sign that White has a move more than in the analogous variation of the Grünfeld. This move enables him still more than in the usual Grünfeld to seize the initiative in the center. White threatens to take 7 PxQP, and if Black retakes with his Knight, by 8 P–K4 White can reach a clear majority in the center. On the other hand, if Black retakes with his Pawn, White can at some time exchange Pawns on Black's QB4 and thus isolate Black's QP. This last variation is known in chess literature as the Rubinstein Variation of the Queen's Gambit and usually arises after 1 P–Q4, P–Q4; 2 P–QB4, P–K3; 3 N–KB3, P–QB4; 4 PxQP, KPxP; 5 P–KN3, N–QB3; 6 B–N2, N–B3; 7 O–O. In both cases, White attains some superiority in the center.

6 ...   P–QN3?

A very bad move, for (a) it allows White to weaken the Black center by exchanging both center Pawns; (b) it weakens the diagonal already controlled by the White KB; (c) it also weakens the Black diagonal K1–QR5.

After 6 ... PxBP; 7 Q–R4, B–Q2 (necessary in order to avoid the consequences of the triple attack against Black's QN by N–K5); 8 PxP, BxP; 9 QxP, White has a good game, but Black's position is not definitely inferior.

On the other hand, after 6 ... PxQP; 7 NxP, White's position is certainly preferable, because he threatens to weaken the Black Pawn structure by 8 PxP and if 8 ... NxP, then 9 NxN.

7 PxQP

This exchange and the following one destroy White's center, it is true, but in order to give the White pieces the opportunity to attack the remaining Black center Pawns.

7 ...   KPxP

The Black center Pawns now become very weak. A little better was 7 ... KNxP. Apparently, the amateur is not acquainted with hanging Pawns, or he does not realize their significance.

8 PxP   PxP

(*See diagram on page 91*)

Black played 8 ... PxP instead of 8 ... BxP to avoid an isolated Pawn, but he might better have played 8 ... BxP, for after 8 ... PxP, he has what are known as hanging Pawns, and hanging Pawns can be looked at, so to speak, as isolated Pawns, for each of the hanging Pawns is, so to speak, isolated in itself.

There *are* situations in which hanging Pawns are tenable and even strong (see Introduction to Game 12), but at this point they are so exposed that there is no question as to the fact that they are weak.

Hanging Pawns can be an asset when the side holding them has the initiative with many developed pieces. In this position, that is definitely not the case. It is difficult to protect the Pawns, whereas it is the easiest thing in the world to attack them.

9 N–B3

A preparatory move that develops a White piece and exerts pressure on the Black center.

9 ...   B–N2?

Better was 9 ... B–K2, but the following line, a more or less logical sequence, shows that Black's difficulties could soon become insuperable in that case also, owing to the fact that his center Pawns are so vulnerable: 9 ... B–K2; 10 B–N5, B–K3 (10 ... P–Q5; 11 NxP); 11 Q–R4, Q–Q2 (the obvious moves on both sides); 12 QR–Q1, O–O; 13 BxN, BxB; 14 NxP, BxN; 15 P–K4, BxNP;

16 RxB, Q–N2; 17 RxP, winning a Pawn in the end.

If 9 ... B–K3; 10 B–N5, P–Q5 (10 ... B–K2 leads to the above variation); 11 N–K4!, which is certainly not better for Black.

After 9 ... P–Q5, 10 NxP wins by the force of White's KB: 10 ... PxN; 11 BxN ch, B–Q2; 12 BxR.

10 B–N5

Indirectly attacking Black's QP. At this early stage of the game, the amateur is already coming into a lost position, and even with the best defense in the world, he cannot save the game any more.

10 ...   P–Q5

Practically forced, since moves like 10 ... N–QR4 or 10 ... N–QN1 could be answered by 11 N–K5, with more pressure against Black's QP.

11 N–K4

This opens possibilities of attack against Black's QBP in conjunction with R–QB1 and also threatens to double Black's KBP.

11 ...   B–K2

This does not prevent the doubling of Black's KBP, since the Bishop is needed to protect the QBP. But Black has no better move.

12 BxN

To give Black a double isolated Pawn. In general, this is sufficient reason to give up the Two Bishops. Moreover, Two Bishops are to be feared only when they become aggressive. In the present position, Black's Two Bishops act as defensive pieces.

12 ...   PxB

If 12 ... BxB; 13 NxP.

At this point, Black is in a hopeless position. All his Pawns are weak. But how should White continue so as to take advantage of these weak Pawns?

It is neither necessary nor possible for White to take advantage of the Black QBP directly. If 13 R–B1, Q–N3; 14 Q–B2, N–N5, and Black gets some counterchances.

13 N–R4!

An excellent move, because from this square the Knight can occupy the KB5 square in front of the doubled Pawns and thus paralyze the entire K wing.

An isolated Pawn has a double disadvantage: (a) It cannot be protected by other Pawns and can therefore be more easily attacked. (b) The opponent can post a piece in front of the isolated Pawn, and that piece cannot be driven away by Pawns. This means that this square in general is a strong square (compare p. 78, top of column 1)

13 ...   Q N6
14 N–B5

With the possibility of 15 QN–Q6 ch, exchanging the Black QB, thus bringing the Black Queen on the diagonal of White's fianchettoed Bishop. Besides, it is clear that whenever he wishes, White can strengthen his pressure on the QBP by exchanging the KB.

14 ...   R–Q1

He prevents QN–Q6 ch.

If instead 14 ... O–O, White wins the attack by 15 Q–B1, threatening 16 Q–R6. For instance, 15 ... K–R1; 16 Q–R6, R–KN1; 17 NxKBP and wins.

14 ... QxP? would lose a piece after 15 R–N1.

15 Q–B1

Attacking Black's QBP (White threatens NxB and the capture of the QBP) and, moreover, threatening 16 Q–KR6 (which prepares the penetration Q–N7, driving away the Rook) and 16 Q–KB4 (which revives the threat N–Q6 ch).

15 ...   B–QB1

Imperative! The Knight on B5 is so strong that it is a matter of life and death to force the Knight to declare its intentions immediately. By this move, the amateur has defended pretty well in his hopeless position.

16 NxB

The simplification which to boot, since 16 N–N7 ch, K–Q2 (16 ... K–B1 is not recommendable on account of 17 Q–R6); 17 Q–KB4, threatening mate with B–R3 allows the strong defense ... N–K4, after which no clear-cut win is in the position.

Choose the line that leads to the clearest favorable continuation. Even if, as in this game, the advantage attained is "only" a plus Pawn in the endgame, one must realize that mating combinations are in general possible only against weak defense.

16 ...   KxN
17 QxP ch

White forces the exchange of Queens, thus cutting down the little initiative Black has, leaving him with a wretched Pawn position. After 17 NxQBP, Black would retain some initiative. Whenever it is a question of whether or not to trade off pieces, consider the Pawn position when the pieces are removed. If that Pawn position favors you, make the trade.

This is the end of the hanging Pawns. White wins a Pawn and maintains a positional advantage in the bargain, for Black remains with a pair of double isolated Pawns and three other isolated Pawns.

17 ...   QxQ
18 NxQ

The game is now entering a new phase. Black not only is a Pawn down, but he has a great many Pawn weaknesses.

18 ...	N–K4
19 QR–B1	

To take advantage of the open file.

19 ...	B–B4
20 KR–Q1	

Obliging the QR to remain where it is and perform the double function of guarding the QP and defending the King against attacks on his second rank, which will be necessary after the White Knight has withdrawn. The Black Rook is an overworked piece. It is too bad that the KR is not at its Q1 and the QR available for guarding the QB file.

20 ...	P–Q6

Loses a Pawn immediately, but the position could not be held in any case. For instance, after 20 ... R–Q3; 21 N–N3 (threatening R–B7 ch and attacking Black's QP a second time):

(1)

21 ... KR–Q1; 22 R–B7 ch,
(1a) 22 ... KR–Q2; 23 RxR ch, winning the QP.
(1b) 22 ... K–K1; 23 RxRP.

(2)

21 ... P–Q6; 22 PxP,
(2a) 22 ... NxP; 23 R–B7 ch, K–K3 (23 ... R–Q2; 24 RxR ch wins a piece); 24 RxRP, NxNP?; 25 R–K1 ch wins a piece.
(2b) 22 ... BxP; 23 R–B7 ch, winning at least a second Pawn.
(2c) 22 ... RxP; 23 RxR, NxR; 24 R–B7 ch, K–Q3; 25 RxBP, with the same result—White wins a second Pawn and has a sure win.

21 PxP	NxP
22 NxN	RxN
23 RxR	BxR
24 R–B7 ch	Resigns

With two connected passed Pawns to the good, White must win.

After 24 ... K–K3; 25 RxRP, Black could try a counterattack with 25 ... R–QB1 (threatening 26 ... R–B8 ch). However, after 26 B–N7, R–B8 ch (26 ... R–B2?; 27 B–Q5 ch); 27 K–N2, B–B8 ch; 28 K–B3, Black cannot do much more (28 ... R–B7; 29 B–R6!).

Game 11

The Queen's Gambit is one of the most popular openings in tournament play, because it is more difficult for Black to realize equality in that opening than in most others. If Black plays exactly, he will eventually attain equality, but if he does not, White has various means at his disposal to increase his slight initial advantage, depending on how Black plays.

Because of the move 2 P–QB4, White has the possibility in most of the variations of the Queen's Gambit Declined of opening the QB file by an exchange of Pawns. Black can answer White's QBPxQP by ... KPxP, after which White gets a half-open QB file and Black a half-open K file (compare Game 13). But if Black has previously moved ... P–QB3, as he usually does, he could also answer White's QBPxQP by ... BPxP, in which case both White and Black would have a completely open QB file.

The strategy of playing on the open file is quite different from that of playing on the half-open file. In case of the open file, the advantage is to the side that controls the open file and is able to prevent the opponent from gaining control of it. The means of attaining this end is the occupation of the file by as many heavy pieces as possible.

Once the hegemony of the open file is secured, one can think of making full use of his advantage. The indicated strategic method is to try to penetrate the hostile position along the 7th and 8th ranks. In view of the fact that Pawns are most vulnerable to horizontal attacks and attacks from behind, this penetration is the most efficient way of using the open file in the endgame. Penetration can also serve to support from the side a frontal K-side attack. The one and the other are the theme of this game.

Queen's Gambit Declined: Classical Variation

Master	Amateur
White	*Black*
1 P–Q4	P–Q4
2 P–QB4	

The Queen's Gambit.

Of the various chess openings, there is none in which the ideas behind the opening can be more clearly delineated.

White immediately contests Black's bid for center control. This move has a number of implications:

(a) It invites Black to play 2 ... PxP (Queen's Gambit Accepted) and thus exchange a center Pawn for a side Pawn. Chess theory shows that in the long run, Black cannot hold the extra Pawn, and if he tries, he is likely to get into a bad position.

(b) It threatens 3 PxP followed by complete control of the center for White, e.g., 3 ... QxP; 4 N–QB3, Q–QR4; 5 P–K4.

(c) By 3 PxP it also threatens to open the QB file for action by White.

| 2 ... | P–K3 |

Black does not have a great choice of effective moves here. He must meet White's threat of 3 PxP. He can play:

(a) 2 ... P–K3, the text, supporting the QP while at the same time building up a solid position. This move has the disadvantage of shutting in the Black QB, but since Black's QNP would be very vulnerable without the protection of the QB, this QB does better in many cases to stay on its original square at this time. Therefore, the fact that it is shut in is not too serious.

(b) 2 ... P–QB3, the Slav Defense (see Game 14).

(c) 2 ... N–KB3(?); 3 PxP, NxP; 4 N–KB3 followed by 5 P–K4, and White gets complete control of the center.

(d) 2 ... PxP, the Queen's Gambit Accepted. A line often chosen is 3 N–KB3, N–KB3; 4 P–K3, P–K3; 5 BxP, P–B4 (a very important move by which Black tries to neutralize the center); 6 O–O, P–QR3, and Black gets certain counterchances on the Q side in exchange for his slight minority in the center.

| 3 N–QB3 | |

By developing his Knight to its QB3, from which point it exercises some control over the K4 square, White threatens under certain circumstances to take possession of this square by 4 P–K4. This Knight move also increases White's pressure on his Q5 square, which is already being threatened by White's QBP.

| 3 ... | N–KB3 |

A developing move that neutralizes White's pressure on both the White K4 and Q5 squares.

4 B-N5

By pinning Black's Knight, White nullifies the pressure which that Knight exercised on the center. He also develops an important piece to a powerful square.

In addition, White threatens 5 BxN and
(a) 5 ... QxB; 6 PxP, PxP; 7 NxP, winning a Pawn; or
(b) 5 ... PxB; 6 PxP, which leaves Black with double isolated Pawns, a serious weakness, as we have seen in Game 10.

4 ...   B-K2

By 4 ... B-K2 Black unpins his Knight and also clears the way for castling. This is the logical place to develop the Bishop in light of Black's aims for control of the center. It prevents White from carrying out the above threat.

By 4 ... B-N5 (the Manhattan Variation), Black prevents White from carrying out the threat of BxN by pinning his Knight. The game could continue: 5 P-K3, QN-Q2; 6 PxP, PxP; 7 B-Q3, later followed by N-K2 to support the pinned QN. The Manhattan Variation is considered less solid than the classical variation of the Queen's Gambit Declined, because on its QN5 the Black Bishop does not have a great deal of significance if White can defend his QN well.

If Black should play instead 4 ... B-Q3, a move which is sometimes made by amateurs with the idea that from Q3 the Bishop can be used for an eventual attack on White's KThen White can carry out his threat: 5 PxP PxP; 6 BxN, followed by 7 NxP, winning a Pawn. But White must not transpose moves and play 6 NxP?, NxN; 7 BxQ B-N5 ch; 8 Q-Q2, BxQ ch; 9 KxB, KxB, winning a piece.

5 P-K3

A sound developing move that strengthens the center and opens a diagonal so that the White KB can defend the gambit Pawn. Moreover, made at this point, it does not shut in the QB, which is already developed.

Equally good is 5 N-B3.

At this point or soon after, amateurs sometimes play 5 BxN with the erroneous idea that a Knight is more powerful than a Bishop. Statistics indicate that on the contrary there are more positions in which the Bishop is stronger than the Knight than the reverse, and this means that before exchanging a Bishop for a Knight a player should have positive arguments for doing so. By the same token, a player might well exchange his Knight for a Bishop unless there are positive reasons for not doing so.

Over and above these general reasons for not making the exchange, we must examine the specific position, a procedure that is always mandatory. By 5 BxN the White Bishop disappears from the board, and Black, without any loss of time, brings his KB to a much more powerful square, where it exerts pressure along a main diagonal.

5 ...   QN–Q2

On this square the QN has two distinct functions, depending on the continuation of the game:

(a) It supports the KN, and its presence in this respect can be of importance if White has developed his Bishop to Q3 and his Queen to B2, and after Black has castled K-side, White threatens BxN followed by BxP ch. Moreover, from Q2 the QN is sometimes moved to KB1 to support its KR2.

(b) At Q2 it constitutes one of the necessary preparations for the freeing of the Black game.

Black, as the second player, has less freedom of movement and a less open game than White. In order to attain equality, Black must at some point open his position so as to obtain the same degree of freedom that White enjoys from the very beginning. Usually this opening of the game is accomplished by what is known as a *freeing move* or a *liberating move*, that is, a Pawn move in the center that forces an exchange by one of the two sides, thereby creating an open or a half-open file.

When we consider the text position, we note that if Black can in some way succeed in playing ... P–K4 without disadvantage to himself, it will give him (a) equality in the center; (b) freedom of movement for his minor pieces, and in particular for his QB, which is as yet hemmed in. We further note that under certain circumstances, ... P–QB4 might be considered the freeing move. The problem of freeing the game becomes clearer after Black has completed his development on the K side and is faced with the necessity of bringing his other pieces into play.

It now becomes evident that 5 ... N–B3, a move that beginners often make, is usually inferior, partly because at the QB3 square the QN does not support the KN and partly because it blocks the development of the QBP, which is detrimental in one way or another to the freeing of Black's game.

6 N–B3

The KN must be developed, and this is the natural square to which to develop it, since it is the square at which the Knight has the greatest radius of influence. From its KB3, the Knight exercises a measure of control over its K5 square and makes Black's freeing move harder to attain, and from its KB3 the Knight may later go to its K5, from which it will exert a powerful restraining influence on Black's movements.

6 ...   O-O

Black now completes his development by bringing his King to a safer place and his Rook to a square from which it can more easily enter into action.

7 R-B1

This is an important strategical move. By later playing PxP, White has the possibility of converting the QB file into a half-open file. With his Rook dominating the file, he can play along it in various ways: double the Rooks, play the Queen to QB2, etc.

If the control of the open QB file is so desirable, one might ask why White does not play 7 PxP, so as to get the open file immediately. White, who can open the file at any time, waits to see if Black will play ... PxP in order to free himself, which would be better for White. If White makes the exchange, he helps Black in his effort to free himself. In comparison with the actual continuation, 7 PxP, NxP! would mean a few tempi in favor of Black. Yet in the Queen's Gambit Declined, White sometimes does play 3 PxP (see Game 13).

7 ...   P-B3

Theory recommends this move as the proper preparation for the freeing plans in conjunction with ... P-K4. The significance of the move will become clear from what follows.

8 B-Q3

White finally develops his KB, and to a square in the center of the board where it exerts pressure along two diagonals and where it aims particularly at Black's KR2. Up to now he has delayed playing the KB in the hope that Black would play ... PxP so that he could reply BxP without losing a tempo.

8 ...   PxP

Black plays ... PxP at this time (a) to make White lose a tempo; (b) to vacate his Q4 square for his KN; (c) as the beginning of a series of moves to free his position.

9 BxP   N-Q4

The second step toward freeing his position.

If Black did nothing to free his position, he would remain so restricted that White would have no trouble in bringing all his pieces into active positions.

Now it is clear that 9 ... N-Q4 would not have been possible without Black's preparation 7 ... P-B3.

10 BxB

The natural move, since 10 B–B4 obviously entails certain disadvantages: after the exchange 10 ... NxB, White will have isolated and doubled Pawns which, however, are compensated for by other advantages.

10 ...   QxB
11 O–O

White puts his King into a safer position and brings out his Rook for action. In most cases it is better to bring the King to safety before taking measures in the center.

If 11 P–K4, Black would continue by 11 ... NxN; 12 RxN, P–K4, with pressure against White's center, because White's KP would be in the air. And if White should play 13 P–Q5, the advance of the QP would not mean much; e.g., 13 P–Q5, PxP; 14 PxP, N–N3; 15 B–N3, B–N5, and White's passed Pawn is weak and strong at the same time, weak because it is isolated, and strong because it is a passed Pawn.

11 ...   NxN

Black wants to free his game by ... P–K4, and he cannot do so as long as his Knight remains on Q4. Therefore, he exchanges.

12 RxN

We have now reached the standard position in this opening. At this point, Black's strategic aim is (a) to neutralize White's center; (b) to free the Black QB.

The game usually continues: 12 ... P–K4 (Black's freeing move), which (a) makes a bid for control of or elimination of the center; (b) opens a diagonal for Black's imprisoned QB; (c) leads to the simplification that makes it difficult or impossible for White to realize the strategic aims in which the Queen's Gambit Declined is strongest. There are several continuations:

(a) 13 PxP, NxP; 14 NxN, QxN (at which point the neutralization is complete); 15 P–B4 (to mobilize the White Pawn majority), Q–B3 (to restrict White's advance); 16 P–B5 (to limit the scope of the Black Bishop), with some difficulties for Black—his QB is hemmed in, for instance;

(b) 13 Q–B2 (White chooses to let Black take the initiative in the center and himself to attack along the QB file), P–K5 (13 ... PxP gives White play along the K file and on the K wing); 14 N–Q2, N–B3; 15 B–N3, B–B4; 16 P–B4, to fix the position. The general opinion is that White is a little better off, because he has play along the half-open file.

(c) 13 Q–N1, P–K5 (13 ... PxP has the same disadvantages as

in (b) above); 14 N–Q2, N–B3; 15 P–QN4, also with some play for White. There are several continuations, although the results of theoretical research have not yet led to the judgment of a definite advantage for White in any of these lines.

12 ...   P–QB4

This is the chief deviation from the orthodox line of the Queen's Gambit Declined. It entails some difficulties for Black, but they are not insurmountable.

By this move Black attains his strategic aim of neutralizing White's center, but not that of freeing his QB. The first disadvantage of the text move is that White obtains control over the QB file.

Therefore, 12 ... P–K4 is somewhat stronger and more in line with Black's indicated strategy.

13 Q–B2

White assumes command of the QB file and threatens, for instance, 14 B–Q3, attacking both Black's KRP and his QBP.

13 ...   PxP

To destroy the White center and to parry the threat mentioned.

White now has to decide whether to take the Black Pawn with his KP or his Knight. This is a weighty decision, because it could be a matter of life and death. Let us consider the advantages and disadvantages of each course:

(a) 14 PxP: advantage—more freedom for White, especially the possibility of bringing the Knight to K5, the QR to the K wing; the Black KP is prevented from advancing; disadvantage—the isolated Pawn, which might become weak, and the square in front of the isolated Pawn, which might be occupied by the opponent.

(b) 14 NxP: a good move with all sorts of possibilities but with the disadvantage that White no longer occupies one of the four center squares with a Pawn and that the Pawn position of the two sides is quite symmetrical. In such positions you can acquire an advantage, but it may be temporary in character, because it is not based on Pawn position. Advantages based on Pawn position are much more permanent in character than those based on the position of the pieces, since the pieces move from place to place and Pawn structure remains constant for a number of moves.

White judges it more advantageous to have greater center control and plays

14 PxP   N–B3

It is important to bring the Knight to the K side for the protection of Black's KR2. If 14 ... N–N3; 15 B–Q3 (with tempo), P–KR3; 16 R–B7, and the extra tempo gives White time to seize the 7th rank.

15 B–Q3

Without tempo.

White's aim will now be to exploit the QB file, which is open and which White completely dominates. Black's efforts will be directed toward finding some way of opposing White's domination and toward freeing his QB.

Since, as we see in the next move, Black could equalize the game by 15 ... P–KN3, it should be asked whether the obvious move 15 R–K1 would have been better here. After 15 ... Q–Q3, White might sacrifice a Pawn by 16 N–K5, QxP, in order to start an attack by 17 R–KR3 or 17 R–KN3 or even 17 R–B3.

15 ...   P–QN3

A plausible move, but as we shall see from the continuation of the game, this method is too slow. Let us look for others.

(a) 15 ... P–KR3 (to prevent N–N5); 16 R–B7, Q–Q3; 17 N–K5 (establishing a powerful outpost in enemy territory), N–Q4 (if 17 ... QxP; 18 NxP, RxN; 19 RxB ch); 18 B–R7 ch, K–R1; 19 NxP ch, and one already sees (1) the force of control of the 7th rank; (2) that Black in this variation

does not succeed in preventing White's domination in a simple way.

(b) 15 ... P–KN3!; 16 R–B7, Q–Q3; 17 N–K5, N–Q4 leads to nothing for White. Therefore, before occupying the 7th rank, White must make preparations so that Black cannot play ... N–Q4 and throw the White Rook back. Correct in this case is 16 B–K4. Now Black cannot continue this development, and even after 16 ... NxB; 17 QxB, he is for the moment at a loss as to how to continue so that White can now play KR–B1 and continue his open-file strategy or, under some circumstances, bring the Knight to K5 or even to N5, just to continue the attack on the now weakened King position.

The text indicates that the amateur probably did not realize the importance of the penetration of the 7th rank by the White pieces. Perhaps he expected to be able to drive back the penetrating Rook without too much trouble. The continuation proves that he is wrong.

16 R–B7

White seizes control of the 7th rank, which is the logical consequence of the control of the open file.

16 ...   Q–Q3

Black moves to the most active square possible under the circumstances. To draw the Queen back to the 1st rank would be too passive. To cover the Queen by 16 ... B–Q2 would create a self-pin, which White would immediately try to exploit by moves such as N–K5 and B–N5.

Now that White has the 7th rank, what can he do with it? How can he increase his advantage? This is a part of the middle-game technique that cannot be compressed into a general rule. But the method can be described through example.

In the position at hand, White notices that if he could bring his Bishop to K4 and thus force Black's QR to vacate the QR1 square, he could then play RxRP, winning a Pawn. But Black's Knight guards White's K4 square. Therefore, White looks around for a way to eliminate the Knight. He plays

17 N–N5

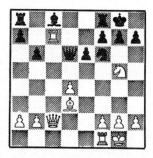

White's move puts his Knight into a position where in one more move it can attack Black's Knight with tempo; it also forces Black's reply by threatening to win his KRP. In addition, it attacks Black's KBP, which, although it is defended by both the King and the KR, could be taken, because Black's KR also has to protect its Bishop.

After 17 R–B1, threatening 18 RxB (18 ... RxR; 19 QxR, RxQ; 20 RxR ch), Black parries by 17 ... P–N3 (creating a hole) and then threatens to drive back the White Rook by 18 ... N–Q1.

17 ...   P–KR3

If 17 ... P–N3; 18 NxBP! (command of the 7th rank), QxP? (better 18 ... RxN; 18 RxB ch, etc., and Black is a Pawn down); 19 BxP!, with an overwhelming attack.

18 N–R7

Simpler would have been the combination just mentioned: 18 NxBP, RxN (18 ... QxP is risky because of 19 R–Q1); 19 RxB ch, etc., but White hopes to get a greater advantage from his control of the 7th rank.

Also 18 N–K4, NxN; 19 BxN comes to practically the same position with this difference, that the Black King is now on N1 instead of R1. Since the King is better on N1 than on R1, considered from the Black side, the direct N–K4 does not take advantage of all the possibilities of the position.

With the text, White will eliminate the Black Knight, partly so as to be able to bring his Bishop to K4 and force the Black QR from QR1, partly because if the Black Knight should move to Q4, it could lead to very complicated play.

Black could still make an attempt to clear the 7th rank by 18 ... N–Q4. From this move arise great complications as a consequence of certain tactical finesses that are in the position. The following variations give an idea as to the problems: 18 ... N–Q4; 19 R–B6,

(a) 19 ... Q–K2; 20 NxR, N–N5 (the point of Black's counterplay); 21 RxB, NxQ; 22 N–N6 dis ch, RxR; 23 NxQ ch, etc.;

(b) 19 ... Q–N1; 20 NxR, N–N5; 21 Q–B4, NxR; 22 QxN, B–N2 (22 ... KxN; 23 B–K4); 23 Q–Q7, KxN; 24 R–B1, B–Q4; 25 R–B7, Q–K1; 26 QxQ ch, KxQ, and White has absolute command of the 7th rank, which will give him good winning chances, since the command of the 7th rank is in general an important advantage.

18 ...   NxN

After the exchange of this Knight, White need not fear that his Rook will be driven back any further, but rather he can be sure of his pieces on the 7th rank. Now that Black's strategic defeat is a fact, the amateur begins to defend himself with great inventiveness and stubbornness. The master has to play with refinement to maintain his advantage and accumulate still more.

19 BxN ch   K–R1
20 B–K4

According to plan.

If Black now answers 20 ... B–R3; 21 R–B1, QR–B1, and White wins by 22 RxR, BxR; 23 QxB! Here it is a question of exploiting the 8th rank.

20 ...   R–QN1
21 RxRP

The first tangible result of control of the 7th rank. Not only does White win a Pawn; he also widens his scope on the 7th rank, which will lead to a possibility of maneuvers along that rank.

21 ...   QxQP

Black maintains material equality, but not for long.

22 R–Q1

An interesting position. Notice how White increases his domination of squares, and by a move made with tempo.

22 ...   Q–K4

Guarding the QR, which would otherwise be loose and a prospect for a possible combination; e.g., 22 ... Q–B3; 23 Q–B7!

The reply 22 ... Q–B4 offers an interesting sequence. White notices that after 23 QxQ, PxQ, Black's KR is committed to the protection of the King along the 8th rank. White can therefore continue 24 RxP, winning the Pawn and more! Black cannot reply 24 ... RxR on account of 25 R–Q8 ch, etc. From here on, the domination of the 8th rank definitely enters.

If 22 ... Q–N5; 23 P QR3 (White could not play 23 RxP?; RxR; 24 R–Q8 ch, R–B1 and White loses a Rook), Q–N4; 24 RxP.

In chess positions, and especially in middle-game positions, there is often a recurring theme that can be found in a number of variations arising from the same position. In this position the recurring theme is the necessity for protecting the Black King along the 8th rank by its KR. This theme is also present in the main line.

23 RxP

Triumph along the 7th rank! Black's KR is an overworked piece charged with two tasks: (a) the protection of the KBP; (b) guarding the 8th rank. The KR cannot perform both of these tasks.

23 ...   B–R3

Black clears the rank in order to free his KR.

24 KR–Q7

Notice that White does not exchange Rooks, which would relax the tension, but rather maintains and increases the pressure along the 7th rank by sending the other Rook down there to support its colleague.

24 ...   RxR

Black naturally exchanges, to cut down the attack and to relieve the pressure. If Black had played either Rook to B1, White could have replied Wi H=R7 and avoided any counterattack.

25 RxR   K–N1

It is important to eliminate the threat of mate along the 8th rank. Black was in a mating net, as appears after 25 ... R–QB1?; 26 QxR ch, BxQ; 27 R–B8 mate.

26 R–B7

The Rook returns to the QB file, where it is supported by the Queen, and again it controls the file, as well as exercising continued pressure along the 7th rank.

Questionable is 26 R–R7? because of 26 ... R–QB1, and Black wins after 27 Q–N1, QxB.

26 ...   R–Q1!

Threatens both ... QxB! and ... QxR!, and White cannot retake because of 28 ... R–Q8 ch, followed by mate. Note the important role played in this game by the 8th rank both for Black and for White.

The amateur shows improvement in finding this move.

27 P–KR3   R–Q5

A counterattacking move that acts like a boomerang. The Black Rook cannot afford to leave the 8th rank.

28 B–R7 ch

White now forces Black to move his King either to the B square, where it will be out in the open and more subject to attack along open lines, or to the R square, where it will be more vulnerable to mate along the 8th rank.

28 . . .   K–R1

If 28 . . . K–B1; 29 R–R7, after which the Bishop has no good squares. And 29 . . . R–B5 is refuted by 30 Q–Q1 (threatening mate), R–Q5; 31 Q–B3 ch, etc. Apparently the Black King is not safe on KB1. But neither is it safe on KR1. White looks for a way to exploit his control of the 8th rank and finds a move with a double threat that he can play with tempo.

29 R–R7

Threatening both 30 RxB and 30 R–R8 ch.

29 . . .   B–B1

Black need not fear 30 QxB ch because of 30 . . . KxB.

30 R–R8

Threatening RxB followed by mate. White still has to play carefully. His Queen cannot move freely because of Black's threat of mate on the 8th rank. Moreover, the White Queen has to protect his Bishop.

30 . . .   R–Q1

Here is a type of position that is often of the greatest frustration to the chess player. White has a won game in effect, for if nothing better appeared, he could exchange pieces and win by his plus Pawn. He knows that at this point there must be a shorter and more elegant win, but he cannot find the proper continuation. What should he do?

Now that the Black King is hemmed in and almost in a mating net, White must visualize the possible mate by saying: "*If* the White Bishop were on its KN6 and the White Queen or Rook on QB8, mate would be assured." So White moves

31 B–N6

White now actually threatens 32 RxB, or even 32 QxB.

31 . . .   Q–QB4

Forced. White cannot carry out his model mate, but the threat of it has forced Black to move to a less advantageous position where he himself no longer threatens mate to White.

32 QxQ

Once White can exchange Queens with a favorable Pawn position, he does so, obtaining a powerful passed Pawn far from Black's King. White has traded an advantage in space, which was temporary, for an advantage in Pawn structure, which is permanent. For a discussion of trading advantages, see the introductory remarks to Game 1 on page 1.

32 ...   PxQ

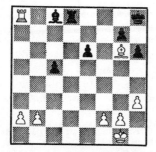

Black is now completely tied up: his Bishop cannot move, his Rook cannot leave the first rank, his King has no effective moves, his Pawn advances have no meaning. In contrast to Black's paralysis, White has a passed QRP and a Pawn plus.

33 P–QR4

Following the principle of advancing the Pawn that is entirely free.

33 ...   K–N1
34 P–R5   K–B1

Hurry!

35 P–R6   K–K2
36 RxB!

Other moves win as well, but this is the most elegant sequence. For instance, 36 P–R7, B–N2 is not so convincing.

36 ...   RxR
37 B–K4

This move threatens to win the Black Rook by 38 P–R7 and 39 P–R8.

37 ...   R–B2
38 B–N7!   Resigns

Black cannot prevent 39 P–R7 followed by 40 P–R8[Q].

Game 12

An early R–QB1 in the Queen's Gambit Declined

How to handle . . . P–QN3 in the Queen's Gambit Declined

The creation of hanging Pawns for an opponent

The attack on the hanging Pawns by the adversary

The weaknesses and strengths of hanging Pawns

The importance of accurate analysis of tactical possibilities

Both Game 10 and the present game illustrate the vulnerability of the hanging-Pawn formation. But in Game 10, hanging Pawns came about as a result of an error on the part of the amateur, whereas in the present game they arise as the logical development of the natural strategy growing out of the opening.

In the present game, the Black Pawn formation PQB4–PQ4 is so dynamic that the hanging Pawns constitute at the same time a serious weakness and a potential source of strength for Black. As the game develops, there is illustrated the exceedingly effective technique of attacking the hanging-Pawn formation. This technique is crowned with success only through an accidental tactical factor: Black's N(K2) is *en prise*, which gives White the opportunity to simplify to his advantage. But for the moment, enough of the weaknesses of the formation.

Hanging Pawns also contain within them two elements of strength: the possibility of opening files through the advance of the hanging Pawns and of increasing the space controlled by the possessor of the hanging Pawns, and the possibility of controlling key squares that can become outposts for the Knights and Bishops of the side with the hanging Pawns.

Position after 21 P–QN3

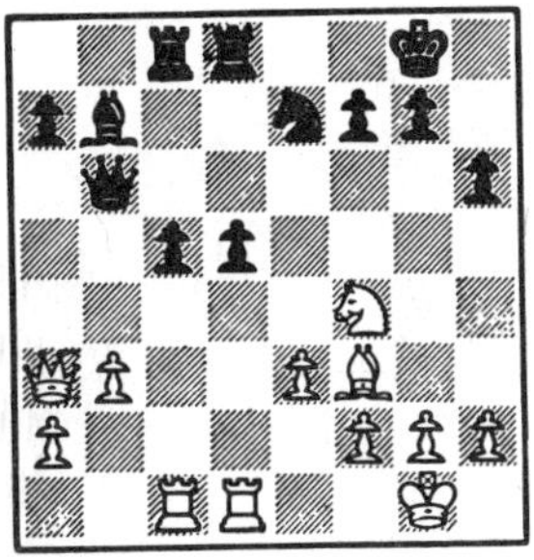

The diagram shows the position in the game that follows, had White played the plausible 21 P–QN3 (instead of 21 N–Q3!). In this position, by pushing his QP, Black would have the possibility of opening a file, with all the risks and advantages it might entail. Let us play 21 . . . P–Q5!; 22 BxB

(for White cannot permit the mutilation of his K side by 22 ... BxB;
23 PxB), QxB, and

(a) 23 RxBP, PxP! followed by
   (1) 24 RxQR, PxP ch, and Black has more mobility, and the White
   King is unsafe;
   (2) 24 RxR ch, RxR; 25 PxP, Q–K5, winning back the Pawn, and
   Black again has more mobility.
(b) 23 PxP, PxP, and Black has more mobility.

This, then, is an illustration of how a player can use hanging Pawns to
open lines, control more territory, and increase his mobility.

If, instead of 21 P–QN3, White plays 21 N–Q3 (as he actually does
in the game), 21 ... P–B5 (forced); 22 N–B4 (more cautious than 22

QxN), then Black answers 22 ... R–B4
(diagramed position). Now Black's QP is
practically backward, since it cannot easily
advance, and Black's QBP forms a point of
support so that the Black Knight might sooner
or later be able to go to its Q6 square, where
it would exercise phenomenal pressure on the
whole White position. On his part, White
could bring his Knight to his Q4 square, but
should he try to, it would increase the possibility of the Black maneuver N–N3–K4–Q6.

Position after 22 ... R–B4

For the moment, more important than the pos-
sibility of Black's posting his Knight on his Q6 square is the weakness
of White's Q wing, for once Black protects his Knight, he threatens
R–R4. So in exchange for the weakness on his Q5 square, Black has
reasonable mobility and possible attacking chances.

Queen's Gambit Declined: Tartakover Maneuver

Master	Amateur
White	*Black*

1 P–Q4	P–Q4
2 P–QB4	P–K3
3 N–QB3	N–KB3
4 B–N5	B–K2
5 P–K3	

So far, the moves are exactly
the same as in Game 11, where
the ideas of these moves are discussed.

| 5 ... | O–O |

Black normally castles early in
the Queen's Gambit Declined, and
he can do it at this point instead
of playing 5 ... QN–Q2, as he
did in Game 11.

Of course, if White now played
6 BxN, Black could not end up
with a Knight on his KB3, for he
could not recapture with his QN,
but White rarely makes this ex-

change, since it leaves Black with the Two Bishops. The only reason that White might play 6 BxN is to reach a sort of exchange variation by transposition (see Game 13): 6 ... BxB; 7 PxP, PxP; 8 Q–N3, P–B3; B–Q3, and White has an easy game, inasmuch as he has no problem developing and has a prescribed strategy of minority attack. But Black's Two Bishops will count in the long run.

6 R–B1

White now develops his QR to its natural square—the one from which it will command the QB file, which can be opened as soon as one side or the other exchanges center Pawns.

The text move is an attempt to meet both 6 ... P–B4 (a sort of Tarrasch Variation, in which Black tries to open the game early) and 6 ... N–K5 (the Lasker Variation, in which Black tries for an easy draw through simplification by exchange). The following variations will show how the text meets each of these moves:

(a) 6 ... P–B4; 7 BxN (to force ... BxB and deprive Black's QBP of the protection of his KB), BxB; 8 PxBP (not 8 PxQP, because of 8 ... PxQP(5)));

(b) 6 ... N–K5; 7 BxB, QxB; 8 PxP, NxN (forced); 9 RxN, PxP; 10 Q–B2, P–QB3; 11 B–Q3, P–KR3; 12 N–K2.

To those familiar with the Lasker Variation, it will be evident that in the above variation, White has gained a few tempi and now stands ready for the minority attack (Game 13).

6 ...   P–KR3

This move is advantageous to Black in two ways: (a) it removes his RP from the KR2 square, where it could become the object of attack by White's Queen at QB2 and his Bishop at Q3; and (b) it forces White to make a choice between the following three moves, the first two of which could be slightly disadvantageous to him:

(a) White could exchange his Bishop for Black's Knight, which would leave Black with the Two Bishops;

(b) White could withdraw his Bishop to his KB4, thus removing his indirect pressure on the center;

(c) White could withdraw his Bishop to KR4, thus continuing to exert indirect pressure on the center.

For Black, 6 ... P–KR3 could have the disadvantage of slightly weakening the castled K position. Once a Pawn in front of the King has been moved, it becomes a possible target for attack.

7 B–R4

White chooses to maintain indirect pressure on the center, which
is relatively best.

If he had played 7 B–B4, and
then later opened the QB file by
PxP, the combined action of his
QR and QB on his QB7 might have
become embarrassing for Black.
Therefore, Black would answer 7
B–B4 by an immediate 7 ... P–
QB4, the standard reply in such
positions.

    7 ...   P–QN3

The Tartakover Maneuver.

The development of the QB is
one of Black's most serious problems in the Queen's Gambit Declined. In this game, he proposes
to fianchetto the QB.

    8 PxP

White almost always plays PxP
when Black fianchettoes the QB in
such positions. Not only is it to
White's advantage to open the file,
which he already controls with his
QR, but also, if Black answers 8
... PxP, the fianchettoed Black
QB is rendered relatively ineffective on the closed diagonal. But
White also had to calculate the
possibilities of the alternate move
that Black now plays.

    8 ...   NxP
    9 NxN

The same position is obtained
after 9 BxB, QxB; 10 NxN.

    9 ...   PxN

Forced, for 9 ... BxB would
lead to the loss of the exchange
after 10 NxBP.

    10 BxB   QxB

The first phase of the game is
now over.

White has only one piece and
two Pawns developed, and his uncastled King is open to attack. On
the other hand, he dominates the
open QB file with his QR. His
strategy will therefore be to attack
on the Q side.

Black has castled and has opened
lines for his QB. In view of the
fact that his QBP is practically
backward, his strategy will be to
push his QBP to B4 as soon as
possible and perhaps try to get
some attack against the uncastled
White King.

Once the Black QBP is at its B4,
hanging Pawns on Black's Q4 and
QB4 will result, and they will then
constitute a theme for further
strategy.

White now looks around for a
plan based on Black's weak points:
the QBP and the QP. He sees the
possibility of attacking the Black
QP by playing B–K2–B3, followed
by either N–K2–B4 or N–K2–B3,
the former being preferable because it does not close the QB file
at any time. He also looks into
ways of protecting his King against
premature attacks. So he plays

11 B–K2!

But suppose that, instead, White had decided to attack the weak Black QBP and had played the plausible 11 Q–B2(?): 11 ... P–QB4; 12 PxP, P–Q5! This is dangerous for White: (a) 13 N–B3, PxP; 14 B–N5 (to prevent ... R–K1), N–R3, and (1) 15 PxNP?, Q–N5 ch, winning a piece; (2) 15 BxN?, BxB, and White cannot castle, the threat of PxP ch hangs over him, and Black's Rooks have free play on his first rank; (3) 15 O–O, NxP; 16 KR–K1, PxP ch; 17 QxP, Q–B3, and White has no serious compensation for the Pawn: (b) 13 B–Q3, PxP; 14 B–K4, PxP ch; 15 KxP, R–K1; 16 BxR, Q–K6 ch; 17 K–B1, B–R3 ch, winning.

11 ...　　　　　R–Q1

The continuation 11 ... P–QB4; 12 B–B3, B–N2; 13 N–K2, R–Q1 leads to the position of the text. But if instead 13 ... P–B5, then 14 P–QN3, P–QN4; 15 N–B3 gives White a positional advantage, as can be shown by tournament play. The point is that in the present situation, Black cannot take advantage of the possibilities that would solve the problem of the hanging Pawns and even establish a Q-side majority for him.

At this point, Black must have also looked into the possibility of simplifying the game by 11 ... Q–N5 ch; 12 Q–Q2, QxQ ch; 13 KxQ, P–QB3. Note that Black is forced to protect his QBP in such a way that his Knight is tied down

to the defense of the weak Pawn. The game might continue: 14 N–B3, B–N2; 15 N–K5!, R–QB1; 16 P–QN4, and Black's position is inferior, because he cannot develop his Q side and because his pieces are tied down to the defense of the QBP.

Since analysis shows that 11 ... P–QB4 leads to the same position and that the simplifying process by 11 ... Q–N5 ch gives him a poor position, Black decided to support his QP by the text move in view of the oncoming attack.

12 B–B3

Black's QBP is backward as long as it remains on its QB2, and since it has to advance at some time or other, Black decides to advance it now. The fact that this advance will result in hanging Pawns for Black does not mean that the move is erroneous, for as has been pointed out in the introduction to the game, hanging Pawns are sometimes a strength, sometimes a weakness, depending on other factors on the board.

12 ...　　　　　P–QB4
13 N–K2

According to plan.

White could play 13 PxP here. It could lead by transposition (13 ... PxP) to the text, but Black could also try to take advantage of White's arrear in development, e.g.: 13 ... B–N2; 14 N–K2, P–Q5; 15 BxB, QxB; 16 O–O, PxBP, and the complications are not un-favorable for Black.

13 ...   N–N0

To develop his QN to its natural square and to bring pressure against White's Q4 square.

14 O–O

The King must be brought to safety, in any case.

White delays PxP, for the later he makes this exchange, the less Black can profit from the opening of the QN file. Yet in one respect, delaying PxP *could* be unfavorable to White, namely, if Black could establish advantageously a Q-side majority with ... P–B5. But we have already seen in the note under Black's 11th move that this advance at that time leads to an advantage for White.

14 ...   B–R3(?)

Instead of using his Bishop to protect his QP, Black places it more actively on an open diagonal where it pins the White Knight and thus exercises indirect pressure against White's Q4 square. Tacti-cally, Black was hoping for 15 Q–R4, BxN!; 16 BxB, NxP!

But his Bishop is loose at its QR3, and since the White Queen gains time attacking this loose Bishop in the 17th move, 14 ... B–N2 would have been better.

15 R–K1

Unpinning in order to proceed with his attack against the Black QP.

15 ...   Q–Q3

Maintaining the protection of his QP, supporting his unprotected Knight, and vacating his K2 square for the Knight.

If 15 ... P–B5; 16 N–B4, Black has the problem of protecting his QP, e.g., 16 ... N–N5; 17 P–QR3, N–Q6; 18 NxN, PxN, which is good for White.

If 15 ... BxN; 16 RxB, and now 16 ... PxP fails against 17 RxN.

16 N–B4

Continuing his plan to bring pres-sure against the QP and forcing the Black Knight to a defensive post.

16 ...   N–K2

The only move.

17 Q–R4

White places his Queen on a square where it has wider range and controls more squares, makes a place for his KR on the Q file, which will soon be opened, and attacks the unprotected Black Bishop, forcing it to lose a tempo and to assume a defensive role.

17 ...   B–N2
18 PxP

At last the time for the Pawn exchange has come. It now gives White the maximum advantage, for now the Black QR is tied down to the defense of its QRP, and there is no possibility of Black's taking advantage of the ensuing open QN file.

18 ...   PxP

Black now has a pair of hanging Pawns, and—as was noted in Game 10—hanging Pawns *can* constitute a weakness, but they do not necessarily do so. It depends on how much activity the light pieces have.

Hanging Pawns require a special kind of strategy on the part of the opposing player. Various resources to be used against hanging-Pawn formations are listed on page 92. Let us see how White exploits their weaknesses in this game.

19 KR–Q1

First, he puts his KR on the best possible square—the one from which it brings additional pressure to bear on the Black QP.

19 ...   Q–QN3

In general, a Queen is too valuable a piece to be left on a file on which there is an enemy Rook, even when a piece or a Pawn of either color intervenes. By moving his Queen to QN3, Black gets his Queen out of line with the White

Rook and also protects his QRP, thus freeing his QR for action. He also attacks White's QNP.

20 Q–R3

White now turns his attention to the other hanging Pawn—a maneuver typical of hanging-Pawn technique. This is the continuation of the direct attack, which began with 16 N–B4.

20 ...   QR–QB1

Thus far, Black has been able to protect both of his hanging Pawns, but all his pieces are occupied in doing so. He has no possibility of undertaking anything else.

21 N–Q3!

The Knight's work on B4 having been accomplished, it now joins in the attack on the other hanging Pawn. The purpose of this attack is to force Black to weaken his position—the very essence of positional play.

Note that White had to act immediately, since Black threatened to free his game by ... P–Q5. For instance, see the analysis on pages 111-112. But after the text move, since Black is unable to protect his QBP for a third time, he is forced to advance it.

21 ...   P–B5

In general, the horizontal position is the safest one for a pair of adjacent Pawns. As soon as one of such Pawns is forced to advance, the resultant diagonal line of Pawns has inherent weaknesses, among others the fact that it makes available to the opponent strong squares on which to post pieces In this position, White obtains the strong Q4 square. On the other hand, the diagonal formation also has some advantages for its possessor, as is pointed out in the introduction to this game.

If there were no tactical details to consider at this point, no threats, White would probably try to maneuver so as to occupy his Q4 square or perhaps bring greater pressure to bear against the weakened Black QP. And Black, on his part, would probably bring pressure to bear against White's QNP or even try to maneuver his Knight to Q6, although this would be a slow process. But since both White and Black Knights are *en prise*, White must first of all analyze tactically and especially ask whether after ... PxN, the ensuing Black passed Pawn will be strong or weak, for if the Pawn should prove to be strong, it will be *very strong!*

22 QxN

In view of the possible strength of Black's PQ6 (after 22 ... PxN) and the mobility of all Black's pieces except his Bishop, this move required a very precise analysis. This analysis had to include an evaluation of Black's possibilities once he attained PQ6, namely, (a)

what PQ6 itself could do; (b) what would happen after ... QxNP; (c) what would happen after ... R D7, (d) what chances White had of winning Black's PQ6; (e) White's own attacking chances, which prove to be very important, but which are quite accidental in that normally it would be surprising that only a Queen and a Bishop could be dangerous to a well-protected K side, but that here several accidental circumstances, such as the vulnerable Rook, the fact that the Queen must protect the Bishop and that it also has other functions that prevent it from moving freely, strengthen White's attacking chances. As a matter of fact, Black can easily parry White's attack, but then he loses his valuable QP.

Actually, White did not have any other really convincing continuation. He could have carried on the attack with 22 N–B4 (see analysis on page 112), but success is not certain.

22 ...   PxN
23 RxR

Both to prevent ... RxR and to keep the KR on the Q file where it can attack and stop the Black Pawn.

23 ...   RxR
24 P–QN3

First, White must protect his QNP.
If 24 B–N4, R–B2, followed by some surprising combinations: (a)

25 Q–K8 ch, K–R2; 26 B–B5 ch,
P–N3; 27 BxQP, QxP!, etc.; if (b)
25 Q–Q8 ch, K–R2; 26 B–B5 ch,
P–N3; 27 BxQP, R–B8!!

24 ...   Q–R3

Attacking White's QRP and protecting his own advanced QP.

25 B–N4!

A powerful move—it attacks the
Black Rook, which cannot afford to
leave the first rank because of Q–
K8 ch, and it puts the Bishop in
a position where it can go to its
KB5, where it threatens to win
Black's advanced QP and possibly
also to participate in an attack
against the Black King. A quiet
move in such a position would be
very risky. Black is threatening R–
B7 and control of the 7th rank
and eventually P–Q7.

25 ...   P Q7

Black thinks that he can take
advantage of his passed Pawn and
his control of his QR3–KB8 diagonal. He threatens ... Q–K7 whenever the White Bishop leaves its
present diagonal.

Preferable was 25 ... R–B1,
but then White wins the dangerous passed Pawn by 26 B–B5. The
game might have continued 26 ...
Q–QB3; 27 BxP, P–Q5; 28 P–K4.
Bad would have been in that case
26 ... B–B1; 27 BxP, QxP; 28 B–
R7 ch!

26 BxR   Q–K7

Threatening mate both by 27
... QxR and 27 ... Q–K8 ch, etc.
If Black can escape a forced move
just once, he himself can mate.

If 26 ... BxB; 27 Q–Q8 ch, K–
R2; 28 QxP.

White now has a forced continuation and announces mate in 7:
27 Q K8 ch, K–R2; 28 B–B5 ch,
P–N3; 29 QxP ch, K–R1; 30 Q–B6
ch!, K–N1; 31 B–K6 ch, K–R2; 32
Q–B7 ch, K–R1; 33 Q–N8 mate.

The game was well played by
the amateur, and if the master had
not himself made each move at the
proper time, the amateur might
well have obtained counterchances.
Only Black's 25th move was weak
and accelerated the loss. This move
was prompted by a common psychological impulse—Black sees that
he must lose a Pawn, so he tries the
impossible.

But it is probable that this line
of the Queen's Gambit Declined
is not the strongest for Black, and
that with accurate play, White will
always get some advantage.

Game 13

Although it is much more difficult to generalize as to middle-game play than about opening or endgame play, as has already been pointed out in Game 10, which featured hanging Pawns, there *are* a certain number of middle-game type positions that lend themselves to a standard strategy. Of these, one of the best known is the minority attack.

First played in the late 1920s, the minority attack is most often applicable in positions arising from the Queen's Gambit Declined, in which White has a half-open QB file and Black a half-open K file, and in which Black's QBP is on its 3rd square, as illustrated in the diagram.

After suitable preparations, White advances his QNP until it comes in contact with Black's QBP. It usually results in some type of weakening of Black's Pawn position, which White subsequently exploits.

The minority attack is subtle and very difficult for Black to meet, even for a master player against another master player. Usually the defender loses the opportunity to obtain a counterattack, after which the attacker can carry out his purpose at ease and all the more forcefully. Naturally the minority attack becomes stronger and more effec-

Typical Pawn position in the minority attack: On the Q side White has 2 + 1 against Black's 4 Pawns.

120

tive if the opponent doesn't defend but looks for safety in counterattack. Everything may depend on who comes first in these conflicting strategies. Considering the fact that in general this type of position does not offer Black much opportunity for a K-side attack, the minority attack will normally win out.

In chess literature there are very few examples in which Black wins a game where White has launched a minority attack.

Queen's Gambit Declined: Exchange Variation

Master	**Amateur**
White	*Black*
1 P–Q4	P–Q4
2 P–QB4	P–K3
3 PxP	

One might be surprised to find White playing 3 PxP here, since this allows Black to answer 3 ... PxP, freeing his QB, the development of which is normally a major problem in this type of opening (see Game 11). There is, however, a factor in this exchange that explains White's strategy.

White makes the exchange in order to have at his disposal the half-open QB file. A half-open file is one on which the Pawn of one side has been removed, but the Pawn of the other side still remains. Since open files are often useless to either side because both

sides can control them with Rooks, the possession of a half-open file is often more important strategically and more promising than a fruitless attempt to control an open file from which Pawns of both sides have been removed.

In the position at hand, White can operate along the half-open QB file, Black along the half-open K file. But practice has shown that it is far easier for White to work along the QB file than Black along the K file.

This game will show what it means to possess a half-open file and how such a file can be exploited.

3 ...	PxP

The alternate 3 ... QxP would be answered by 4 N–QB3, thus gaining a tempo for White and allowing an early P–K4. True, after 4 ... Q–Q1; 5 P–K4, Black might make an attempt to break up White's center by 5 ... P–QB4, but after both 6 P–Q5 and 6 N–B3 White has an excellent game.

4 N–QB3	N–KB3
5 B–N5	B–K2

All these are normal developing moves that aim to control the four center squares.

    6 P K8

For Black there are two dangerous types of attack lurking in a position of this sort: (a) a combinational attack against Black's K side, which as a rule involves White's castling on the Q side; (b) the *minority attack*, as seen in this game, which is of a positional nature.

        6 ...   O–O

In positions where the White Queen is on its Q1, the White KB on or able to play to its Q3, the White QB on its KN5, the White KN on its KB3, and where the Black KN is on its KB3, as in the present game, it is wise for Black to play ... P–KR3 as soon as possible in order to give White less choice. In the comments after Black's 10th and 11th moves, we shall explain the meaning of this more clearly.

In itself, the advance of the Black KRP means a slight weakening of the K side, but this slight weakening has to be accepted if one has a special purpose for making the move. Besides, only under special circumstances can such a weakening be exploited, as for instance, if White can successfully advance his KNP, and such circumstances are scarcely present here.

    7 Q–B2

By placing his Queen on QB2, White stakes a claim both on the half-open QB file and on the diagonal QN1–KR7.

        7 ...   P–B3

This move was necessary at some time or other in order to protect Black's QP.

    8 B–Q3

White now threatens 9 BxN and 10 BxP, winning a Pawn.

        8 ...   QN–Q2

Black could also have played 8 ... P–KR3, and after 9 B–R4 he would have come to the same line as noted after Black's 6th move.

    9 N–B3   R–K1

If White decided to make the combinational attack on Black's KRP, he could now castle on the Q side, then advance his K-side Pawns. The game might then continue: 10 O–O–O, and

(a) 10 ... N–B1; 11 P–KR4, B–K3; 12 QR–N1, R–B1; 13 BxN, BxB; 14 P–KN4, or

(b) 10 ... P–KR3; 11 B–R4, N–K5; 12 BxB, QxB; 13 BxN, PxB; 14 N–Q2, P–KB4; 15 P–KN4.

10 O O

By his castling on the K side rather than on the Q side, it is clear that White has chosen the positional handling of this game. As soon as possible White will try to take advantage of his chances on the Q side.

10 ...   P–KR3

If Black had played this move when it was first suggested (6 ... P–KR3; 7 B–R4, O–O; 8 Q–B2, P–B3; 9 B–Q3, QN–Q2; 10 N–B3, R–K1; 11 O–O ...) or even at move 8, he could now have continued by 11 ... N–K5, liberating his game, whereas in the actual game 10 ... N–K5 would lose a Pawn. Compare the move ... N–K5 in the actual game and in the above-mentioned variation:

Actual game: 10 ... N–K5?; 11 BxN, BxB; 12 BxRP ch, losing a Pawn.

After 10 O–O, inserting the moves 10 ... P–KR3; 11 B–R4; 11 ... N–K5!; 12 BxN, BxB, with a reasonable position for Black.

On the other hand, if Black had played 6 ... P–KR3, White might have preferred O–O–O to O–O, thus choosing the attack against Black's K side as a plan.

11 B–KB4

White had the choice of playing 11 B–KB4 or 11 B–R4. If Black had played 6 ... P–KR3, White could have already withdrawn his KB to KR4, and there would not have been any choice. One might ask: "If it is as important to have the QB on KB4, why not play it there at once? The explanation would go deep into opening theory and cannot be taken up here. In general, 11 B–KB4 is preferable, for from that square the Bishop controls several important squares on the Q side and can collaborate in the minority attack that White will soon launch. On the other hand, it should be examined whether Black, after B–KB4, can exchange the Bishop for the Knight with advantage. So after B–KB4, White has to take into consideration the move ... N–KR4, which threatens to exchange his valuable Bishop. For that reason, in many cases White plays P–KR3 as soon as possible in order to open the square KR2 for the retreat of his QB.

11 ...   N–B1

In this special case it does not matter that White has not yet played P–KR3, for 11 ... N–R4 is refuted by the well-known combination 12 NxQP, and if 12 ... PxN; 13 B–B7, winning the Queen.

12 P–KR3

In order to retain the QB after
... N–R4

13 ...   B–Q4

Black does well to exchange
Bishops, on the one hand to clear
the field and possibly start a K-
side attack, on the other in order
to eliminate White's QB and to
relax its pressure against Black's
Q side.

13 BxB   QxB

White has not been able to retain his QB, but he still has a slight
edge, since he has exchanged his
Bad Bishop, the Bishop that was
on squares of the same color as
are his advanced Pawns, for Black's
Good Bishop, namely, the Bishop
that was on squares of the opposite
color of those on which his advanced Pawns stand.

14 QR–N1

Preparing for the minority attack!

The minority attack is so called
because White, with a 2–5 Pawn
formation, attacks Black with a
4–3 Pawn formation along the
half-open QB file. In this attack,
Black's QBP is always on its R3.
The force and consequences of this
minority attack will soon become
clear.

14 ...   B–Q2

Black might have played 14 ...
P–QR4, but White would have
replied 15 P–QR3, with the same
general result.

15 P–QN4

The first active thrust against
Black's QBP.

15 ...   Q–K2?

Black aims to increase his control of space and to continue by
16 ... N–K5, which combines a
freeing maneuver with an attack.

In general, little can be done
against the minority attack. A move
such as 15 ... P–QR3 would be
answered by 16 P–QR4, and then
if 16 ... P–QN4; 17 PxP, and
after 17 ... RPxP, Black remains
with a backward QBP, or after 17
... BPxP, with an isolated QP and
a backward Pawn on QR3.

But here Black does miss the opportunity to slow down the speed
of White's attack by not playing 15
... QR–B1. In that case, the White
Queen would stand unfavorably
posted in the line of Black's QR,
and White would have to make
several preparatory moves, such as
KR–B1, before playing P–N5, since
now an immediate P–N5 would
fail against ... PxP, BxP ... N–
K5.

16 P–N5

The purpose of the minority attack is to weaken the hostile Pawn formation.

There are now four possibilities: (a) If Black exchanges, his QP will be isolated. (b) If White exchanges and Black retakes with his Pawn, Black will have a backward Pawn on the half-open QB file. (c) If Black recaptures with his Bishop, his QP will be isolated as in the first case. (d) If the Black Pawn bypasses the White NP, White can exchange with the result: a Black isolated Pawn on the Q file and a strong square on White's Q4 for the White Knight. Thus, no matter which way the minority attack goes, Black ends up with an inferior Pawn position, a weakness which White can then set about to exploit.

16 ...   N–K5

This is not a bad move. It aims to secure more freedom for Black and to exert a little pressure on the White position. It limits White's freedom of action to the extent that it obliges him to keep his Knight protected. Moreover, we have already seen that Black cannot do much to counter White's strategy of weakening Black's Q-side Pawns.

17 N–K5

Threatening to win a Pawn by cutting the communication of Black's Knight with its base and exchanging at White's K4, as well as intensifying the pressure on the Black Q2 square.

17 ...   NxN

There isn't anything better. No relief is afforded by 17 ... P–B3, for after 18 NxB, NxN; 19 PxP, PxP, the resultant position is very powerful for White, who could continue, for instance, 20 NxN, PxN; 21 B–R6, and the Black BP has become very weak. Or after 18 ... QxN; 19 PxP, QxP (19 ... PxP; 20 NxN loses a Pawn); 20 NxP wins a Pawn (20 ... QxN??; 21 B–B4), QxQ; 21 BxQ, N–Q7; 22 N–B7, and White maintains the Pawn.

Thus White can either weaken the Pawns or win a Pawn.

After 17 ... N–Q3; 18 PxP, BxP; 19 NxB, PxN; 20 N–R4, the attack against the weakened Pawn has begun, just as in the game.

18 QxN

Black now has several possibilities:

(a) 18 . . . PxP; 19 NxB, NxN, 20 RxP, N—N3; 21 Q—N3, followed by P—QR4 and P—QR5 with all sorts of chances for White, since both Black's QP and QNP are weak;

(b) 18 . . . P—QB4; 19 NxB (19 QxP, QxQ loses the Knight) comes into consideration. After 19 . . . NxN; 20 PxP, Black has an isolated QP. But he is not too badly off, for all his pieces are in action;

(c) 18 . . . KR—B1, which he plays.

18 . . .   KR—B1

By threatening . . . P—QB4 and . . . PxP, Black presses White to make a decision. The decision will, however, be favorable to White, since Black will soon find himself with a backward QBP—one of White's high-priority desiderata in the minority attack.

19 PxP   BxP

19 . . . PxP is met by 20 R—N7, with additional pressure on the 7th rank.

20 NxB

Now Black gets his backward Pawn.

20 . . .   PxN

Forced, for if 20 . . . RxP; 21 Q—N3, losing a Pawn.

At last we have the definite Pawn configuration toward which White has been working. Black has a backward Pawn on his QB3, and a new phase of the game is about to start. How can White take advantage of Black's backward Pawn? White cannot accomplish much simply by attacking, because Black will be able to defend. White must apply pressure on two fronts, that is, he must be able to attack Black's QB3, the vital point, and also be able to start action somewhere else. This is the secret of realizing positional advantage. When pressure is brought to bear from two directions, Black will find it difficult to defend on both fronts, and he should eventually crumble before White's double pressure.

21 KR—B1

It is logical for White to exert more pressure along the QB file and to prevent Black from liquidating his weakness by . . . P—QB4. Also, by pressing against the QBP, White can more easily maintain his superiority on the QN file. Black

cannot oppose this pressure by ...
QR–N1, because White would ex-
change Rooks and then win the
QBP.

21 ...   Q–K3?

Black leaves the 7th rank in
order to protect his QBP. Thus he
offers White the second front,
namely, the possession of the 7th
rank.

Black should have played 21 ...
R–B2. In that case, White would
have continued 22 Q–QR5, Q–Q3;
23 Q–R6, threatening 24 R–N7.

22 Q–B2

Threatening to win the exchange
by B–B5. White could also have
played 22 R–N7 at once, in which
case Black should have continued
22 ... N–Q2. With the text, White
first tries to get possession of the
diagonal KB5–QB8.

22 ...   Q–Q3

No better would have been 22
... P–N3; 23 R–N7.

23 R–N7!

The force of this move is such
that Black can no longer move any
of his heavy pieces. For instance,
23 ... R–B2 loses a Pawn by 24
RxR, QxR; 25 QxP. Or 23 ...
QR–N1; 24 RxRP. The Black pieces
are completely tied up to the defense of their Pawns.

23 ...   N–K3

The only piece that can move.
The idea of the text is to advance

... P–QB4 and in this way get
rid of the weak BP. The BP is not
only a weakness, but also an obstacle. It hinders the Rooks and
the Queen from moving freely. If
Black can get rid of his BP, the
QP will be weak, but it will not
be an obstacle.

After 23 ... P–QR4 (or ... P–
QR3), White wins the BP by 24
R–N6. The sally 24 ... Q–R6
(putting pressure on the White
Bishop and QRP) does not work.
White simply answers 25 RxBP,
RxR; 26 QxR, and the remaining
Black Rook is attacked so that
Black has no opportunity to take
White's Bishop.

Black could consider making the
sally at once: 23 ... Q–R6. White
has several answers, but the simplest is 24 Q–B3!, QxQ (24 ...
QxP? loses the Queen after 25 R–
R1); 25 RxQ, and we get positions similar to those in the game;
e.g., 25 ... N–K3; 26 B–B5, K–
B1; 27 BxN, PxB; 28 P–N3, and
Black is in *Zugzwang*.

Finally, 23 ... N–Q2 does not
ease the position either, because
of 24 B–B5.

24 B–B5

This prevents Black from carrying out his plans. White can exchange a Knight and win a Pawn if Black advances his BP

Black is now in a kind of Zugzwang on a full board. This is amazing. He cannot move a single piece without losing at least a Pawn. Let us examine the position closely:

(a) 24 ... K–R1; 25 RxBP

(b) 24 ... K–B1; 25 BxN, followed by 26 Q–R7

(c) 24 ... Q–R6; 25 BxN, PxB; 26 Q–N6, Q–B1; 27 QxKP ch, winning two Pawns

(d) 24 ... Q–Q1 or Q–B1; 25 BxN, PxB; 26 Q–N6, Q–B3; 27 QxQ, PxQ; 28 R–K7, winning a Pawn

(e) 24 ... QR–N1; 25 RxRP

(f) 24 ... KR–B2; 25 RxR, followed by 26 QxP

(g) 24 ... other KR moves; 25 QxP

(h) 24 ... N moves; 25 BxR

(i) 24 ... P–QR3 or P–QR4; 25 R–N6, winning the QBP

(j) 24 ... P–B4; 25 BxN, and
(1) 25 ... QxB; 26 PxP, or
(2) 25 ... PxB; 26 Q–N6

(k) 24 ... P–B3; 25 BxN ch, QxN; 26 Q–N6, followed by mate

(l) 24 ... P–N3; 25 BxP, PxB; 26 QxP ch, with an early mate

(m) 24 ... P–KR4; 25 P–KR4, and Black is again in *Zugzwang*

(n) 24 ... P–N4 (the text)

24 ...   P–N4

The only move that does not lose material at once. Literally speaking, there is no longer a state of *Zugzwang*, because the Black King can now move.

25 B–N4

Making room for the Queen and maintaining a virtual *Zugzwang* as far as the Black pieces are concerned.

25 ...   K–N2

The only move, as can be seen from the different possibilities listed after White's 24th move.

26 P–N3

At this point White could have played 26 Q–KB5 at once, but that move is still stronger when the Black King is on its KN1. Therefore, White makes a waiting move, which does not alter his situation and which forces Black into a less favorable position.

26 ...   K–N1

The only move.

27 Q–KB5

White relieves the pressure on Black's QBP, because he sees that he can get a decisive advantage on the other wing.

27 ...   N–Q1

After 27 ... R–B2, which has now become possible because, by moving his Queen, White gave up the double threat on the QB file, White wins a Pawn just the same by 28 RxR, NxR (28 ... QxR leaves Black in a hopeless position after 29 Q–B6, threatening both QxRP and BxN); 29 Q–Q7, and Black is bound to lose his QBP after all.

28 R–Q7   Q–K3

Other moves by the Queen are no better. For instance, 27 ... Q–R6; 28 R–B2, or 27 ... Q–B1; 28 RxQP, etc.

29 Q–B3

White could also have won a Pawn by 29 QxQ: 29 ... PxQ; 30 R–K7, K–B1; 31 R–R7, but the text is still stronger.

29 ...   Q–K5

Other moves lose a Pawn immediately. For instance, 29 ... Q–N3; 30 RxQP.

30 Q–B6

Attacking the Black KRP and forcing back the Black Queen.

30 ...   Q–N3

After 30 ... Q–R2, White wins immediately by 31 R–K7, threatening both R–K8 ch and BxR.

31 QxQ ch   PxQ
32 RxQP

Also possible is 32 R–Q6.

32 ...   PxR
33 BxR

Since White's Rook is stronger than Black's, White prefers to leave it on the board, rather than play 33 RxR. We'll see the power of this Rook in what follows.

33 ...   R–N1

The reply 33 ... K–B2 to bring the King out of captivity will be met by 34 R–B7 ch, K–B3; 35 B–N7, NxB; 36 RxN. White has maintained his positional superiority and will not have much trouble in realizing his plus Pawn. Still, this would have been slightly better than what follows, for after the text continuation White wins a second Pawn by force.

34 R–B7

By attacking Black's QRP, White prevents the Black Rook from attacking the White QRP, after which ... RxP could follow.

34 ...   P–QR4

The Black Knight cannot play, since 34 ... N–B2 is answered by 35 B–K6.

35 R–B5

Although attacking two unprotected Black Pawns, White cannot take either of them before bringing his Bishop to safety. But on the other hand, except for ... R–N8 ch, the Black Rook cannot leave the first rank, for in that case White can take one of the Black Pawns at once, while after K–N2 and a move such as B–N4, White will win one of the Black Pawns, for Black cannot protect them both.

35 ...   P–R5

After 35 ... K–B2; 36 B–R6 or B–N4 wins the Pawn.

36 B–Q7

White now attacks both Black's QRP and his QP.

36 ...	R–N7
37 BxP	RxRP
38 B–N3	

Black's QP is now doomed.

38 ...	R–R8 ch
39 K–N2	K–B1
40 BxP	

The Black Knight is now encircled by the White Bishop so that it cannot move without being taken or exchanged, leaving White with a won ending in either case, since he has two passed Pawns.

40 ...   Resigns

When there are no counter-chances at all, the only thing the Black player can do is to wait and be prepared to meet the blow. That is what happens in this game. One can scarcely tell whether it is a master or an amateur who is handling the Black pieces, except at Black's 21st move, in which he offers his opponent a second front. Certainly a master would not have done that. But apart from Black's 21st move, it can only be considered as bad luck for the amateur that he gets into a position that is so hard to defend.

Game 14

The theory of the Slav Defense of the Queen's Gambit Declined

Finding a plan for the middle game

The importance of centralization

Motives for the exchange of pieces

The disadvantage of getting a piece out of play

Holes in the position

The exchange of Rooks in the endgame

Paralyzing the opponent's pieces in the endgame

The role of the King in the endgame

One of the most challenging problems in chess is the choice of an effective middle-game strategy. Such strategy must be based on the characteristics of the position, and when there are no enemy weaknesses to attack, it must often be aimed simply at neutralizing the opponent's attempts to build up power, to free himself, etc.

An error of judgment in strategy is not as easily punished as a mistake in tactics. For that reason, even when a player has not chosen the best strategic line at a given point, he is not necessarily irretrievably lost, and often by proper subsequent play he can recoup and arrive at a position where his slightly superior opponent finds himself hard put to get anything better than a draw out of the game.

The possibility of converting a somewhat unfavorable position into a drawish line exists both in the middle game and in the endgame. The play that follows shows that in the critical phase of the game where it is necessary to make plans, the amateur fails, but it also shows that at various points in this same phase the amateur might have converted the position into lines in which even a master would have found it difficult to get more than a draw from it.

Queen's Gambit Declined: Slav Defense

Amateur	Master
White	*Black*
1 P–Q4	P–Q4
2 P–QB4	P–QB3

The Slav Defense of the Queen's Gambit Declined. We have seen in Game 11 how in the classical line of the Queen's Gambit Declined 2 ... P–K3 shuts in the QB and how much energy must be expended later in order to open lines for the Bishop.

In the Slav Defense 2 ... P–QB3 supports the center and retains for Black the privilege of playing out his QB later if he desires.

3 N–KB3

If Black now accepts the gambit by playing 3 ... PxP, White regains the gambit Pawn in the usual way: 4 P–K3, P–QN4; 5 P–QR4, P–K3; 6 PxP, PxP; 7 P–QN3, etc.

At this point, White often plays 3 N–QB3, which leads to other variations. If Black accepts the gambit, he cannot hold the Pawn either, for after 3 ... PxP,

(a) 4 P–K4!

(1) 4 ... P–QN4; 5 P–QR4, P–N5 (5 ... P–QR3?; 6 PxP, BPxP; 7 NxP); 6 N–R2, winning either Black's QBP or QNP, and if 6 ... P–N6; 7 N–QB3, B–R3, White recovers the Pawn by N–B3, followed either by N–K5 or, after some preparations, by N–Q2.

(2) 4 ... P–K4; 5 N–B3, PxP; 6 QxP, QxQ; 7 NxQ, P–QN4; 8 P–QR4 P–N5; 9 N–Q1, B–R3; 10 N–K3, always regaining the gambit Pawn.

(b) 4 P–K3, P–QN4; 5 P–QR4, P–N5; 6 N–R2, again winning either Black's QBP or QNP.

3 ...	N–B3
4 N–B3	PxP

Here Black seemingly violates the principle of retaining control of the four center squares by exchanging the center Pawn on his Q4 for White's side Pawn on QB5. However, Black has compensation. He threatens to retain the extra Pawn by playing 5 ... P–QN4. To recover the Pawn, White usually weakens his position by playing 5 P–QR4, thus surrendering his QN4 square to Black. By playing ... B–QN5 later, Black will pin White's QN and gain control over White's K4 square, so that White cannot at some later time make use of his majority in the center.

Often at this point amateurs (and up to around 1930, masters also) play 4 ... B–B4, which has the disadvantage of weakening Black's QNP; e.g., 5 PxP, PxP (the lesser evil for Black would be 5 ... NxP, which leaves the center to White); 6 Q–N3, and Black is in trouble, since the move attacks Black's QNP and exerts pressure against Black's QP. At this point, best to defend the QNP is 6 ... B–B1 (as Capablanca played against Alekhine in 1927—but this shows how bad 4 ... B–B4 really is). Other moves: (a) 6 ... Q–Q2; 7 N–K5 wins either Black's QP or QNP; (b) 6 ... Q–N3; 7 NxP, QxQ; 8 NxN ch, KPxN; 9 PxQ, with a plus Pawn for White, who, however, has some difficulties to overcome.

5 P–QR4

After 5 P–K3, which is also playable, but certainly not better, 5 ... P–QN4; 6 P–QR4, P–N5, and either (a) 7 N–QN1, B–R3, whereupon Black keeps the Pawn for a while and gets counterplay by ... P–B4 whenever White regains the Pawn; or (b) 7 N–R2, P–K3, and it will cost an extra move to bring the White QN into an active position.

The continuation 5 P–K4, P–QN4 is a gambit, for after 6 P–QR4, P–N5, Black maintains his plus, since White's KP is lost.

5 ...   B–B4

With this move Black exerts pressure on the center, thus controlling White's K4 and preventing White from playing P–K4.

6 P–K3

Often 6 N–K5 is played here. This is a playable move, but it is against the principle of moving the

same piece only once in the opening. Black would then continue with 6 ... P–K3 and get in his thematic KB pinning move, all the same: 7 NxP(B4), B–QN5. If White tried to get the center by P–B3 and P–K4, Black could sacrifice: 7 P–B3, B–QN5; 8 P–K4, BxP; 9 PxB, NxP, with a difficult position for both sides.

6 ...   P–K3
7 BxP   B–QN5

With this pin Black exerts pressure on the White center, and White is prevented from pushing his KP. By this type of center control Black should gain superiority in space.

At this point each side has three pieces developed, but it is *White's* QB which is undeveloped. Both of Black's Bishops are well developed, which is some compensation for White's numerical majority in the center.

8 O–O   O–O

We have now reached a position in the middle game where White must find a good plan. He

notices Black's loose KB and unprotected QNP and plays

9 Q–N3

White hopes to force the exchange of the Black Bishop or to
win Black's QNP

Since White does not obtain positive results by 9 Q–N3, he should
play according to the general strategic principle: *centralization in the
opening phase.*

White should therefore try either
9 Q–K2 (followed by P–K4) or
9 N–K5 (preparing P–B3 and P–
K4). The latter move is answered
by 9 ... P–B4, with neutralization of the White center. Compare
the position at the end of these
two lines:

  (a) 9 N–K5, P–B4; 10 N–R2, B–
      R4; 11 PxP, QxQ; 12 RxQ, B–
      B7 (even).
  (b) However, after 9 Q–K2 Black
      cannot equalize in the same
      way: 9 Q–K2, P–B4? (better
      is 9 ... B–N5 or 9 ... N–
      K5); 10 N–R2, B–R4; 11 PxP,
      N–B3; 12 R–Q1, Q–K2; 13 N–
      Q4, KR–Q1; 14 P–QN4! and
      White wins:
      (1) 14 ... BxP loses a piece
          after 15 NxN, PxN; 16 NxB.
      (2) 14 ... NxP; 15 B–Q2 is
          complicated but loses material
          as well: 15 ... QxP (15 ...
          N–B3; 16 NxN and 17 BxB);
          16 N–N3, Q–N3; 17 NxB, etc.

9 ...   Q–K2

By the same move Black protects his KB and his QNP, which
is necessary, since after 10 ... P–

QR4; 11 N–R2! is strong and forces
the exchange of the Black KB.

White has erroneously expected
Black to play 9 ... BxN. There
are a number of reasons for Black's
not exchanging here. Strategically,
he should not exchange for the following reasons:

  (a) Never exchange a Bishop
for a Knight unless there are important considerations for doing so.
  (b) Do not strengthen your opponent's center (9 ... BxN; 10
PxB! and White has a stronger
center).
  (c) Do not open lines for your
opponent (9 ... BxN; 10 PxB!
and the White QB, now inactive,
can play to R3! Later, the opening
of the QN file to the Rook can
also become important).

There is also a tactical reason
for not playing 9 ... BxN, namely,
10 QxP!.

10 B–Q2

This is a complex position whose
consequences are not easily evident
to the amateur. For instance, after
the obvious 10 ... QN–Q2, very
strong would be 11 P–K4! and (a)
11 ... NxP loses a piece after 12
NxN; (b) 11 ... BxP also loses
a piece after 12 NxB; (c) 11 ...
BxN; 12 PxQB, BxB; 13 NxB, PxP;
14 QxP is favorable for White.

At this point 10 N–R2 would
be answered by 10 ... B–Q3 on
the principle of centralization. Black
can play this, because now his
QNP is protected.

10 ...   P–QR4

By protecting the KB twice, this move prevents White from playing 11 P–K4.

11 KR–Q1?

This is the type of erroneous move often made by the amateur. The text is just a waiting move without any exact goal. Does the White KR stand better on Q1 than on KB1? That is doubtful. In some variations the pin of White's KN by ... B–KN5 could become difficult for White.

The position is critical, and both sides try to clear the situation in the center in their favor. 11 KR–Q1 does not accomplish anything, and is therefore a waste of time.

In some positions it might be preferable to make a waiting move to see what the opponent is going to do, but never in a *critical* position in which certain aims must be realized.

Had White played 11 KR–K1, threatening 12 P–K4, things would have been quite different. Good or bad, this move would have been according to the characteristics of the position. After 11 ... QN–Q2; 12 P–K4, B–N5; 13 P–K5, N–Q4; 14 B–KN5, chances are difficult to

appraise. This does not mean that 11 KR–K1 would have been the right line—it would merely have been one of the possible lines and merits study.

A closer examination of the position leads to the conclusion that the following strategic line is best:

(a) White should plan to bring his QN to KN3, where it also controls the center, where it cannot be exchanged, and where it can cause trouble for the Black Bishop on its KB4;

(b) White should mobilize his QB by placing it at its QB3. White's rough strategic plan will be 11 N–K2, 12 N–N3, 13 B–B3.

Note that 11 N–K2 results in a position in which Black has no advantage: (a) He could answer 11 ... QN–Q2, but after 12 BxB, PxB, Black's QNP(5) will eventually become weak. (b) White also gets a satisfactory position after 11 ... B–Q3; 12 N–N3, B–N3 (12 ... B–KN5; 13 N–K5 is advantageous for White because of 13 ... BxN; 14 PxB, KN–Q2; 15 QxP!); 13 B–B3, and White has a satisfactory position. Now 13 ... QN–Q2 fails against 14 QxP (note the difference between this move and 13 QxP after 12 ... B–Q3 in the present game), although Black has a draw in hand after 14 ... KR–QN1; 15 QxP, R–QB1; 16 Q–N5, QR–N1; 17 Q–R6, etc. Instead, Black would have to continue after 13 B–B3 with 13 ... P–B4 followed by 14 ... N–B3.

11 ...   QN–Q2

This move develops the QN, prepares 12 ... P–K4, and connects the Rooks. Connected Rooks occupying the 1st rank are useful for defensive and offensive purposes.

12 N–R2(?)

White plays thus in order to induce the exchange of Bishops. But the QN is now completely out of play on QR2.

Much better is still 12 N–K2, B–Q3; 13 N–N3, B–KN5; 14 QxP, and Black is obliged to force a draw by 14 ... QR–N1; 15 Q–R6 (15 QxP?, R–N3!), R–R1, etc.; or 14 ... KR–N1; 15 QxP, R–QB1 (not 15 ... R–N3? because the QR is *en prise*); 16 Q–N5, KR–N1; 17 Q–B6, etc.

Compare the position of the Knight at QR2 in the game with the same Knight at KN3 after 12 N–K2.

12 ...   B–Q3

Black will now be able to obtain a clear superiority in the center. He controls his K5, and White cannot prevent his playing ... P–K4. However, his advantage, like so many positional advantages in this type of opening, is minimal.

At this point White must look around for some way of equalizing. Note that 13 QxP? (which leads to a draw after 12 N–K2) fails here against 13 ... KR QN1; 14 QxP, B–K5!; 15 P–Q5, BxN; 16 PxB, N–K4.

Since there is no possibility of White's preventing Black's threatened ... P–K4, which will eliminate White's KN and expose White's K side to a forceful attack, White decides to bring his relatively inactive KB to Q3, which after the exchange 13 ... BxB; 14 QxB will bring the Queen into the center for defense and strengthen the square K4. So he plays

13 B–Q3

White might have done better, however, to play the likewise attacking move 13 B–B3, which would lead to a general exchange after 13 ... P–K4; 14 PxP, NxP; 15 NxN, BxN; 16 BxB, QxB, after which there is not much left in the position, since Black's KB has been exchanged as well. In order to avoid this extreme simplification, Black could have played 13 ... N–K5, after which he might first exchange his Knight for the White Bishop, then push the KP, thus avoiding the general simplification on his K4.

13 ...   BxB

Black makes this exchange for several reasons:

(a) After 13 ... B–KN5 or 13 ... N–K5, the possibility of 14 QxP revives. See the line under move 12 beginning 12 N–K2.

(b) Black does not wish to lose his influence over his K5.

(c) Black is perfectly willing to exchange White's Good Bishop on Q3, but he would be unwilling to exchange the Bad Bishop on White's Q2. Compare this to Black's 12th move, where he withdraws the Good Bishop.

14 QxB	P–K4

The freeing or liberating move. Let us study its effect on the position:

(a) With it, Black occupies a center square, K4, whereas up to now only White had a Pawn in the center, on his Q4.

(b) It forces an exchange of Pawns and pieces in the center, which improves the mobility of the Black pieces.

(c) It enables Black to control more space.

(d) In this special position it does *not* liberate Black's QB, which is already free and exchanged, but it does in many other variations.

(e) It weakens White's defense, since it leads to the exchange of White's KN, the rock of White's defense.

Note that if White did not exchange Pawns, Black could do so himself. But still more effective is Black's threat ... P–K5. After 15 Q–K2, P–K5; 16 N–K1, the White Knight is driven from its strong position, and Black can build a convincing attacking position by 16 ... N–Q4 and something like 17 ... P–KB4.

For those reasons White wisely makes the exchange.

15 PxP	NxP
16 NxN	

This exchange forces the weakening of White's K side.

Possibly preferable was 16 Q–K2, NxN ch (if 16 ... KR–Q1; 17 B–B3 simplifies); 17 QxN, N–K5 or 17 ... Q–K4; 18 Q–N3, and the weakening of White's K side cannot be forced.

16 ...	QxN

White is now obliged to weaken the Pawn formation in front of his King in some way. He has a choice of playing 17 P–B4 or 17 P–KN3. If he plays 17 P–B4, Black replies 17 ... Q–K2, remaining in control of his K5, which is very serious, since White has the Bad Bishop, which is hampered by its own KP and KBP, and as long as Black controls his K5 square, White cannot play P–K4. We further notice that 17 P–B4, Q–K2; 18 BxP? would be answered by 18 ... RxB;

19 QxB, QxQ; 20 RxQ, RxP, and the ensuing pin on the QR file is killing.

17 P–KN3

In a position of this sort there are holes on the White K side. This means that the White squares KB3 and KR3 are weakened in such a way that they might be occupied by a Black Queen, Bishop, or Knight. In the present game, Black might be able to bring his Queen to KR6 and his Knight to KN5.

Note how useless White's Knight is on QR2.

At this point, however, White threatens to win a piece by 18 B–B3. The threat is all-important in the middle game especially, and each side must see which threats it can make and which threats it must parry.

17 ...   N–K5!

This is an especially good move, since it accomplishes so much: (a) it parries White's threat 18 B–B3, which would win Black's Bishop; (b) it prepares N–N4–B6 or –R6; (c) it protects the Black Bishop; (d) it frees Black's KB3 square

for the Queen, from which square the Queen will attack White's KBP.

18 N–B3

White plays to get his Knight into the active conflict.

However, there is a sharper line: 18 B–B3, NxB; 19 QxB (19 NxN, B–N5 is a little better for Black), QxQ; 20 RxQ, NxN; 21 RxN, QR–Q1, with a somewhat superior ending for Black, who will be in possession of the Q file.

18 ...   N–B4

Black cannot exchange because after 18 ... NxN; 19 BxN, he would lose his Bishop. Also, he does not wish to exchange for strategical reasons—his Knight will be useful in White's weakened Pawn position.

The alternative, 18 ... N–N4 (to penetrate on the K side), loses a piece because of 19 P–B4 and (a) 19 ... N–B6 ch; 20 K–N2, Q–R4; 21 Q–K2 (not 21 QxB?, QR–Q1, followed by 22 ... NxB) or (b) 19 ... N–R6 ch; 20 K–N2, Q–K3 (20 ... Q–R4; 21 QxB); 21 P–B5, Q–R3; 22 P–K4, Q–R4; 23 QxB.

Note that the White squares in White's position are weak; there are holes on both sides. Here one feels the importance of having a Good Bishop to protect these White squares.

19 Q–B2

White wishes to prevent Black from occupying his QN3.

If instead, White had played 19

Q–B1, Black could strengthen the pressure by 19 ... N–N6 or, still better, by 19 ... KR–Q1.

19 ...   Q–K3

Black's strategy at this point is to penetrate White's position via N6 or Q6. Pressure on White's position may lead to the occupation of the Q file or to the winning of a Pawn, and we see in the game how because of this pressure White cannot avoid losing a Pawn or leaving the Q file to Black.

20 K–N2

White wishes to prevent Black from playing Q–R6. This is not one of Black's aims for the moment, but it might become an aim at any time.

If White clears the Q file by playing 20 B–K1, Black answers 20 ... KR–Q1, and now Black is ready for ... Q–N6. White cannot stop Black's penetration of the Q side, but he might soften the consequences. Best here would be 20 N–K2, in order to bring the Bishop to a more active post at B3 and then possibly to bring the Knight into the game via Q4.

20 ...   KR–Q1

Black could have played 20 ... Q–N6 immediately, but first he strengthens his position on the Q file.

21 P–K4(?)

Strategically this move enables White to eliminate weaknesses from his K side (P–B3 is still necessary)

and to free his Bishop, but as we shall see from the continuation, the move practically leads to the loss of a Pawn.

With 21 B–K1, White could have avoided the loss of a Pawn; e.g., 21 ... Q–N6; 22 Q–K2.

21 ...   Q–N6

All lines now seem to lose a Pawn for White:

(1)

22 Q–N1, B–K4
  (1a) 23 R–R3, Q–B5!
    (1a1) 24 P–B3, BxN, followed by ... Q–K7 ch
    (1a2) 24 P–N3, Q–N5; 25 N–N5, QxP ch
    (1a3) 24 B–K3, RxR; 25 QxR, NxKP
  (1b) 23 P–B4, BxN
    (1b1) 24 BxB, RxR; 25 QxR, QxQ; 26 RxQ, NxRP; 27 BxRP, NxP!
    (1b2) 24 PxB, Q–B5, and the threat 25 ... Q–K7 ch makes it impossible for White to defend his KP.

(2)

22 KR–QB1, B–K4; 23 P–B3 (23 R–R3, QxQ; 24 RxQ, BxN; 25

BxB, NxKP), QxQ; 24 RxQ, N–
N6; 25 R–Q1, BxN; 26 PxB,
R–Q6; 27 R–N2, N–B4, and
Black will win at least a Pawn.
For instance.

(1a) 28 R–R1, QR–Q1, 29 K–
B2, NxRP, etc.

(2b) 28 K–B2, NxRP; 29 RxP?,
NxP, etc.

So White plays

22 QxQ   NxQ
23 QR–N1   BxP

The discovered double attack on
the White Bishop leads to the winning of a Pawn.

24 RPxB

Worth considering was 24 B–N5.
Black would continue 24 ... RxR;
25 RxR, B–K4.

24 ...   NxB

Black does not take with the
Rook, because his Rook is better
than the White Rook, and he wishes
to keep it.

25 QR–B1   N–N6

At this point White has three
possibilities:

(a) Exchange no Rooks at all:
26 R–QN1, K–B1. This is probably
best.

(b) Exchange both Rooks: 26
RxR ch, RxR; 27 R–Q1, RxR; 28
NxR. Black then has to play this
ending very carefully to take advantage of his extra Pawn. This variation will be examined after the
27th move.

(c) Exchange one Rook, but this
leaves the Q file to Black, which
gives him an additional advantage.

In Rook endings the stronger
side will exchange all Rooks if in
the ending with minor pieces his
King is better placed than the
hostile King. This will certainly be
the case if his King can penetrate
the hostile position, which is impossible as long as the Rooks remain on the board.

26 RxR ch   RxR

Supposing that White now forced
the exchange of the remaining
Rook by threatening to command
the Q file: 27 R–Q1, RxR; 28 NxR.
In this position it appears that the
Black King could walk straight
down. But let us examine the situation a little more carefully.

(a) 28 ... K–B1; 29 K–B3?,
K–K2; 30 K–K3, K–Q3, and the
White King cannot come any
nearer, since 31 K–Q3 loses a second Pawn after 31 ... N–B4 ch,
and Black wins easily. However,

(b) 28 ... K–B1; 29 N–K3!
(the counterattack), and, for instance, either 29 ... N–B4; 30 N–
B4!, NxRP; 31 NxP, NxP; 32 NxP,
or 29 ... K–K2; 30 N–B5 ch, and

the King must defend his KNP, and after 30 ... K–B3, there follows 31 N–Q6. The Pawn exchanges do not lead to a clear win.

(c) 28 ... N–B4!; 29 N–B3, K–B1 (after having first tied up White's Knight).

(29 ... N–Q6; 30 N–Q1 could be played as well, but it amounts to the same thing, since the Black Knight has to withdraw after K–B3–K3) 30 K–B3, K–K2; 31 K–K3, K–Q3; 32 K–Q4, N–K3 ch; 33 K–B4. The White King has to go too far from the K wing in order to keep the Black King from penetrating on the other wing. Notice how badly the White Knight is placed for counterattack; this is the result of Black's 28th move. 33 ... P–KN4! (threatening ... P–R4, followed by ... P–R5). In Knight endings, the farther passed Pawn often decides. After 34 P–KN4 the Black King could penetrate on the K side: 34 ... K–K4, etc.

All in all, after the exchange of all Rooks, Black still has serious difficulties to overcome.

But White chose the least advantageous of the three possibilities listed after Black's 25th move, exchanged only one Rook, and then played

27 R–B2

It is important to note that Black now has *two* advantages: an extra Pawn and a file controlled by a Rook. It is difficult to defend against two weapons at the same time. In chess, a + a > 2a, that is,

two advantages are greater than twice one advantage.

| 27 ... | P–B3 |
| 28 P–B3 | R–Q6 |

Threatening to win a Pawn by the combination 29 ... RxP; 30 KxR, N–Q5 ch.

| 29 R–B2 | N–Q7 |

Black's plan is very simple: first he will tie up as many White pieces as possible, then he will advance his King. The text move attacks White's KB3 and opens possibilities like N–B5 and N–K6 ch. The White Knight can move only to QR2, where it is powerless.

30 P–KN4

Had not White played this move, Black could continue by ... P–R4 and ... P–KN4 in order, after further simplification, to create a passed Pawn.

| 30 ... | N–B5 |
| 31 K–N3 | N–K4 |

The Black Knight is better placed on its central K4 square, where it ties up the White pieces and prepares eventually to occupy its KB5.

Black must not play 31 ... NxP; 32 RxN, RxN; 33 RxNP. This would free White's game and give him counterchances. The secret of the endgame for the weaker side is counterattack! In positions such as there, even a big advantage is reduced very much by giving the opponent any initiative.

32 K–N2   P–KN4

This move secures Black's KB5 for him. Black visualizes N–N3–B5 ch, forcing the White King to N3; then mating possibilities arise, as will later become evident.

33 K–N3   N–N3

Black could have advanced his King immediately, but it does not make much difference. It is just a matter of which way Black ties up the White Rook, whether directly by attacking the BP or indirectly by mating possibilities.

34 N–R2

White now begins a series of repetitive moves that illustrate eloquently how completely Black has tied him up.

34 ...   N–B5

With the Black Knight posted here, the White Rook can never come to a counterattack as long as Black has the threat of ... R–Q7 and ... R–N7 mate.

35 N–B3   K–B2

With the K side immobilized, Black now brings in the King to work on the Q side.

36 N–R2   K–K3

Before moving his King to the center, Black had to examine 37 R–R2, K–K4!; 38 RxP, R–Q7; 39 R–R2, N–K7 ch; 40 K–R3 (otherwise ... N–B8 dis ch), RxP; 41 N–B3, N–N8 ch; 42 K–N3, RxR; 43 KxR, NxP ch, and wins.

37 N–B3   N–N3

In order to answer 38 R–R2 by 38 ... N–R5.

If 37 ... K–K4(?); 38 R–R2, K–Q5; 39 RxP, R–Q7 (analogous to the former variation), but the saving move 40 R–Q7 ch is possible.

38 N–R2   K–K4

Now the King can advance, for in the case of 39 R–R2, N–R5.

39 N–B3   K–Q5
40 N–R2   K–B5

Notice that the Rook is always indirectly tied up, since any move on the part of White's Rook could be answered by either ... N–R5 or ... N–K4, and also the counterattack against Black's RP is prevented.

40 ... K–K6 would be answered by 41 N–B1, giving White some counterchances.

41 N–B3	K–N6
42 K–N2	N–K4
43 K–N3	N–B5

Black now wins the QNP and probably the RP.

44 Resigns

Just one variation to show how close together a win and a draw are: 44 R–R2, NxP; 45 N–K2.

(a) 45 ... NxP??; 46 N–B1 ch
(b) 45 ... R–Q7?; 46 N–B1 ch, K–B7; 47 RxR ch, KxR; 48 N–N3 ch, with drawing chances.
(c) 45 ... KxP?; 46 N–B1, R–Q8; 47 RxN, RxN; 48 RxP, with drawing chances.
(d) 45 ... R–Q2!, which wins easily, for Black has paralyzed the counterattack on the KR file, and White can no longer prevent the loss of his QRP (46 N–B1 ch, K–R6), after which Black has a plus of three passed Pawns on the Q side.

In this game the principal difference between the amateur and the master lies in the degree to which each handles the position immediately after the opening. The amateur fails to make plans of his own, does not realize what the master's plans are, and does not meet the master's plans in the right way.

Game 15

The theory of the Caro-Kann Defense

Planning the middle game

Exploiting the loose piece

Sharply calculated tactics in order to maintain the lead

Weakening the hostile King position

Planning the middle game

Deflecting a piece from a critical open line

In almost every chess game there comes a time when one phase of the game is over, when another is about to begin, when there are no pressing tactical problems, and when the player must ask himself, "What shall I do next? In which direction should the game go now?" Such a point might be called a moment of decision, a time when some plan must be decided upon, a plan that is often purely strategical, sometimes also tactical.

By decision we mean the formulation of a general plan of continuing the play. The decision is usually made at a time when things are relatively quiet, with no pieces *en prise,* no enemy threats, no tense tactical situations that claim priority.

Sometimes it is possible to formulate a plan for the entire game, but usually a decision is taken for only a given phase of the game, say for from five to ten moves.

Once a player has decided that the moment of decision has come, he must study the position carefully from all angles. He must evaluate his own strengths and weaknesses and those of his opponent and must weigh the details of the position, such as Pawn distribution, location of the opponent's King, existence of open and half-open files, etc.

At the base of the plan will be one or more general ideas—aims toward which to strive. Only by establishing aims can a player go forward in a meaningful manner. Those who fail to make a plan wander aimlessly

144

from move to move, or depend on purely tactical opportunities of the moment to gain their advantage. Not that a plan should be unalterable, once it is made. What one's opponent does and the tactical requirements of the moment must always make a player ready to reconsider, to modify, to change entirely, if circumstances warrant. But to have objectives and a plan to attain them is important.

Sometimes the position is such that a single plan imposes itself—no other continuation is as logical. Other times—and these are, of course, the more complicated cases—several possible plans may be feasible, and in that case the plan finally adopted will depend somewhat on the comparative merit of the various possibilities, somewhat on the temperament of the player—whether, for instance, he prefers an attacking game involving risks and sacrifices or a positional solution that will crush his opponent more slowly, but more surely.

Caro-Kann Defense

Master	Amateur
White	*Black*

1 P–K4

After 1 P–K4, Black has a number of choices. He can

(a) also occupy the center with 1 ... P–K4 (preliminary to many openings);

(b) after suitable preparation play for ... P–Q4 (French, Caro-Kann);

(c) disturb White's KP by 1 ... N–KB3 (Alekhine Defense);

(d) start independent counteraction on the Q side and in the center by 1 ... P–QB4 (Sicilian);

(e) do nothing at all about White's occupation of the center (fianchetto).

1 ...   P–QB3

The Caro-Kann opening. Black prepares to hit at White's center by ... P–Q4.

Black could also hit at the center immediately by 1 ... P–Q4 (the Center Counter Game), but not without some disadvantage to himself. Or he can interpose a preparatory move (1 ... P–K3 [French Defense] or 1 ... P–QB3 [Caro-Kann]). The Caro-Kann has the advantage over the French of not shutting in the QB after 2 ... P–Q4. It has the disadvantage of taking from the Black QN its natural square QB3 and of losing a tempo for development. By development is to be understood one of the following types of moves: (a) bringing out a piece; (b) castling; (c) making a Pawn move that opens a line for a Bishop. Thus 1 ... P–K3 is a tempo for development, but 1 ... P–QB3 is not.

2 N–QB3

White usually replies 2 P–Q4. With this traditional reply, he takes possession of the center squares.

He occupies his own Q4 and K4 squares with Pawns and gains control of the QB, Q, K, and KB squares on the 5th rank.

The more recent variation, 2 N–[illegible] is based on the idea that White does not need to occupy his Q4 square at this moment and that by deferring this move he gets a considerable development of pieces, which allows him more activity at an earlier stage of the game and in some cases a very important tempo (see comment after 4 NxP).

2 ...   P–Q4

Black contests White's attempt to occupy the center.

3 N–B3

This continuation is more flexible than the classical line, which could still be reached by 3 P–Q4. As will be shown after Black's 4th move, the text continuation prevents the Black Bishop from developing to ... KB4, as it does in an important branch of the classical line.

If Black should now reply 3 ... P–Q5, then 4 N–K2, P–QB4; 5 P–Q3, followed by 6 P–KN3, etc.

This gives the King's Indian Reversed, with two tempi plus for White: (a) because he is White, (b) because of the loss of tempo caused by playing ... P QB4.

Black now looks for a suitable continuation. He reasons: (a) 3 ... N–B3 is possible but not easy after 4 P–K5, N–K5; (b) 3 ... B–N5 is satisfactory; after 4 P–KR3 (not 4 ... B–R4; 5 P–KN4, B–N3; 6 PxP, PxP; 7 P–KR4!, P–KR3; 8 N–K5, etc.—very instructive, but) 4 ... BxN; 5 QxB, and White has the Two Bishops, but this is not an open game where the Two Bishops are most effective; chances are even; (c) 3 ... P–K3 blocks the QB; (d) 3 ... PxP breaks the tension but brings the White QN into a better position. In general, amateurs do not like unsolved situations on the board. Therefore, our amateur chooses

3 ...   PxP
4 NxP

Now, what shall Black play?

In the classical line (1 P–K4, P–QB3; 2 P–Q4, P–Q4; 3 N–QB3, PxP; 4 NxP), Black often continues effectively with 4 ... B–B4 and then 5 N–N3, B–N3; 6 P–KR4, P–KR3; 7 N–B3, N–Q2!, preventing 8 N–K5.

But in the text, 4 ... B–B4 would be bad at this point, because White has already developed his KN, which would not yet have been developed in the above classical line. The text would then continue: 5 N–N3, B–N3; 6 P–KR4,

P–KR3; 7 N–K5 (impossible in the classical line), B–R2; 8 Q–R5, P–KN3; 9 B–B4!, threatening mate. White has tremendous development, the Black Bishop is useless on KR2, and White has other threats that will further disrupt the Black position. This line should be compared with the above classical line.

Theory gives, among other moves, 4 ... B–N5, which would be followed by 5 P–KR3, BxN.

Theory also gives the text continuation:

4 ...   N–Q2

This is Salo Flohr's idea, and a good one. Black will next play 5 ... KN–B3, thus preventing White from doubling the Black Pawns by NxN ch. The problem of the undeveloped QB will be solved with a timely ... P–QB4, ... P–QN3, and ... B–QN2.

5 B–B4

Or 5 P–Q4, followed by 6 B–Q3.

With the text, Black's KB2 is particularly vulnerable, and if Black does not play ... P–K3, he may get into trouble sooner or later on his KB2 or K3; e.g., 5 ... P–QN3??; 6 BxP ch, KxB; 7 KN–N5 ch, K–K1; 8 N–K6, winning the Queen. The move 5 ... N–N3 might lead to trouble as follows: 6 BxP ch, KxP; 7 N–K5 ch, K–K1; 8 Q–R5 ch, P–N3; 9 NxP and (a) 9 ... PxN; 10 QxR, or (b) 9 ... KN–B3; 10 NxN ch, PxN; 11 NxR ch. Even after 5 ... N–KB3,

White has the possibility of starting an attack by 6 KN–N5, P–K3; 7 NxBP, KxN; 8 N–N5 ch. It is not certain that the White attack will succeed, but with his King in a vulnerable position, Black will surely have certain problems to solve.

So White's B–B4 more or less forces Black to shut in his QB by playing

5 ...   P–K3
6 O–O   KN–B3
7 N–N3

Before making this move, White had to weigh the advantages and disadvantages. *For:* the exchange of Knights favors Black, since exchanges favor the side controlling the least territory. *Against:* the move loses a tempo, since the Knight is certainly not better posted on KN3 than on K4.

7 ...   B–K2
8 P–Q4

The right move at the right time. White develops this important Pawn, occupies the center, gains control over his QB5 and K5 squares, and liberates his QB. Up to this time it was important to bring a number of pieces into the struggle. Now it is time to occupy the center. A good example of modern thinking.

8 ...   O–O
9 Q–K2

The White Queen brings pressure to bear on the K file, guards her own 2nd rank, vacates the 1st rank for free movement of the Rooks, and cedes the Q square to the Rook.

9 ...   P–QB4

Black has moved his QBP a second time, but the loss of time could not be avoided. The initial 1 ... P–QB3 was necessary to control Black's Q4 square; now 9 ... P–QB4 is important in order to neutralize the White center.

A tempo in the middle game is, in general, less important than in the opening, and if the broken double-move has two different aspects, it should be considered. It must be kept in mind also that this move forces the opponent in a special way, and one could imagine that under certain circumstances this might result in the win rather than in the loss of tempo. Let us try to illustrate this concept.

From the initial position, play 1 P–Q4, P–Q4; 2 P–QB4, N–QB3; 3 N–QB3, P–K4; 4 PxQP, NxP. White now has the move. Compare the following continuations: (a) 5 P–K4; (b) 5 P–K3, N–B4; 6 P–K4, N–Q5. The position after (a) is exactly the same as after (b), with one essential difference in the situation: after (a) Black has the move, but after (b) White has the move. Therefore, we must conclude that in (a), where White has played P–K4 in one move, he has *lost* a tempo, whereas in (b), where White has played P–K3–K4 in two moves, he has *won* a tempo.

10 R–Q1

The Rook can exercise great pressure on the Q file, the more so because the Black Queen is still on that file.

10 ...   P–QN3

According to the Flohr plan mentioned after Black's 4th move.

White's development is practically completed. The middle game has been reached. One of the most difficult points in a chess game is here. Sometimes White can base his next move on a well-formulated long-range plan; other times he must choose his move on the basis of general principles. But in any case, he must mentally go through a number of steps to find the best move or at least a playable move.

First he asks, "Does Black have any tactical threats?" In the position at hand, Black has nothing more than 11 ... PxP. Second he asks, "What is Black's probable strategy?" It appears that Black will continue his development with ... B–N2 and ... Q–B2. Third, he asks, "What are the apparently best moves for me, and where will they lead?" In this position he considers the following possibilities:

(a) 11 B–B4, B–N2; 12 PxP, BxP; 13 N–K5, Q–K2. This seems to lead to a satisfactory game for Black.

(b) 11 B–KN5, trying to bring pressure against Black's Q2 in view of the possibility BxN, BxB, in order to rob the QN of its protection by the Black KN. An example: 11 ... B–N2; 12 PxP, PxP; 13 N–K5, and Black is in great difficulty. White threatens 14 BxN and 15 NxN. After 13 ... Q–B2, White wins a piece all the same by 14 NxN, and 13 ... Q–K1 is met by 14 B–N5 or by 14 NxN, NxN; 15 BxP!, a sham sacrifice that wins a Pawn (15 ... PxB; 16 QxP ch, etc.) In order to relieve the pressure, Black does best to play 11 ... P–KR3, after which 12 BxN, BxB; 13 PxP, PxP; 14 B–N5, Q–K2 seems to overcome the difficulties.

(c) 11 N–K5 is also a strong try. It threatens to strengthen the pressure by 12 N–B6 and exchanging the Black KB. Some of the obvious answers do not seem to work:

(1) 11 ... B–N2; 12 PxP, PxP (or 12 ... BxBP); 13 B–QN5, and wins;

(2) 11 ... Q–B2 seems good. But 12 NxP! (one of the goals of White's last move), KxN (12 ... RxN; 13 QxP, and White wins the Rook); 13 QxP ch, K–K1 (13 ... K–N3; 14 Q–B5 mate); 14 N–B5 is awkward for Black, because mate is threatened: 14 ... N–QN1; 15 B–N5 ch, K–Q1; 16 PxP dis ch, etc.

(3) A little better would be to exchange Knights: 11 ... NxN; 12 PxN, N–Q2 (12 ... N–Q4; 13 N–B5 is troublesome for Black); 13 N–K4, Q–B2; 14 N–Q6, BxN, and both after 15 RxB and after 15 PxB, White has maintained pressure that is certainly comparable with the pressure White obtained in the game.

(4) Perhaps Black's best answer after 11 N–K5 would be: 11 ... B–Q3, after which (a) 12 NxP does not seem to work: 12 ... RxN; 13 QxP, Q–K2 (exchange and two Pawns for a piece, but Black has a good development then); (b) 12 PxP does not work either: 12 ... BxN and (c) 12 NxN, BxKN consolidates the Black game (13 PxP, BxP; 14 B–KN5, B–K2).

(d) 11 PxP, which seems the most favorable of all, for it brings into play the pressure of the Rook on the Q file, immediately creating tactical possibilities that are not otherwise available.

11 PxP   BxP

Here 11 ... PxP would not have been too bad, since Black's KB would then have continued to protect Black's KB3 square. In many types of games Black's KB renders greater defensive service at its K2 than offensive service at its QB4.

It will appear in the game that Black needs protection of his KB3. The fact that after 11 ... PxP Black has two isolated Pawns does not count as positive him should which is rather curious.

12 N–K5

The strength of White's previous 11 PxP now becomes clearer. It opened the Q file and allowed White to take advantage of his greater control of space, and especially of the pinned Black QN.

12 ...   Q–B2

Black must break the pin immediately or court disaster. After the plausible 12 ... B–N2, for instance, 13 B–QN5 is very powerful.

Since Black must move his Queen, he chooses the best square to which to move it. At QB2 the Black Queen protects its QB3 from invasion by the White Knight, attacks the White Knight at its K5, and guards its QN2 square in order to answer a possible Q–B3 by ... B–N2.

13 B–B4

The Black Queen is again submitted to an indirect attack that embodies the double threat (a) 14 NxN and (b) 14 N–N6.
Note that 13 NxP, RxN; 14 QxP would not have accomplished much after 14 ... N–B1.

13 ...   NxN
14 BxN   Q–K2

White had many possibilities of hitting the Black position, and it was Black's problem to reduce them to a minimum. In several respects he has done a good job, and only one vulnerable spot remains—his KB3, which we shall see from the continuation.

The present position is very important in the game at hand and very instructive in methods of chess analysis. Let us consider it.

If White allows him time, Black will play ... B–N2, contest White's control of the open Q file with his KR– or QR–Q1, and what will White have? Possibly nothing more than equality. His advantage will have evaporated. He must, therefore, look for some way of taking advantage of his superior development before Black can catch up with him. How can he do it?

In all positions where one side has superior development, it is important for that player to investigate carefully some means of capitalizing on that superior development before the opponent completes or evens up his development.

In the position at hand Black's Rook is *loose*, that is, unprotected. A loose piece is always a sign to look for a possible combination. Even if the loose piece can be protected, this will consume time, which gives the attacking player one extra move.

White now investigates the following line:

15 Q–B3 (attacking Black's QR), B–N2; 16 BxN, BxQ; 17 BxQ, BxR; 18 BxR, and White is a piece up, for if 18 ... RxB; 19 RxB, or if 18 ... BxQBP; 19 BxB. White sees that he wins with this line. He therefore investigates further, for Black probably has more favorable variations. He reasons, "With 15 Q–B3, B–N2; 16 BxN, Black will have to answer 16 ... PxB to avoid the loss of a piece. Thus White will have wrecked Black's Pawn position and laid open Black's K side."

With this idea in mind he moves

15 Q–B3

Notice that the attack on the unprotected Black QR forces Black's reply, which assures White of the continuation of the play along the lines contemplated above.

15 ...   B–N2
16 BxN   PxB

White has now attained his strategic objective of doubling Black's KBP's and mutilating his K-side Pawn protection. The question now arises, "Was the strategy sound? Will Black's broken K side lead to a successful mating attack by White, or will Black's half-open KN file give him counterchances, especially in conjunction with his Bishop at QN2?"

White's problem is how to exploit Black's weaknesses, which consist of a weak King and a weak KBP(3). It is of importance to combine an attack against these two weaknesses.

White sees two ways of continuing the attack: (a) 17 Q–R5 and (b) 17 Q–B4. First we'll examine 17 Q–R5. A few possibilities:

(a) 17 ... K–R1?; 18 B–Q3, P–B4; 19 NxP, PxN; 20 BxP, P–B3; 21 R–Q7, and wins;

(b) 17 ... P–B4; 18 Q–R6 leads to the game.

(c) 17 ... KR–Q1!; 18 Q–R6, K–R1; 19 N–R5, R–KN1, and Black has counterchances.

On comparing these variations with the continuation of the game, we come to the conclusion that 17 Q–B4 is indeed preferable.

17 Q–B4

Maintaining pressure against the Black KBP(3) and leaving the R5 square free for the Knight.

17 ...   P–B4

The defense 17 ... K–R1 amounts to about the same thing as the game: 18 P–N4, BxP; 19

R–Q7 (see the game). Other possibilities are inferior:

  (a) 17 ... P–K4?; 18 Q–R6
(threatening both 19 N–R5 and
19 N–R5);

  (b) 17 ... KR–Q1; 18 N–R5
(threatening 19 Q–N3 ch and
mate in a few moves), K–R1;
19 NxP, Q–B1 (to prevent 20
Q–R6); 20 P–KN3, and White
has a plus Pawn and good attacking chances. By comparing
with (c) under Black's 16th
move, we see that 17 Q–B4
(instead of 17 Q–R5) has made
this defense less effective.

18 Q–R6

Now White threatens the powerful 19 N–R5, and 19 ... P–B3
is not adequate because of 20 BxP
ch (20 ... QxB?; 21 Q–N7 mate).
Therefore, although of interest is
18 ... BxP ch; 19 KxB, Q–B4 ch;
20 K–K1, QxB; 21 Q–N5 ch, K–
R1; 22 Q–B6 ch, K–N1; 23 R–Q4
and N–R5 soon wins, Black's next
move is practically forced.

18 ...   K–R1

So that 19 N–R5 can be answered by 19 ... R–KN1 with

counterchances along the KN file.

Here is another critical position.
White must find a forcing reply
now, and not one move later, for
if given a move, Black can consolidate by ... R–Q1 or ... R–
KN1.

Let us consider the combination
19 R–Q7, QxR; 20 Q–D0 ch, K–
N1; 21 N–R5, threatening mate.
But Black can save himself by 21
... Q–Q5 or 21 ... B–Q5. This
explains the move that follows:

19 P–QN4!

To divert the Bishop from access
to his Q5 square.

19 ...   BxP

Forced. If 19 ... B–Q3; 20
RxB! wins as follows: 20 ... QxR;
21 Q–B6 ch, K–N1; 22 N–R5,
and Black must sacrifice his Queen
to parry the mate: 22 ... Q–Q5;
23 QxQ, P–B3.

20 R–Q7!

White wishes to continue with
21 Q–B6 ch and 22 N–R5. Just as
he did not want Black to be
able to play ... B–Q5, defending
against mate, he now wishes to
divert the Black Queen from protecting its KB3 square. The Queen
must accept the Rook sacrifice or
be taken.

20 ...   QxR
21 Q–B6 ch   K–N1

Now follows a series of forcing
moves.

22 N–R5   B–QB6 (forced)

The only try.

| 23 QxB | P–B3 (forced) |
| 24 BxP ch | |

The Black Queen must be forced from its 2nd rank, and White sacrifices a second piece to do so. But in a mating combination any number of pieces may be sacrificed, provided that there is a forced win by the pieces immediately involved in the mating net.

24 ...	QxB (forced)
25 Q–N3 ch	K–B2 (forced)
26 Q–N7 ch	K–K1 (forced)
27 QxB!	Resigns

This wins in all variations with White's consecutive threats of 28 N–N7 ch followed by 29 R–Q1 ch. For instance: (a) 27 ... R–Q1; 28 N–N7 mate; (b) 27 ... Q–K4; 28 N–N7 ch, K–Q1; 29 R–Q1; ch, etc.; (c) 27 ... Q–B1; 28 R–K1 ch, K–Q1; 29 Q–K7 mate.

Here, as in many of the previous games, the amateur failed because he did not see profoundly enough at the moment of decision, and this most often comes immediately after the opening.

In this game, we can criticize Black's 11th move, but we cannot criticize his play without a plan. On the contrary, his strategy is very clear: first develop, next neutralize the opponent's center, then bring all the pieces to maximum activity. It proved to be extremely difficult for the master to counter these plans and to execute the plans he himself had devised. In the long run, however, the amateur's resistance, although brave and stubborn, was hopeless, because of the many brilliant moves of the master opponent.

Game 16

The theory of the Sicilian Defense

The Dragon Variation of the Sicilian

Opening lines

Taking possession of open lines

The strength of the Black KB on White's Q side

Combined attack against White's Q wing

Neutralizing the opponent's moves

Command of the 7th rank

Cutting the opponent's lines of communication

The irresistible passed Pawn

No chess opening is so strong that the opposing side cannot attain equality with the proper moves, but to do so one must understand the ideas behind the opening and know what the opponent is striving for.

This is especially true in the case of the Sicilian Defense, which is one of the more subtle chess openings. In most variations of the Sicilian, Black does not seek direct control of the center, and he almost never attempts an attack against the King castled on the K side.

The ideas behind the Sicilian Defense look mysterious, but in reality they are very clearly defined. Black plays for unspectacular but none-theless telling advantages on the Q side. First he opens his QB file; then he usually brings pressure to bear on this half-open QB file by his Queen and one of his Rooks. He often plays his QN to QR4 in order to exert pressure on or to occupy his QB5 square. In the Dragon Variation of the Sicilian he fianchettoes his KB, which then exerts pressure along its entire diagonal and becomes particularly potent as it presses on White's QR1, QN2 and QB3 squares.

This strategy is so subtle that it often brings about the collapse of

White's Q-side structure without his being able to do anything about it even with best play and full realization of what is taking place.

Sicilian Defense: Dragon Variation

Amateur	Master
White	*Black*
1 P–K4	P–QB4

The Sicilian Defense—one of the most intriguing replies to 1 P–K4. It has a modern character that makes it very difficult for White to realize the type of game he normally does in the 1 P–K4 opening.

Instead of meeting White's occupation of the center with a counterplay for the possession of the center, Black attempts to secure play on the other side of the board. By 1 . . . P–QB4 Black (a) commands his Q5 square; (b) is prepared to open the QB file for counterplay on the Q side after White plays P–Q4.

2 N–KB3

White wishes to contest Black's control of White's Q4 square. An immediate 2 P–Q4 would be followed by 2 . . . PxP; 3 QxP, N–QB3, which wins a tempo for Black, since White has to lose a move in order to bring his Queen out of danger. White therefore makes the preparatory move 2 N–KB3, exerting pressure on his Q4 and threatening to gain control of it by 3 P–Q4. Moreover, 2 N–KB3 develops the White KN to its natural square.

2 . . .   N–QB3

Black increases the pressure on his Q5 square.

Often 2 . . . P–Q3 is played at this point. The function of 2 . . . P–Q3 is to prevent an eventual P–K5 by White. It is interesting to study the difference between a Sicilian with an early . . . N–QB3 and one with an early . . . P–Q3.

(a) 2 . . . N–QB3; 3 P–Q4, PxP; 4 NxP, N–KB3; 5 N–QB3, P–Q3; 6 B–KN5.

(b) 2 . . . P–Q3; 3 P–Q4, PxP; 4 NxP, N–KB3; 5 N–QB3, P–KN3.

In (a), Black cannot realize his K-side fianchetto at the 5th move, since 5 . . . P–KN3?; 6 NxN, followed by 7 P–K5, and the Black pieces get into disorder. Neither can he play P–KN3 on his 6th move, since 7 BxN, PxB would mean a serious weakening of his Pawn structure; in (b) Black can realize his K-side fianchetto, because he has postponed the development of his QN.

3 P–Q4

White takes possession of his Q4. If now 3 . . . PxP; 4 NxP, NxN; 5 QxN, the White Queen could not be driven away, as it could have been after an immediate 2 P–Q4.

3 . . .   PxP

Black does not wish to permit White to build up a strong center.

If Black did not take, White could continue 4 P-Q5, gaining space.

Besides, this is the most important point of the Sicilian buildup: Black has played his QBP to his B4 so as to be ready to exchange a side Pawn for a White center Pawn, thus creating a potential majority in the center. After the exchange, Black has a KP and QP, whereas White has only a KP.

The question of when to maintain tension in the center by allowing the status quo and when to exchange is an important one in chess. In general, you take, if

(a) you would lose a tempo by not taking; e.g., 1 P-K4, P-Q4; 2 P-K5? loses a tempo you would not wish to lose, whereas 2 PxP wins a tempo; or

(b) you do not wish to accept other difficulties; e.g., 1 P-K4, P-Q4; 2 N-QB3, P-Q5.

In the text, Black takes, in order to prevent 4 P-Q5. Moreover, he exchanges a side Pawn for a center Pawn and opens the QB file.

4 NxP

White's Knight is now in the center of the board, but Black can and sometimes does drive it away by ... P-K4 (see Game 18).

If, however, Black should now exchange Knights with 4 ... NxN; 5 QxN, White would be considerably ahead in development. Therefore, Black usually replies

4 ...   N-B3

Black attacks White's KP, forcing him to protect it. But he is forcing White to protect his Pawn in the most economical way, namely, by 5 N-QB3, and by so doing prevents White from later playing P QB4, which would give him a very strong grip on the center square Q5.

5 N-QB3

As was pointed out after Black's second move, White is now threatening 6 NxN followed by 7 P-K5. For that reason Black must do something to prevent it.

Notice that this Pawn push was not possible one move earlier, as 5 NxN, NPxN; 6 P-K5? is met by 6 ... Q-R4 ch.

5 ...   P-Q3

Here 5 ... P-KN3 is refuted by 6 NxN, NPxN; 7 P-K5, and the Black Knight has no good place to go.

The beginning of another system for developing Black's KB is 5 ... P-K3. If now 6 NxN, NPxN; 7 P-K5, then 7 ... N-Q4 is possible. So the game usually continues 6 KN-N5 (best for weakening the effect of the pin that follows), B-N5; 7 P-QR3, BxN ch; 8 NxB, P-Q4; 9 PxP, PxP, and although Black now has an isolated Pawn, his chances are not bad, because White cannot prevent the advance of Black's QP to his Q5, which gives him considerable possibilities of increased activity.

6 B–K2

In the Sicilian Defense the K2 square is a good place for White's KB. From here it guards its KN4 square, discouraging Black from coming there with his Knight.

Another good square is QB4, which especially in recent times is preferred for the Bishop: 6 B–B4, P–KN3?; 7 NxN, PxN; 8 P–K5!! In a Schlechter-Lasker game there followed 8 ... N–N5 (not 8 ... PxP??; 9 BxP ch!); 9 P–K6, P–KB4, and Black could hold his own only with great effort.

In the Sicilian, the Q3 is not a good square for the White KB, partly because of the presence of a Pawn at K4, partly because White's Knight at Q4 needs the protection of the Queen.

The Richter attack 6 B–KN5 forces Black to the K3 system: 6 ... P–K3; 7 Q–Q2, B–K2; 8 O–O–O, and White has a wonderful game, but Black is not without counterchances.

6 ...   P–KN3

The Dragon Variation. Black will develop his KB to N2, from which point it will exert strong pressure along the diagonal.

Or 6 ... P–K3, which leads to the Schevenigen System, the idea of which is to maneuver along the QB file and eventually advance in the center.

Or 6 ... P–K4, which leads to the Boleslavsky System (see Game 18).

7 B–K3

White brings his QB to a square from which it strengthens White's Q4 square, which may be necessary after Black's next move, which indirectly attacks White's Q4.

Also at this point is played 7 N–N3, the simplest way of relieving Black's pressure against White's Q4 square—even before Black has developed his Bishop to its KN2. The move 7 N–N3 has the advantage of controlling White's Q5 square and, after careful preparations (White first has to protect his KP), N–Q5 followed by P–QB4 can become very strong.

7 ...   B–N2

In the course of the game, White must be careful to neutralize the pressure of the Black KB along the diagonal. He must also keep an eye on his QR, which, although separated from the Black KB by a number of pieces, will never be entirely safe as long as it remains on QR1.

8 O–O   O–O

9 P–KR3(?)

To prevent ... N–KN5, which entails the exchange of a Bishop for a Knight; but nowadays this move is considered superfluous. After 9 Q–Q2, N–KN5; 10 BxN, BxB; 11 P–B4 is very strong: 11 ... B–Q2 (to save the Bishop from trouble after P–B5); 12 QR–Q1, R–B1; 13 R–B2, to be followed by N–Q5 and later, after due preparation, by P–KN4 and P–B5, gives White a strong initiative and chances for attack. Black's Two Bishops do not mean much in his rather cramped position.

9 ...   B–Q2

Develops the Bishop and makes way for ... R–B1. From its Q2 the Bishop can eventually go to QN4 or QR5. From Q2 the Bishop also protects the Black QN, so that Black eventually can play ... P–QR3 and ... P–QN4.

10 Q–Q2

Clearing the 1st rank and making possible at some later time the move B–R6 to force the exchange of the strong Black KB and to

create weak Black squares for Black. An immediate B–R6 would lose a piece after ., , NxN

10 ...   P–QR3

A thematic move in the Sicilian — the beginning of a Q-side attack by P–QN4–QN5 or P–QN4 followed by N–QR4. By preventing N–N5 it also prepares the way for ... Q–B2.

11 P–B4

To increase White's superiority in the center and to prevent a later ... N–K4. The P–B4 serves in part to control the White K5 square, in part to prepare for B–KB3 without blocking the KBP. Moreover, under special circumstances the White advance P–KN4, P–B5, P–N5 could become dangerous for Black.

On the other hand, White's position becomes more vulnerable, as we shall see later. His K4 square can no longer be protected by his KBP.

Note that White's Pawn on KR3 serves the positive purpose of preventing ... KN–N5, but it creates a hole at White's KN3. This hole will not be serious in most cases, but on the other hand it sometimes does constitute a problem. Note further that at this time 11 B–R6 would lose a piece, because the White Queen must then protect both the QB and the N(Q4).

11 ...   R–B1

In the Sicilian the QR normally goes to QB1, principally to start building up pressure along the half-open QB file, but also to some extent to get off from the long diagonal, where it would be in line with White's KB if the latter should go to its KB3, as it often does.

12 B–B3   Q–B2

Black increases his pressure along the QB file. The purpose of this pressure will become apparent presently.

White's plan of development looks very harmonious: PK4 + PKB4, and behind these Pawns the Bishops and the Knight ready to go into action, and now the Queen on Q2 completes the harmony. It has taken half a century to demonstrate that this formation is *not* harmonious but, on the contrary, very vulnerable.

13 QR–K1(?)

Better would be 13 QR–Q1, since after 13 ... N–QR4 (threatening ... N–B5); 14 Q–Q3, N–B5; 15 B–B1 (as occurs in this game), it is very important for White to have an additional support for his N(Q4). This occurs in the game.

13 N–Q5 would be tremendous if White's QB2 were adequately protected, but at this point that move loses a Pawn: 13 ... KNxN; 14 PxN, NxN; 15 BxN, BxB ch; 16 QxB, QxP.

13 QR–B1 would be quite good to prepare for 14 N–Q5, but in that case Black answers 13 ... N–QR4; 14 N–Q5, NxN; 15 PxN, N–B5; 16 Q–K2, NxB or 16 ... NxNP.

13 ...   N–QR4

Another thematic move in the Sicilian. It threatens 14 ... N–B5, thus posting the Knight in a very commanding position. This threat cannot be parried by 14 P–QN3, because White would lose his Knight. At its QR4 the Knight increases pressure on the QB file.

14 Q–Q3

In anticipation of 14 ... N–B5. If White did not move the Queen here, after 14 ... N–B5, Black would exchange ... NxB, which would be very awkward for White, since his QB protects the vital Q4 square, and after this exchange the Black KB would become very powerful by such an elimination. Moreover, if 15 Q–B1, Black would also have 15 ... NxP; 16 QxN, QxN.

But perhaps better was 14 Q–B2 so that after 14 ... N–B5; 15 B–B1, Black cannot pin by 15 ... Q–N3, as he does in the game.

14 ...   N–B5

Black has obtained an ideal position in the Sicilian. He has (a) control of the half-open QB file; (b) an attack against White's QN2; (c) a threat of pressure on White's QB3 square, since in order to drive away the Black Knight, White would have to play P–QN3, in which case the White N(QB3) would be *en prise;* (d) the possibility of P–QN4–N5; (e) the possibility of ... P–K3 followed by ... P–Q4.

15 B–B1

The White QB is compelled to leave its centrally posted spot and go back to defend the attacked QNP, all the more serious because this Bishop is very vital for maintaining the central White position against attacks of various kinds.

If White tries to defend by 15 P–QN3, Black wins a Pawn by 15 ... N–N7; 16 Q–Q2, QxN; 17 QxQ, RxQ; 18 B–B1, N–B5.

15 ...   Q–N3

Threatening both 16 ... NxNP and 16 ... P–K4, winning a Knight after 17 PxP, PxP, followed by 18 ... PxN. Moreover, there is the indirect threat of the

Black KB against the White N(Q4)!

16 P–QN3

Now the position looks tremendous for Black, since White's N(Q4) cannot move and could at any time be subject to an additional attack from Black's KB. Still, there is only one way to obtain only a small advantage. Let us consider the possibilities:

(a) 16 ... NxP?; 17 RxN, P–B4; 18 RxP, QxN ch; 19 QxQ, BxQ ch; 20 K–R1, BxN; 21 RxB, N–R4; 22 B–R3, and White has nothing to fear.

(b) 16 ... N–K4?; 17 PxN, PxP; 18 B–K3, PxN; 19 BxP, and White stands well.

(c) 16 ... P–K4?; 17 PxN, PxN; 18 N–Q5, and White is all right.

(d) 16 ... N–N5? It seems as if Black could afford to put his Knight *en prise*, because White's N(Q4) is also *en prise.* After 17 N(3)–K2, two Black Knights are *en prise.* The attempt to save things by 17 ... KN–K4; 18 PxN, NxP fails after 19 Q–K3 (unpinning), NxB ch; 20 NxN.

In complicated middle-game positions, all possibilities must be explored, but one cannot be certain of finding something. However, often there is a motif that indicates along which lines the best move might lie. Here, it is the double consideration: (a) that the Black Queen pins the White N(Q4); (b) that Black's KB is also on a diagonal with that Knight. Black therefore plays

16 ... N–KR4

By clearing the diagonal, Black now attacks White's N(Q4) twice.

17 N(3)–K2!

White protects his N(Q4) a second time. Nonetheless, Black's pin remains, which is annoying.

It is curious that although Black's N(5) is *en prise*, if White takes it, he loses an extra piece because of the priority of check: 17 PxN?, QxN ch; 18 QxQ, BxQ ch, followed by 19 ... BxN.

17 ... N–N6!

Attacking the defender. White's N(K2) is an overworked piece. It has to guard both its KN3 and Q4, which is too much.

Other continuations do not work: 17 ... P–K4; 18 PxN, PxN; 19 BxN, PxB, and Black has attained nothing.

18 NxN

If 18 PxN, NxR?; 19 KxN loses material for Black. Correct is 18

... NxN ch and 19 ... QxN ch, winning a Pawn.

18 ...   QxN ch
19 QxQ

After the preferable 19 K–R1, Black replies 19 ... QxQ; 20 PxQ, N–R4, and Black is also a little better off, because his Rook has the open file and his Bishops are well directed.

19 ...   BxQ ch
20 K–R2   N–R4

One phase of the middle game has come to an end; another is about to begin.

White's position is characterized by the vulnerability of his Q-wing Pawns and the impossibility of consolidating his position by P–B4, as the game will show. Black's position is characterized by a concentration of pieces on the Q side.

21 P–B4

White is practically forced to make this move. In general, such a move would be very good for White, but in this particular case Black can exploit it.

If White tries to protect his

QBP by 21 R–K2, then 21 ... B–
B6, threatening 22 ... B–N4, winning the exchange, or 21 ... P–
QN4, and the White QBP remains
weak.

21 ...   P–QN4!!

A very important strategical
move. It opens files and diagonals.
White's QBP is now attacked three
times, defended only once.

When a player opens a line, he
must be sure that he will obtain
more benefit from it than his opponent. Here is a typical example
of taking possession of the half-
open file—an overwhelming attack
against the hostile Pawn that shuts
the file. In this position, Black's
strategical aim is to penetrate via
the 7th rank.

22 PxP

Black can answer 22 B–Q2 by
22 ... B–N3, and then White faces
the same problem. Then 23 BxN,
BxB; 24 R–B1 is not a satisfactory
way out, because of 24 ... B–Q7
followed by 25 ... BxP.

22 ...   BxP

Black now dominates the QB
file with his Rook and the important diagonals with his Two Bishops. White dominates nothing at all.
Still, Black will not have everything his own way.

23 B–K2

Naturally, White seeks to reduce
Black's control. By exchanging a
Bishop that dominates nothing for
a Bishop that dominates important

squares, White reduces his disadvantage.

23 ...   R–B7

Black cannot prevent White from
eliminating one of the Two Bishops,
but he increases his hold on the
position from another angle: control of the 7th rank, which is the
ultimate purpose of the open file.
After 23 ... BxB; 24 RxB,
White would have attained two
goals: (a) elimination of one of
the Bishops; (b) preventing the
occupation of the 7th rank by the
Black Rook.

24 BxB   PxB
25 R–K2

White continues his strategy of
neutralizing Black's hold on the
open lines and ranks.

25 ...   KR–QB1

By doubling Rooks Black maintains his grip on the 7th rank.

26 B–R3

White must move his Bishop out
of danger, and in so doing he also
frees the KR for other work.

26 ...   B–R2!!

Threatens 27 ... RxR; 28 NxR, R–B7, winning the White QRP. Black could not play this as long as his Bishop was on his Q5.

But 26 ... B–N3? leads to a draw after 27 B–N4, RxR; 28 NxR, R–B7; 29 BxN, BxB; 30 N–B1, B–Q7; 31 N–Q3!, RxP; 32 R–B2.

The superiority of 26 ... B–R2 over 26 ... B–N3? will become clear after a few more moves.

27 B–N4

If 27 R(1)–K1, B–B7; 28 RxR, RxR, and Black has complete control of the 7th rank. White can no longer defend his QRP, for if 29 R–QR1, B–Q5.

27 ...	RxR
28 NxR	R–B7!

Instead of 28 ... N–N2, placing his Knight in an inactive position, Black prefers to give it to White in exchange for White's more actively placed Knight. Black would prefer ... N–B3 to ... N–N2, since QB3 is a much better square for the Knight, but after 29 R–B1, Black's Knight would not be advantageously placed on its QB3. So first 28 ... R–B7, and then the Knight can go—if it still can go—to its QB3.

29 BxN

If 29 N–B1, N–B3 wins a Pawn after 30 N–Q3, RxRP. He wins even more after 30 B–R3, P–N5 or 30 B–K1, RxN.

29 ...	RxN

Threatening both the QRP and the KP. Note that Black could not take this Knight if his Bishop were on its QN3. He would then have to play 29 ... BxB, in which case the Knight could go to its QB1, protecting White's QRP. This is the big difference between 26 ... B–R2 and 26 ... B–N3.

The total result of Black's strategy is the winning of one Pawn, which is the direct consequence of his control of the open file and of the 7th rank.

30 R–B1

Since he cannot protect his KP, White takes command of the QB-file. Black would best answer 30 P–K5 by 30 ... PxP; 31 PxP, B–N1.

30 ...	RxKP

This centralizes and gives Black a passed and a half-passed Pawn. 30 ... RxQRP would also have given Black a Pawn advantage, but it would have been much more difficult to make this Pawn advantage felt, and in this case the tactical situation would have given White more counterplay: 30 ...

RxRP; 31 R–B8 ch, K–N2; 32 B–
B3 ch, P–B3; 33 P–K5, QPxP; 34
PxP, and White has the threat PxP
ch and R–B7 ch. After 34 ... PxP;
35 BxP ch. K–B2; 36 R–KR8, the
situation is not clear. Especially in
the endings with Rooks and minor
pieces, one should avoid the opponent's obtaining the initiative.
Usually the initiative is worth almost one Pawn.

31 R–B8 ch	K–N2
32 B–B3 ch	P–B3
33 K–N3	

After 33 P–N3 there follows 33
... R–K7 ch; 34 K–R1, RxP.

| 33 ... | R–K6 ch |
| 34 K–R2 | |

White must not take his King
into the open field and into enemy
territory. If 34 K–N4?, P–R4 ch;
35 K–R4, RxB!; 36 RxR, B–B7 ch;
37 P–N3, K–R3, followed by 38
... P–N4; 39 PxP, PxP mate.

| 34 ... | B–B4 |

To cut the communication line
of the White Rook and to remove
the Black Bishop from a vulnerable
spot, since White's R–B7 could be
annoying.

| 35 B–R5 | |

For after 35 B–Q2 or 35 B–N2,
35 ... R–K7 wins the White QRP.

| 35 ... | P–N5 |

The White Bishop is cut off from
its K1 square, and the position of
the Black Bishop is strengthened,
since White can no longer play P–

QN4. Furthermore, the White QRP
is immobilized, and Black threatens
to win it by R–K7. Note how both
of White's pieces are now seriously
restricted.

| 36 R–N8 | |

But White double-attacks Black's
QNP.

| 36 ... | R–K5 |

Protects the NP and attacks the
BP.

| 37 K–N3 | |

If 37 P–N3, (a) 37 ... R–K7
ch; 38 K–R1, RxP; 39 BxP, B–
B7; 40 P–N4, B–N6; 41 P–B5,
PxP; 42 PxP, R–KB7; or (b) 37
... P–R4, to break the White
Pawn chain by ... P–R5.

In all these cases not only does
Black get two plus Pawns, but
White's King is very unsafe.

| 37 ... | K–B2 |

Both White and Black will attempt to bring their Kings to the
center, especially White, in order
to drive the Black Rook from his
central point.

| 38 R–N7 | |

This move does not have much point, but White has to do something, and if he tries to bring his King to the center, again some very attractive combinations emerge: 38 K–B3, R–K6 ch; 39 K–N4, P–R4 ch; 40 K–R4, R–KB6!; 41 P–N3 (White must not fall into the mating net 41 PxR?, B–B7 mate), RxP ch!; 42 PxR, B–B7 mate.

38 ...   K–K3
39 B–Q8

White double-attacks Black's K2.

39 ...   P–Q4

By this single move Black protects his KP and Rook, makes possible ... B–Q3, and advances a passed Pawn.

40 B–B7

To prevent ... B–Q3, followed by the win of White's KBP.

40 ...   P–Q5!
41 R–N5   P–Q6!

At this point Black can afford to sacrifice the Bishop in order to queen. If 42 RxB, P–Q7.

42 P–B5 ch

In order to open White's B4 square for his Bishop and thus stop the Black passed Pawn.

42 ...   PxP
43 B–B4   RxB!
44 Resigns

If 44 KxR, P–Q7, nothing can prevent Black from queening.

Black won by his plus Pawn, his centralization, the greater mobility of his Rook and Bishop, and by White's vulnerable King position.

In this game the amateur does not give evidence of the shortcomings so typical in previous play. He develops strategic plans immediately after the opening, he shows initiative, he is aware of the hostile threats, which he parries as well as possible, and he does not stop offering the greatest possible resistance, even after he has begun gradually to lose terrain because of the consistently strong play of his master opponent. The only weakness displayed by the amateur can be found around the 10th move, when he is a little too optimistic in his judgment of his chances to seize the initiative, but this is easily understandable in an opening such as the Sicilian, where the Black forces stay in the background for a long time and come into action only later, which can easily give White the impression that he has the best of it. In a game between two strong opponents where one of the opponents overrates his position, it is easy although dangerous for him to try to avoid the drawish lines that might have been the best under the circumstances.

Game 17

Attacks against unweakened King positions normally require far more time to prepare than attacks against weakened King positions. If in a game both sides are playing for an attack against a castled King, time is usually the deciding factor, and in view of what has been said, weaknesses in the King position can weigh very heavily.

In the Sicilian Defense, while Black is making the moves necessary to the Q-side positional thrust described in the previous game, White often launches a strong K-side foray. Such a K-side attack stands good chances of becoming dangerous, especially in the Dragon Variation of the Sicilian, where Black slightly weakens his K-side Pawn formation in order to fianchetto his KB, thus giving White a point of attack on Black's KN3. Against such a K-side attack, Black must play vigorously either to develop his own attack or to carry out a counterpush in the center; otherwise White will bring his onslaught to a head before Black's slower attack can get underway.

This game exemplifies a K-side attack by White and a Q-side attack by Black. Featured are the defensive and offensive strength of White's P–KB3, the disastrous result of Black's failure to play actively, and finally White's method of breaking up Black's K-side Pawn formation, of opening the KR file, and of exploiting that file to bring about mate.

Sicilian Defense: P–KB3 Variation

Master	Amateur
White	*Black*
1 P–K4	P–QB4
2 N–KB3	P–Q3

In the Sicilian Defense, 2 ... N–QB3 is often played at this point. For the difference between 2 ... P–Q3 and 2 ... N–QB3, see the remarks under Black's 2nd move in Game 16.

3 P–Q4	PxP
4 NxP	N–KB3
5 N–QB3	P–KN3

With this fianchetto Black indicates his intention of developing his KB to N2 and playing the Dragon Variation of the Sicilian.

6 B–K3

This move places the Bishop on important diagonals, supports White's N(Q4), and helps clear the 1st rank for castling.

Although White has played his Bishop to K3, 6 ... N–N5 does not work at this point, because after 7 B–N5 ch, 7 ... N–QB3 wins a Pawn for White, and 7 ... B–Q2 is followed by 8 QxN, winning the Knight outright.

6 ...   B–N2

Black's fianchettoed Bishop exerts pressure all along the diagonal.

7 P–B3

This move has a very special significance: it strengthens the center and suggests that White's stra-

tegical plan will include castling on the Q side and an attack on the K side that will be introduced by P–KN4, a move made possible by 7 P–B3. Moreover, the possibility of the sally ... N–N5 is eliminated.

7 ...   N–B3
8 Q–Q2

At its Q2 the Queen clears the way for castling long and, at a favorable time, permits the Bishop to go to KR6, where it can force an exchange of Black's fianchettoed Bishop, thus creating weak Black squares on the Black K side.

This maneuver is not possible immediately, however, since the Queen also has the task of guarding the N(Q4). If 9 B–R6, BxB; 10 QxB, NxN, losing a piece.

8 ...   O–O

The Black King cannot safely stay in the center, and the position does not lend itself to castling on the Q side for various reasons, among which are the absence of Black's QBP. Therefore, despite White's obvious intention of making a K-side attack, Black has no better move here than castling.

9 O–O–O

White thus completes his development. He is now ready to carry out his strategy, which consists of (a) advancing the KRP and the KNP; (b) forcing the opening of the KR file; (c) annihilating Black's

KB by B–R6 or B–Q4; (d) developing a mating attack against the Black King.

9 ...   B–Q2

'l'homy says that Black cannot remain passive. He should play 9 ... NxN followed by 10 ... B–K3. The game might go: 9 ... NxN; 10 BxN, B–K3; 11 P–KR4, Q–R4 (threatening the QRP); 12 K–N1, KR–QB1 (threatening 13 ... RxN and 14 ... QxP ch); 13 P–R3, P–QR3, and 14 ... P–QN4. In this variation both sides play; in the game itself only White plays.

10 P–KN4

White starts the attack, which is based on the fact that Black's K wing is weakened by ... P–KN3 and that his King has castled on the opposite side. By advancing the KNP and the KRP, White will soon be able to open either the KR file or the KN file. This possibility of opening a file is naturally of great importance for the attack.

10 ...   P–QR3

A thematic move in most variations of the Sicilian. Black aims for ... P–QN4 followed, under certain circumstances, by ... P–QN5. But here this Q-side demonstration does not work, for White's attack is too sharp, and Black's reply is too passive. Black must take action against White's attack by ... Q–R4, ... QR–QB1, and ... NxN, as in the variations given after Black's 9th move. But Black has already lost a tempo by ... B–Q2,

and a tempo weighs heavily in the struggle for priority between attack and counterattack.

11 P–KR4

White continues his attack against Black's PKN3. In this attack both the KNP and the KRP must advance.

11 ...   P–QN4

Unmindful of the impending attack, Black develops his own attack against White's Q side. Black's system is too slow—he does not defend at all, and, as a matter of fact, he should have chosen defense rather than counterattack.

Black could have defended to some extent by a peculiar-looking move—11 ... P–KR4. It looks strange to weaken the King position voluntarily by advancing one of the defending Pawns. But after some consideration, it will be seen that 12 PxP, NxRP gives Black a new bulwark and also that 12 P–N5 does not advance White's attack. After 11 ... P–KR4, White has to change his strategy; he must try to eliminate Black's KN, which is a tremendous bulwark of Black's defense, for once the Black KN is eliminated, White's PxP will be much more effective, opening the KN file and weakening the Black KRP. The game might continue: 12 N–Q5, followed by

(a) 12 ... KNxN; 13 PxN, NxN; 14 BxN, BxB; 15 QxB, PxP; 16 PxP, and White can prepare in a leisurely fashion the continuation of his violent wing attack with moves such as P–N5 followed by P–R5 (P–R5 at once blocks the position);

(b) 12 ... PxP; 13 NxN ch, BxN; 14 NxN,

(1) 14 ... PxN; 15 P–R5, PxBP; 16 PxP, and White has a strong attack; e.g., 16 ... PxP; 17 B–B4 ch, P–K3; 18 QxQP, R–B2; 19 Q–N3! and wins;

(2) 14 ... BxN; 15 P–R5, PxBP; 16 PxP, and again White's attack is overwhelming; e.g., 16 ... BxKP; 17 Q–R2, BxKNP; 18 B–Q3, or 16 ... PxP; 16 B–B4 ch.

In all these variations the opening of the KR file seems to be decisive.

12 P–R5

The first result of White's strategy: Black cannot prevent White from opening the KR file.

If now 12 ... PxP, White answers 13 P–N5, which leads to the opening of the KR file rather than the KN file. White could also answer 13 PxP, which is likewise very strong; e.g., 13 ... R–K1; 14 R–N1, K–R1; 15 P–R6, B–KB1, and Black's game is not enviable,

but perhaps White would still have to work hard in order to win.

12 ...   P–N5

Apparently, Black is realizing one of his strategic aims: to drive away the White QN, which is a general legitimate Black aim in the Sicilian. But in this game Black plays on general principles without considering the specific position. As a result, the White Knight goes to its Q5, which is to a certain extent part of White's plan of exchanging Black's K-side defenders in order to strengthen the attack.

13 N–Q5

13 ...   KNxN

This exchange is favorable to the attacker, since all the defensive Black pieces disappear, but what was Black to do? If 13 ... N–K1; 14 NxN, BxN; 15 B–R6, threatening PxP, BxB, and Q–R6 ch.

14 PxN   NxN
15 BxN

Now Black's QNP is *en prise*, and White is threatening to win

outright by BxB, PxP, and Q–R6
ch.

15 ...   DxB
16 QxB   Q–N4

Black's first threat, but it is already too late. White's plans have made such progress that White can ignore the threat in order to mobilize all his forces for the final assault.

Where a player's position is so strong and his attack so overwhelming, he can usually afford to figure out the winning combination without losing time for defense.

Here, for instance, 17 K–N1 is answered by 17 ... Q–B4, causing White's Queen to give up a dominating central position, thus considerably diminishing White's attacking chances.

On the other hand, White has to be sure that his attacking move will carry through. If White should play 17 P–R6, threatening mate, 17 ... P–B3 would be an adequate reply, and in that case the whole attack would come to an end for many moves.

So White plays

17 B–Q3

The strength of this move will appear from the continuation of the game. It (a) clears the first rank, thus enabling the QR to act on the KR file; (b) attacks Black's PKN3, threatening under some circumstances PxP, and after ... RPxP or ... BPxP, BxP. It is clear that somewhere later the Bishop posted on Q3 will be able to take an active part in the attack.

17 ...   QxRP

If instead Black now plays 17 ... Q–B4, then 18 Q–KB4, threatening 19 Q–R6 and mate along the KR file; and if 18 ... QxQP; 19 Q–R6 still decides.

18 PxP   BPxP

If 18 ... RPxP??; 19 Q–R8 mate.

19 RxP!

The standard way! White is threatening both 20 Q–R8 mate and Q–N7 mate. But even the standard way should be calculated exactly. A very slight change in circumstances could spoil the combination, and then one should not choose "the standard way."

The alternative move 19 BxNP can lead to the same position as occurs in move 23 of the game after 19 ... PxB; 20 R–R8 ch, K–B2; 21 R–R7, K–K1; 22 Q–N7. The two lines are equally good.

19 ...   KxR

If Black, before taking this Rook, had first sacrificed his Queen for the other Rook just to avoid White's combined attack of Queen and Rook, he would have lost all the same: 19 ... Q–R8 ch; 20 K–Q2, QxR ch; 21 KxQ, KxR; 22 Q–K4, and if 22 ... R–KN1; 23 QxKP ch, R–N2; 24 QxQP, a dead win for White.

20 R–R1 ch   K–N1

21 R–R8 ch!!

Forcing mate in a few moves.

Equally good is 21 Q–R8 ch, which forces mate as follows: 21 ... K–B2; 22 BxP ch, KxB; 23 Q–R7 ch, K–B3 (if 23 ... K–N4; 24 Q–R6 mate); 24 P–N5 ch, KxP (or 24 ... K–K4; 25 Q–K4 mate); 25 Q–R6 ch, K–B4; 26 R–R5 mate.

21 ...   K–B2
22 R–R7 ch   K–K1
23 Q–N7   Resigns

Nothing can prevent slaughter along the 7th rank and an early mate. For instance: 23 ... K–Q1; 24 QxP ch, K–B2; 25 QxB ch, K–N3; 26 Q–B7 mate.

From the White side we see a clear outline of strategy leading to the opening of the KR file, followed by a very straightforward exploitation first of that file and then of the 7th rank.

Black's strategy is perhaps just as straightforward, but much slower and less effective. As a matter of fact, only Black's Queen is attacking White's King position, and despite its threat ... Q–R8 ch, Black has no great power, because after K–Q2 this check leads absolutely nowhere. The point is that Black has no counterplay on the 8th rank and none elsewhere on the board, so that White can carry out his own play almost at will. Still, White must analyze the situation carefully, since under certain circumstances ... Q–R8 ch could be dangerous, and once having sacrificed his Rook, White must be able to go through with the attack or he could eventually find himself in a quieter position with a piece down and no initiative.

This is not a great game on the part of the amateur. At no point could he assert himself. He could not get his own attack started, and he failed to realize how strong his opponent's attack was becoming. Had he understood that White's attack would come so soon, perhaps he could have defended better, but it is always difficult for a player to judge such far-reaching developments. In this special case, the theory of openings has made the valuation for us. It is one of the shortcomings of this amateur in particular, and of amateurs in general, that they miss some of the refinements of opening theory. But since opening theory is extensive and often subtle, we can hardly blame the amateur for being ignorant of all its details.

Game 18

The Boleslavsky Variation of the Sicilian Defense

A new concept of the treatment in the Sicilian of the important center square at Black's Q4

Postponing the blow

Motives for the sacrifice of the exchange

The importance of playing actively even when materially ahead

Attack and counterattack

One of the fascinating features of chess is that players are always discovering something new about its nature and its techniques. What one chess generation looked upon as bad comes in a following generation to be considered as a positive good.

In general, a *hole* is considered as a serious weakness, for it permits the opposing side to post pieces on it. But in the Boleslavsky Variation of the Sicilian, developed in the 1940s, Black deliberately creates a *hole*, knowing that he either will be able eventually to eliminate it to his advantage or will obtain compensation elsewhere.

As a result of his strategy and of a sharply calculated combination, Black finds himself in the middle game with an advantage of two Pawns. Once a player has a material advantage, how should he continue? This game shows the importance of vigorous play even when one has material advantage.

It is surprising that in many cases a player has to win a game twice before he scores his point. First he must beat his opponent strategically by giving him some clear positional disadvantage or by depriving him of a Pawn or more. But since this will not make his opponent resign, he has to beat him tactically as well. In practice, players do not always realize the importance of this second phase of the game. They tend to think that after they have attained a strategic victory, their game should play itself. Often the player with a strategic advantage tends to rest on his laurels and play passively rather than find the most enterprising moves —moves by which he himself retains the initiative. Such do-nothing strategy can be fatal. The initiative is very important in chess. Sometimes it is worth one or two Pawns, sometimes even more.

Sicilian Defense: Boleslavsky System

Amateur	Master
White	*Black*
1 P–K4	P–QB4
2 N–KB3	N–QB3
3 P–Q4	PxP
4 NxP	N–B3
5 N–QB3	P–Q3
6 B–K2	

Another Sicilian Defense. For the theory of these early moves, see Game 16.

6 ...   P–K4

The Boleslavsky System.

This is a strange move dating from not earlier than 1944. Why is it so strange? Because it leaves Black's center square Q4 unprotected, in flagrant contradiction of the usual principles of chess. Just before the war, Reuben Fine wrote of the Sicilian (after 4 NxP, and quite in contradiction of the Boleslavsky concept):

"White now has a Knight in a commanding central position. It can be driven away only by ... P–K4 on Black's part. But ... P–K4 would create an absolute hole at Black's Q4, which is far worse than the temporary disadvantage caused by the strong White KN. As a result, White's Knight can only be gotten out of the way after long preparation, and in the meantime, Black has to submit to a somewhat cramped position."

On the other hand, (a) 6 ... P–K4 wins a tempo for Black by forcing White to play his Knight, and (b) should Black later be able to play ... P–Q4, then *he* has a majority in the center.

Practice indicates that, in most cases, Black reaches his goal, and White has to find ways to compensate.

7 N–N3

Also possible is 7 N–B3, which leads to almost the same continuation as 7 N–N3.

After 7 NxN, PxN, Black would get control over his Q4 square. Still, this is not a bad variation for White. He continues 8 O–O and 9 P–B4.

7 ...   B–K2

At this point the occupation of the weak square by 8 N–Q5 would lose White a Pawn after 8 ... NxP. But even if N–Q5 should become possible later, it would lead to nothing after ... NxN, PxN. Then Black's Q4 square would no longer be weak, since it would be blocked by White's own Pawn.

Strategically, 8 B–KN5 would be a strong move, for followed by 9 BxN it would strengthen White's control over his Q5 square. But tactically after 8 B–KN5, 8 ... NxP equalizes: (a) 9 NxN, BxB; 10 NxP ch, K–K2. The Knight on Q6 is now *en prise* and if (1) 11 N–K4, QxQ ch; 12 RxQ, the position of the Black King in the center is better than it would be on the wing —a general case in the ending; if (2) 11 NxB ch, RxN, and Black has nothing to fear; (b) 9 BxB, NxN, 10 BxQ, NxQ; 11 RxN, KxB; 12 RxP ch, K–K2, and Black is all right.

So White plays

8 B–K3

He simply continues the development.

8 ...   P–QR4

Black plans ... P–R5, and perhaps ... P–R6, weakening the White Q side and giving Black more room on the Q side.

In general, this move is not worth much in the Sicilian, as it can be stopped by P–QR4, but in this game, if White does stop it by P–QR4, it means that Black's QN can then come to its QN5, thus strengthening Black's pressure on his Q4 square.

9 P–QR4

White plays 9 P–QR4 anyway, which means that Black will try to occupy his QN5 in order to be able to play ... P–Q4.

White could have played 9 P–QR3. Then Black would have answered 9 ... P–R5; 10 N–B1, B–K3, followed by 11 ... P–Q4, the strategic aim.

9 ...   O–O
10 O–O   N–QN5!

Now is it almost impossible for White to prevent Black from playing ... P–Q4, and we know what this means.

If White reinforces by 11 B–B3, Black will answer 11 ... B–K3.

If 11 B–KN5, B–K3 (11 ... NxP?; 12 BxB, NxN; 13 PxN, QxB; 14 PxN, would now lose a piece for Black); 12 BxN, BxB; 13 B–B3, Q–N3! is also good for Black, for it threatens a typical combination: 14 ... NxP; 15 QxN, BxN or ... QxN, and therefore White must answer 14 N–Q2 and

Black plays ... KR–Q1 followed by ... P–Q4.

11 Q–Q2

White plans to increase pressure on the Q file by bringing one of his Rooks to bear on the file.

11 ...   B–K3

Preparing for ... P–Q4.

Black could already have played 11 ... P–Q4, which would have given him at least an even game: 11 ... P–Q4; 12 PxP, KNxP; 13 NxN, NxN, and (a) 14 KR–Q1, NxB; 15 QxN, Q–B2, or (b) 14 B–B5, BxB; 15 NxB, N–B5!; 16 QxQ?, NxB ch.

The technique is first to strengthen the pressure along the QB file against Black's QB7 and then to push. This pressure will be realized by moving minor pieces in order to be able to play Black's QR and Queen to the QB file. In general, postponing a blow can constitute a very effective war of nerves against an opponent, since he does not know exactly where to defend. Also see the comments under White's 13th move.

12 KR–Q1

If now 12 ... P–Q4; 13 PxP, KNxP; 14 NxN, NxN; 15 N–B5, and White is well off.

12 ...   R–B1

With the following combination in mind: 13 P–B3, P–Q4!; 14 PxP, KNxP; 15 NxN, RxP!; 16 NxB ch, QxN, and Black wins back his

Knight plus an extra Pawn, because White cannot protect his Knight.

13 QR–B1?

Understandable but not sound, as the game shows. Preferable was 13 B–Q3, after which Black plays 13 ... P–Q4, with a rather satisfactory game. He has his Knights well placed and a majority in space. The move 13 B–Q3 illustrates what you gain by postponing the blow—after 11 ... P–Q4, White would never have had the idea of playing such a passive move. Now it is the only defense, because there are other blows in the air.

13 ...   RxN!!

A surprising four-move combination, not too deep, but absolutely forced.

The combination is based on a number of apparently unimportant circumstances that will be explained as they occur. The *first* is that White's KP was protected by the QN. By eliminating its protector, Black wins at least the KP for the exchange.

14 PxR

After 14 QxR, the same sequence: 14 ... NxKP; 15 Q–K1, NxQBP!; 16 RxN, BxN, or 16 QxP, BxN, with material advantage to Black in both cases.

14 ...   NxKP
15 Q–K1

Forced. The *second* circumstance: limited mobility for the White Queen. The *third* circumstance: the hanging position of the White Knight on N3 (protected by the QBP(2), which will be taken).

15 ...   NxQBP(7)!
16 RxN

Forced again, since 16 Q–B1 would lose *more* material: 16 Q–B1, NxB; 17 PxN, BxN, thus losing White a Bishop more (two pieces in all for the Rook).

The *fourth* circumstance: the diagonal position of the N–R–R. When the Bishop takes the Knight, it will be in a position to win the exchange.

The master sees the characteristic points and tries to give shape to them by a combination. He looks for moves that force the opponent. But for the moment, he does not actually play the moves, only plays them mentally and then judges the results.

16 ...   BxN

Thus Black will regain the exchange and be two Pawns to the good.

17 R–N2   BxR
18 BxB

Such positions are very tricky. Black has won two Pawns, but for the moment they do not count. So for the time being there is a kind of "field equality," and in such positions the player with the greater number of Pawns is inclined to avoid the struggle, believing that he should not take any chances because he is two Pawns up. But he is wrong. He *must* struggle actively. He cannot afford to remain passive. If he plays timidly or indifferently, he is likely to lose his entire advantage.

In this position, Black must defend his attacked QNP, and he can at the same time attack the White QBP. But 18 ... Q–B2 might be unsound for two reasons: (a) B–N6 at some later time; (b) RxNP at a later time would also attack the Queen.

18 ...   Q–B1

This also allows Black the possibility of playing along the diagonal, especially to his K3.

19 B–B3

Apart from being two Pawns down, White is not at all badly off, perhaps even better off than Black. White has the Two Bishops. Black's KB is passive, his QRP and QNP are weak, and even his QP is somewhat weak.

19 ...   P–B4

Notice that the Black pieces are defensively posted; they do not collaborate in aggressive attack.

The merit of the text move is that it neutralizes White's Two Bishops and puts up a struggle for the initiative, which was threatening to pass entirely into White's hands.

After 19 ... NxQBP, Black would lose a piece by 20 R–B2.

White would get fair drawing chances after 19 ... QxP; 20 QxQ (or 20 Q–N1), NxQ; 21 RxP, B–Q1; 22 B–B6.

20 BxN

White makes this exchange partly because White's KB is not effective anyway when obstructed by Black's Knight, partly because the Knight must be removed, since it exerts pressure against several strong squares in the White position. Black has accepted a double Pawn to eliminate one of White's Two Bishops.

20 ...   PxB
21 Q–N1

Attacking Black's QNP and KP simultaneously.

21 ...   QxP
22 RxP   B–B3

By moving his Bishop, Black puts it to work—defensively, it is true—but on its K2 it was simply an unprotected piece.

Look at the change that has taken place in the position! Black is now an equal partner! Even if it should cost one of the extra Pawns—and it does not—it is advisable to "play" in such positions instead of waiting. The battle has not yet been won, but Black now has trumps as well as White.

23 P–R3

As long as Black can mate White, once the White Queen leaves the first rank, White must lose a tempo in this way in order to give mobility to his Queen. For instance, 23 QxP? would have been fatal.

23 ...   P–Q4

Protects the KP and prepares ... P–Q5. Black aims to obtain threats as soon as possible by pushing the Pawns. In such positions it is often a question of who can develop threats first.

24 Q–N5

Of course, White must try to trump up some sort of attack with his Queen.

24 ...   P–Q5

Just in the nick of time.

The QP was *en prise,* and the text is obvious, but in view of what follows, it appears that White has a dangerous attack that can just be parried by counterplay. If this had not been possible, then 24 ... Q–Q6 would have been the right move, since (a) 25 QxQ would lose immediately–giving a strong passed Pawn, and Black has two plus Pawns–but after (b) 25 B–B5, there are problems; e.g., 25 ... QxQ; 26 RxQ (26 PxQ is also good–the White NP becomes dangerous), R–Q1; 27 RxP, P–Q5 (Note the inactivity of the Black Bishop behind its KP and QP. In the middle game, where the Bishop had the important function of defending the KNP, this was all right, but in the endgame all pieces must be active.).

25 B–R6!

White can offer this sacrifice, because if 25 ... PxB; 26 Q–Q7, threatening mate.

After 25 Q–Q5 ch, K–R1; 26 Q–B7 looks good, but Black plays 26 ... Q–B1!; 27 R D7, Q–Q1, and since both the White Queen and Bishop are attacked, White must lose a piece.

25 ...   P–K6!

Black's advance of the KP serves at the same time as a defense and as a counterattack. Black now has a number of threats: 26 ... PxP ch, 26 ... Q–K8 ch, and the sequence 26 ... PxB; 27 Q–Q7, Q–Q6, etc.

After a relatively quiet move such as 25 ... P–Q6, Black must meet 26 Q–Q7 with strong threats. The point is that Black has to speed up his attack–and this is what is accomplished by the text move.

Likewise, an immediate 25 ... PxB would have forced Black to give perpetual check after 26 Q–Q7!

26 Q–Q5 ch

Here 26 Q–Q7 would not mean much after 26 ... Q–K8 ch; 27 K–R2, PxP, winning.

26 ...   K–R1
27 Q–B7

A very strong move for an amateur! White threatens mate in various ways; e.g., 28 QxR mate, or 28 BxP ch, BxB; 29 QxB mate.

27 ...   PxP ch

Note 27 ... RxQ?; 28 R–N8 ch, followed by mate.

28 K–R2

A magnificent and surprising countermove would be 28 KxP, RxQ!; 29 R–N8 ch, B–Q1 dis ch!!

28 ...   R–KN1

The only move, but sufficient. If now 29 BxP ch, 29 ... BxB wins.

29 R–N1

What else?

29 ...   Q–K8
30 Resigns

What a game!

As in the previous game, here the amateur was playing against a strategy with which he was not familiar, a strategy that could not be met by simply making the standard developing moves.

Here the amateur did make the standard developing moves, which were sound moves, and he also was confronted with a disadvantageous psychological factor. He had the impression that his position was completely safe, but if he had had a better understanding of the strange but strong system he was playing against, he certainly would not have overlooked Black's surprising sacrifice on his 13th move.

Apart from that, the amateur played perfectly well, especially in his attempt to obtain counterchances after he had suffered the material loss of two Pawns. The master could force the amateur to his knees only by very sharp master play and deep and exact calculation.

Game 19

The opening theory of the King's Indian Defense

Pawn-chain strategy as applied to the King's Indian Defense

The importance of carrying out an indicated strategy

The open file for attacking purposes

The function of the spearhead Pawn in preventing the King's flight

The accumulation of attacking power

The struggle in the center can lead to a great variety of Pawn formations. On the one hand, it is possible that by exchange one side may lose all his center Pawns, and then the other side has won the first phase of the struggle and now has the duty of taking advantage of the center majority that he has achieved. On the other hand, the tension in the center may be maintained for a part or the whole of the middle-game phase, which means that the struggle for the center was not resolved. Or the Pawns may advance in such a way that they stand diagonally parallel to each other in an immobile formation known as a *Pawn chain*.

The Pawn chain requires a very special type of strategy that consists in attacking the base of the hostile part of the chain. Such an attack can, if properly prepared and executed at the proper moment by an exchange of Pawns, lead to two sorts of advantages: (a) the creation and domination of an open file; (b) creation of a weak Pawn at the base of the opponent's Pawn chain.

In the execution of this strategy, one must always consider the possibility and the wisdom of an extension of the Pawn chain, in which case the base of the opponent's chain is moved one rank lower. The prospect of such an extension requires a very precise comparison between the possibilities before and after the extension.

In this game, which revolves around the Pawn chain, White forces a weak Pawn at the base of the Black chain, but Black, as compensation, gets control of the open file that he creates on the other side of the board. As the game develops, the attack along the open file proves to be more significant than the weak Pawn at the base of the chain.

King's Indian Defense:
Main Variation without Fianchetto of White's KB

Amateur	Master
White	*Black*
1 P–Q4	N–KB3
2 P–QB4	P–KN3
3 N–QB3	

We have already found these moves in the Grünfeld-Indian (Game 9). At this point the Grünfeld-Indian continues 3 ... P–Q4, whereas the King's Indian continues

3 ...	B–N2
4 P–K4	

By this move White prevents Black from ever again playing the Grünfeld.

The move 4 P–K4 is a logical follow-up of 3 N–QB3, since if White does not play 4 P–K4, Black gets a second and still better possibility of playing ... P–Q4, and after PxP, NxP, the opportunity of making the exchange NxN(QB6), followed by an attack against White's central Pawn formation

PQB3-PQ4 from all sides, as in the Grünfeld, for instance (see Game 9). So if White plays N–QB3 in the King's Indian, he should not allow Black the possibility of ... P–Q4 for too long a time.

White now has an imposing array of center Pawns on his 4th rank. They control his QN5, QB5, Q5, K5, and KB5.

How can Black afford to permit White to control so much territory in the center?

The strength of one's center consists of (a) the extent and importance of the squares controlled; (b) the nature and availability of the space behind the center, which can be a base for action. Therefore, in determining the value of one's center one must ask: (a) Do I control more and better squares than my opponent? (b) Can I use the space behind the center for an attack?

White must realize that by playing P–K4 he weakens his Q4 square in a larger sense, for having played P–K4, White will no longer be able to maintain the tension in the center so easily. After Black has played ... P–Q3 and ... P–K4 or ... P–Q3 and ... P–QB4, his Pawn on the 4th rank combines with his KB to bring pressure against White's Q4 square.

In general, if the side that oc-

cupies the center can maintain the
tension, it is advantageous. In other
words, it is good for White to maintain the formation PQB4–PQ4–PK4
against the Black formation PQ3–
PK4. But if White should play
either P–Q5 or QPxKP, he gives up
the tension, which may have some
disadvantages.

At this point, White could also
have played 4 N–B3, but this line
gives him fewer possibilities. Or he
could have played 4 P–KN3, and
Black could have answered 4 . . .
P–Q4, which is a strengthened
Grünfeld for Black, since the K-
side fianchetto does not mean much
for White in the Grünfeld.

4 . . .   P–Q3

To attain some influence in the
center, since it is always somewhat
risky to leave such an excellent
center to the opponent by not having one's squares of the 4th rank
controlled by a single Pawn. The
move . . . P–Q3 is found in a number of openings where Black permits White to occupy the center up
to a certain point, as in the Alekhine Defense.

If Black could afford to permit
White to occupy the 4th rank with
three center Pawns, it might not
be recommendable to allow him to
push on to the 5th rank. Still, Black
could play 4 . . . O–O instead, and
after 5 P–K5, N–K1, Black would
have the possibility of attacking
White's advanced Pawn by . . . P–
Q3 and . . . P–QB4. But this procedure is more difficult. Simpler is
4 . . . P–Q3.

5 N–B3

An important crossroad. Here
White has the choice of 5 N–B3,
5 P–KN3, 5 P–B3, 5 P–B4.

White had to choose how he
wanted to develop his KB, whether
to play 5 N–B3 and use the KB
to protect his QBP, or to play 5 P–
KN3 and fianchetto the Bishop to
KN2. This choice is especially important in resolving the question of
whether or not center tension is to
be maintained. Whatever the
method of developing the KB, this
problem will arise in a few moves.
But the criteria used for the decision will differ with the choice
White makes at this point.

On the other hand, with 5 P–B3,
the Sämisch Variation of the King's
Indian, White says: "I want to attack on the K side by moves such
as P–KN4 and P–KR4–5. First I
have to close the center by P–Q5
and castle on the Q side." For instance: 5 P–B3, O–O; 6 B–K3, P–
K4; 7 P–Q5, QN–Q2; 8 Q–Q2, P–
QR4; 9 P–KN4, N–B4; 10 P–KR4,
B–Q2; 11 P–R5! with a strong attack.

Finally, P–B4 leads to the so-
called Four Pawns Variation of the
King's Indian. The broad center has
certain advantages, but on the
other hand, it is not always easy to
withstand Black's attacks against
such a center.

5 . . .   O–O
6 B–K2

The alternate 6 B–Q3 would entail several disadvantages: (a) the

White Queen would lose direct control along its file; (b) it would be difficult for the KB to perform any special function on Q3, since the QN1–KR7 diagonal is not especially vulnerable with the Black Pawn formation PKB2–PKN3–PKR2, and the KB is blocked by its own KP.

On its K2 the Bishop has no very special function either. It permits castling, it does not shut off the Queen's pressure along the Q file (although at times it prevents White's KR from controlling the K file), and sometimes from K2 it helps guard White's KN4 square, as it does in this game.

6 ...   P–K4

Black now takes possession of a center square himself. It is true that the free range of the Black KB is blocked by 6 ... P–K4, but at the same time the Bishop helps strengthen the pressure along the long diagonal. After an eventual ... PxP, the force of Black's fianchettoed Bishop is increased considerably. On the other hand, if White should play P–Q5, the diagonal would be definitely closed, but this move constitutes a concession on the part of White as well as of Black.

The Black KP is now attacked by White's QP and KN, defended only by its own QP; yet analysis will show that the text move entails only a sham sacrifice on the part of Black. For instance, 7 PxP, PxP; 8 NxP, NxP wins back the Pawn.

It is important for Black to play 6 ... P–K4 at this point in order to allow the Black QN the possibility of going either to B3 or Q2. If Black should play 6 ... N–B3 immediately, White would answer 7 P–Q5, and the Knight would have to return to home base (7 ... N–N1). But after 6 ... P–K4, followed by 7 ... N–B3, if 8 P–Q5, N–K2, where the Knight stands well.

7 O–O

White could also have played 7 P–Q5 here, but it is against the principle of maintaining the tension in the center as long as possible. On the other hand, 7 P–Q5 would have prevented the Black Knight from going to its QB3.

7 ...   N–B3

Threatening to win a Pawn by 8 ... PxP; 9 NxP, NxP; 10 NxQN, NxN; 11 NxQ, NxQ; 12 NxBP, NxNP. The text is much more enterprising than 7 ... QN–Q2, since it tries to force White to a declaration in the center.

8 P–Q5

White decides to close the center. This is an important turning point in the game, for as soon as White plays 8 P–Q5, Black gets his chances on the K side. Before 8 P–Q5, the move ... P–KB4 on the part of Black (naturally after Black's KN has vacated the KB3 square) might have resulted in weaknesses for Black after White plays QPxKP and KPxKBP. At that time, the side attack initiated by ... P–KB4 would have made Black's position vulnerable along the diagonal. After 8 P–Q5, this danger no longer exists.

What other possibilities did White have? Could he have maintained the tension in the center in addition to greater freedom for himself and no counterchances for Black?

White could try 8 B–K3, N–KN5; 9 B–N5, P–B3; 10 B–B1, which certainly would change the entire game. Is 8 B–K3 better than 8 P–Q5? In one respect, yes, since it maintains tension, in another respect, no, since Black gets his chances as well in the form of winning some tempi.

The line 8 PxP, PxP does not give either side an advantage. After 9 QxQ, if 9 ... RxQ; 10 B–N5!, and Black has to play 10 ... R–K1, because of the threat 11 N–Q5, possibly preceded by BxN, and Black's position is not quite satisfactory. Better is 9 ... NxQ; 10 NxP, NxP.

8 ...   N–K2

We are now in the presence of a Pawn chain, already mentioned briefly in Game 8 under Black's 15th move. A Pawn chain is made up of two diagonal lines of interlocked Pawns, one White, one Black. The head of each line is the part projecting farthest into the opponent's territory, the base the part extending farthest back into one's own territory. A Pawn chain may consist of two or more Pawns of each color. In the present position, the White part of the chain consists of the Pawns on White's K4 and Q5, the Black part of the chain, the Pawns on Black's K4 and Q3. The head of White's part of the chain is White's QP, and of Black's part of the chain is Black's KP; the base of White's part of the chain is White's KP, and of Black's part of the chain is Black's QP. The presence of such a Pawn chain requires a very special strategy on the part of each player. Each player should attack the base of the opponent's part of the chain. Thus, White must attack Black's QP, and Black must attack White's KP. This sort of attack is made by advancing one of one's own Pawns to the square where it comes in diagonal contact with the base of the opponent's chain, thus putting the Pawns in a position where either side can exchange. The aim of this type of attack is to create an open file and to deprive the base of the opponent's chain of its Pawn protection. If the file is opened, the Rooks can bring their maximum force into play. If the base of the opponent's Pawn chain is deprived of protection, it may be attacked by pieces and captured. However, the player who succeeds in attacking the enemy base by moving up one of his own Pawns does not necessarily make the Pawn exchange. He has the option of exchanging Pawns and thus creating the open file and depriving the enemy base of its Pawn protection, or of pushing his own attacking Pawn one space more, thus extending the Pawn chain farther into enemy territory and enlarging his control of that territory.

Pawn-chain strategy will be illustrated also in connection with the position arising under White's 9th move of Game 22.

9 N–K1

This move is defensive, in that it allows P–B3 (to protect White's KP after ... P–KB4), and offensive in that it makes possible N–Q3, which would support White's QBP when it goes to B5.

9 ...   N–Q2

This move is defensive, in that it guards Black's QB4 square against White's P–B5 (which is in line with White's indicated strategy), and offensive because it permits Black to play ... P–KB4 (which is also in line with Black's indicated strategy) and in some exceptional cases to play ... N–QB4.

Also good is 9 ... N–K1, but from that square the Knight does not exercise any control over his QB4 square or protect his K4 square; on the other hand, this move does keep open the diagonal for Black's QB.

10 B–K3

An offensive move that prepares a later P–QB5 and is made at this time in order to keep the QB in its aggressive possession of this diagonal by preparing for it a retreat to B2 by playing P–B3. Black, in the meantime, will play P KB4–KB5.

Nowadays, however, 10 N–Q3 is considered better, for (a) White does not lose time by having to play B–B2 after Black's ... P–KB5; (b) the White QB is considered more active when developed to its Q2, from which it can be brought to QN4 or QR5.

Not in harmony with the strategy of the Pawn chain would be 10 P–B4?, for it attacks the head rather than the base of the opponent's Pawn chain. Black would answer 10 ... PxP and obtain his K4 square for his pieces (11 BxP, N–K4). By attacking the head of a Pawn chain, you risk turning over a strong square to your opponent.

But there *are* positions in which an attack against the *head* of the Pawn chain is successful. White's 14th move in Game 8 illustrates this.

10   P KB4

Attacking the base of White's Pawn chain, as the strategy dictates.

11 P-B3

To allow the Bishop to retreat to B2.

The line beginning 11 PxP, which is not a bad move here, is very instructive. Black would not then answer 11 ... NxP, for that would give a strong K4 square to White. Rather, he would play 11 ... PxP; 12 P-B4, and if ... P-K5 (certainly not the best), White obtains the strong Q4 square, which he can occupy by N-QB2-Q4, and Black's protected passed KP is worth nothing, since it is a block-aded passed Pawn (blockaded by White's QB), which is more of a disadvantage than an advantage.

11 ...   P-B5

This is a very important point in the game. The Pawn chain has been extended. White's base now becomes PKB3, rather than PK4, and now Black's strategy is to play for P-N5. At this point, he does not play to weaken the base of White's Pawn chain, which is suffi-ciently protected, but to open the KN file. The farther distant the enemy base, the more difficult it is to attack it successfully. Therefore, Black aims at opening, not weaken-ing. This is a generalization, but special circumstances may prevail. Look at Black's Q3, to be attacked by P-QB5, N-N5, and (if the White QB had remained on the diagonal QB1-K3) B-QN4 (or B-QR3). However, it is clear that White's KB3 can be attacked only a very few times.

Mistaken strategy would have been 11 ... PxP, for White would play 17 NxP and occupy the strong K4 square. Even if White had no Knight to occupy his K4 square, and if he had to answer 11 ... PxP by 12 PxP, the resultant posi-tion would not be good for Black, because he would have attained nothing. The open file is for both Rooks, and now Black no longer has a base to attack, whereas White does have—the Black QP!

12 B-B2   P-KN4

Both sides play according to plan, but it will take considerable time before either can attain his goal.

13 N-Q3

Consistent with White's aim of playing P-QB5 at a favorable time and then opening the QB file and weakening Black's QP by QBPxQP.

13 ...   R–B3

The Rook will go to KN3, where it will participate in the attempt to open the KN file and attack White's castled King.

Some players prefer 13 ... R–B2, which is a little slower, but which defends the 7th rank in case White attacks via the QB file with his QR and QN.

14 P–B5

White, too, is beginning to realize his strategic aim. If he can now force Black to play 14 ... PxP, the QB file will be opened and the Black KP will be weakened.

14 ...   P–KR4

Black ignores White's attack on the base of his Pawn chain and continues his own strategy of trying to open the KN file.

15 PxP

Not bad, but perhaps 15 R–B1 would have been even better, in that it would have afforded the additional possibility of P–B6, as well as preserving the threats PxP and N–N5.

When you have a choice, it is a good policy to leave your opponent in doubt as to which line you are going to follow.

15 ...   PxP
16 R–B1!

A very good move! It takes possession of an open file and threatens an attack along that file by N–N5. It would be very awkward for Black to permit White's QN to jump via QN5 to QB7—and eventually to the strong square K6!

16 ...   P–R3

Forced and weakening. White must now take advantage of this weakening of Black's QN3 square. How can he do it? One way is by P–QR4–R5, N–R4 N6, another simply by N–R4, Q–N3, N–N6—White occupies his QN6 square and then continues his attack along the QB file. True, Black can play P–QN4 at any time in order to refute White's play, but this means a further weakening, which permits White to reply later N–N4–B6.

17 P–QN3

Planning N–N2–B4 or –R4.

This is a third system, also very instructive, but a little slower, and therefore a line that offers less chances in the available time.

17 ...   R–N3

Black can thus afford to ignore the White demonstration on the Q side and place a heavy piece along the file he wishes to open.

18 N–N2

Consistent. White plans to attack Black's QP by N, at the same time preparing a break at his QN6

18 ...   K–R1

Black continues to prepare for the push ... P–KN5. Notice the extremely careful calculations he makes in preparation for the push. He considered an immediate 18 ... N–KB3, but this move has disadvantages. It would leave Black's QN3 unprotected. Also, after Black had realized his ... P–KN5, White could play B–R4, and Black would have no good way to continue the attack. Therefore, Black clears his KN1 square, planning to play N(K2)–KN1–R3, where it will exert pressure on Black's KN5 square.

19 P–QR4

In order to be able to play N–B4 without risking the Knight's being driven back immediately by ... P–N4.

19 ...   N–KN1
20 N–B4   N–R3

So far, both sides have executed their respective strategical plans in the most logical way. Now White could have continued by P–R5 and N–N6 lessening the Black attack. Instead of this, he looked for a defensive line against the Black bulldozer in the form of P–KN4 and P–KR4

21 P–R3?

White cannot prevent ... P–N5 in any case, and to attempt to prevent it by a Pawn move is very weakening. *If* White wishes to stop Black's Pawn advance, he should have done so in some other way:

(a) 21 Q–K1, to continue after 21 ... P–N5 by 22 B–R4! and in that case, Black prepares to counter by ... B–B1 and ... B–K2 (not ... B–B3 at once, because he intercepts the protection of his QP);

(b) 21 P–KN4, PxP e.p., and if 22 PxP, P–N5, or if 22 BxP, P–R5; 23 B–B2, P–N5!; 24 PxP, NxP; 25 BxN, N–B3; 26 P–R3, NxB; 27 PxN, BxP. In both cases, Black is able to continue the K-side attack, but not as effectively as played in the actual game.

21 ...   P–N5

The text seems to cost Black a Pawn, but this is only temporary. Black is now sure to obtain the open N file. One sees how useless White's last move was, only weakening and collaborating.

22 RPxP   PxP
23 PxP   N–B3

With this move Black gives himself the possibility of winning back the Pawn and opening the file.

24 P–N5

A pretty try. White wins the exchange, but loses the game.

Also insufficient are (a) 24 B–N6, Q–K2 and (b) 24 N–N6, R–N1. In neither of these variations can White prevent ... N(B3)xNP, after which there are all sorts of threats similar to those we shall see in the game.

Probably better was 24 B–R4, in which case Black answers 24 ... N(R3)xP, and before he can continue his attack, he will have to make some preparatory moves such as ... Q–B1, since his Knight is pinned.

| 24 ... | RxP |
| 25 B–R4 | N(B3)–N5! |

The Black Rook cannot escape. If 25 ... R–N3; 26 B–R5.

26 BxR

It was not necessary to take at once. Better was first 26 R–B3, in order to gain time for the defense.

Not good is 26 NxQP?, which is answered by 26 ... N–K6.

26 ...   QxB

White has won the exchange, but the Black attack has become very strong. Black is now threatening mate by 27 ... Q–R5 and 28 ... Q–R7 ch.

27 BxN   BxB

If 27 ... NxB, then White can prevent Black from carrying out his threat by 28 R–B3; for 28 ... Q–R5?; 29 R–R3.

28 Q–Q2   Q–N3

So as not to be disturbed by NxQP. If, for instance, 28 ... R–KN1; 29 NxQP, the Knight might even succeed in reaching its KB5 square and constitute a nuisance there.

29 Q–KB2

This enables White to play N–Q2–B3 (defensive) or to continue by Q–R4 or Q–N6 (offensive). So chances look pretty fair for White.

29 ...   R–KN1

Here we are in the presence of the building up of an accumulation of power. Place the pieces into position, and threats will follow automatically.

30 R–B2

Overprotection of his KN2 square —an example of accumulation of defensive power. If White had carried out his original defensive plan, it appears that Black's attack would

grow stronger anyhow: 30 N–Q2,
Q–R4; 31 N–B3, B–B3, threaten-
ing 32 ... B–Q1 followed by 33
... BxN; 34 QxB, B–N3 ch; or 32
... D–R0.

Of offensive moves White could
not think at all, if 30 Q–R4, B–B3;
if 30 Q–N6, B–KB1, threatening
31 ... B–B6!

Black would now like to make
some move with his QB in order
to vacate his KN5 square for his
Knight (... N–N5, ... Q–R7
mate). But on the other hand, he
does not like to take the Bishop
from this square, since it is very
valuable for attack here, and after
30 ... B–Q2; 31 Q–R4 is a good
defense. He now tries to combine
both ideas and plays

30 ...   Q–R4

Black gives up the QP in order
to gain a few tempi and to bring
his KB into action after 31 NxP
by 31 ... B–KB1, under certain
circumstances to be followed by
... B–QB4.

The accumulation of power is
becoming overwhelming. There is
no sufficient defense. White cannot
defend himself, for

(a) the White King is vulnerable
and is defended only by his
KNP;
(b) all the Black pieces are in
action;
(c) Black has the open KN file;
(d) Black's KBP is very strong
on its 5th rank.

This does not mean, however,
that any attacking method would
be sufficient. Black must play carefully; e.g., 31 Q–N6,
(a) not 31 ... B–Q2; 32 N–Q2,
N–N5; 33 N–B3—and Black
has nothing;
(b) not 31 ... B–B3; 32 QxQP,
B–R5; 33 QxKP ch;
(c) but 31 ... B–KB1 (first
clearing the KN file); and
(1) 32 NxQP loses a piece after
32 ... Q–N3; 33 N–B4, QxQ;
34 NxQ, B–B4 ch;
(2) 32 K–R2, Q–R5 ch, and his
King cannot escape because of
Black's strong KBP!
(3) 32 N–Q2, B–K2; 33 QxNP
(33 N–B3 loses a piece), B–
R5; 34 KR–QB1, B–N6; 35 N–
B1; Black now wins by making
use of his forces in the most
effective way. One example just
to illustrate: 35 ... B–B1; 36
Q–N8, N–N5; 37 QxQP, B–R7
ch!; 38 NxB, QxN ch; 39 K–
B1, P–B6!!—the *key move!* The
threat is 40 ... Q–R8 mate.
If White plays indifferently, he
will be mated on the move: 40
N–K2, PxP ch; 41 K–K1, P–
N8[Q] ch; 42 NxQ, QxN ch; 43
K–K2, Q–K6 ch; 44 K–B1, N–
R7 ch!; 45 RxN, B–R6 ch; 46
RxB, QxR ch; 47 K–K1, R–

N8 ch and mate in three. The series of checks is wonderful! Certainly there are many other variations, but to give them would only confuse the reader. The line we have chosen is the most difficult for both sides. Now let us go back to the diagram that follows Black's 30th move and try 31 N–Q2, B–B3 (threatening both ... B–R5–N6 and, under some circumstances, ... B–Q1–N3 ch); 32 N–B3, BxN; 33 QxB, N–N5; 34 Q–R3, QxQ; 35 PxQ, N–K6 dbl ch, winning an entire Rook.

In the game, White played

31 NxQP   B–KB1

Winning a tempo by attacking the White Knight.

32 N–B4

If 32 N–B5, BxN; 33 PxB, N–N5 wins.

32 ...   B–B6!

Consider the accumulation of power! Every piece plays its part: the Rook brings direct pressure on White's KNP and behind it on the White King; the QB adds to the pressure, threatens the win of a Pawn; the KB stands in readiness to go to its QB4, where it could draw the White Queen from its protective post; the Knight can likewise drive the White Queen from its KB2 by N–N5 with the continuation ... Q–R7 ch. The Queen cooperates in the mate on KR7 after N–N5.

33 QxB   B–B4 ch
34 Resigns

For this wins the Queen. If 34 KR–B2 or QR–B2, 34 ... QxQ! And if 34 Q–B2, N–N5! and mate on the next move.

In this game the amateur put up a good fight as long as he activated his Q-side attack against the master's K-side attack. True, he did not choose the quickest way to attack, as pointed out in the remark after Black's 16th move, but even the slower system gives him certain counterchances. The decisive error of the amateur was his 21st move, where he tried to stop an advance that cannot be stopped. Because of that, serious consequences followed.

But for a long time the amateur found the proper defensive move, and the master had to discover a long series of sacrificial variations in order to exploit his advantage.

Game 20

The White K-side fianchetto in the King's Indian

Ways of slowing down Black's equalization in the opening

Procedure when Black seizes the initiative in the opening too soon

Psychological reasons for choosing moves which force the opponent to make a choice

Penetration of the open K side

Opening up the position for attack

The in-between move in combinations

Black's role in the opening is to strive for equality by gradually overcoming his slight initial disadvantage. With best play on White's part, Black can attain equality only through a series of slow and solid moves. If Black attempts to seize the initiative prematurely, he risks ending up with inferiority because of White's slight initial edge.

In order for Black to assume the initiative in the opening, he must normally take some risks and leave certain weaknesses in his position. In such cases White must discover the weaknesses Black has incurred and find the best way to exploit them.

White's refutation of such premature initiative on the part of Black often results in an advance in development for White, as a result of which Black may not be able to castle at the proper time.

As long as the position remains closed, this does not matter too much. Therefore, White will have to use his extra tempi to try to open up the game, and this he will do by bringing his pieces to the front near the Black position.

In the game that follows, this well-known procedure is executed with cleverness, exactness, and inventiveness.

King's Indian Defense: Counter-Fianchetto

Master	Amateur
White	*Black*
1 P–Q4	N–KB3
2 P–QB4	P–KN3

The initial moves of the King's Indian. If White now plays 3 N–QB3, it could lead to the Grünfeld-Indian, which gives Black considerable counterplay on the long diagonal (see Game 9). But by postponing the development of his QN, White avoids the Grünfeld. He rather plays

3 P–KN3

In such positions, in general, White's KB occupies a more favorable place on the wing than in the center, where it often hampers other pieces. From its KN2, the Bishop controls more squares than it would from its K2 or Q3. However, if White is planning to attack Black's castled King's position by P–KR4–R5, the Bishop might be more useful on its K2 or Q3 in order to support this advance.

3 ...   P–B3

In order to play 4 ... P–Q4, with complete equalization in the center. Black, who because he plays second has just a bit less initiative than White, must strive to attain equality in whatever opening he plays. In this position, Black hopes to gain equality by the following moves: 4 B–N2, P–Q4; 5 PxP (difficult to avoid, since White's KB will not be placed so as to maintain the tension at QB4), PxP; 6 N–KB3, B–N2, etc.

Since the above variation leads to a symmetrical position in which Black has virtual equality, White looks for a move that will allow him to retain his slight superiority.

4 P–Q5

With the text move, White sacrifices a tempo in order to obtain a preponderance of space and to increase the activity of his wing Bishop. It prevents Black from playing ... P–Q4, which move would reduce the activity of the White KB considerably. True, being posted behind a White Pawn on Q5, its activity may be reduced in this way as well, but indirectly the Bishop could play an important role. The game itself shows the preventive function of White's KB, for Black never played ... P–K3 in the game for fear of giving his opponent the opportunity of opening the important diagonal on which the White KB was posted.

4 ...   PxP   .

This move is not forced, but Black hopes to obtain an advantage by what follows

5 PxP   Q-R4 ch?

An attempt to obtain the initiative, which is always very dangerous for the second player at such an early stage of the game.

Black should continue by 5 ... P-Q3, or 5 ... B-N2. If White answers 5 ... B-N2 by 6 P-Q6, then 6 ... P-K3, and while White's QP presses, it does not hamper development. Moreover, much later, it might become weak.

Let us see how White refutes 5 ... Q-R4 ch.

6 N-QB3   N-K5?

The weak point in Black's plan —he lays open a diagonal along which he is vulnerable. He intends: 7 Q-Q3 (or 7 Q-B2), NxN; 8 PxN, B-N2; 9 B-Q2, N-R3, with pressure against White's Q wing, and if 10 P-QB4, N-N5!

7 Q-Q4

Attacking the loose Rook. This move does not seem to stop Black's plans either: 7 ... NxN and (a) 8 PxN, R-N1, followed by 9 ... B-N2, with the same result as in the previous note, or (b) 8 QxN, QxQ ch; 9 PxQ, B-N2, with positional advantage to Black. But White has better.

7 ...   NxN
8 B-Q2!

This is the refutation of Black's sally, as is shown by the crucial combination 8 ... QxQP; 9 QxN, N-B3 (forced, since White was threatening 10 QxB mate); 10 QxR, QxR; 11 B-R6. This proves that Black is now forced to weaken his K wing by ... P-B3 or ... R-N1.

What was Black's mistake? He acted contrary to an important general principle: *Do not take the initiative without an advance in development*—and he did not calculate the exact consequences. Note that you can act against principles if your calculations justify it. General principles are main highways, and it is always possible that some byroad may be quicker in a specific case.

White could not have played 8 QxR here, for 8 ... N-K5 dis ch; 9 K-Q1, NxP ch.

8 ...   R-N1

Better was 8 ... P-B3, but Black is dreaming of ... B-N2. Faced with a choice between ... P-B3 and ... R-N1 (as is shown by the analysis following White's 8th move), Black chose the worse of the two, for this move definitely eliminates castling on the K side, and as castling on the Q side does not seem very attractive either (the QB file is open), the prospects of the Black King are far from rosy.

9 BxN   Q–B2

Instead 9 ... Q–Q1 might have saved a tempo.

10 R–B1

Black was still threatening 10 ... B–N2 and 11 ... BxB. After the text, it would not be wise for Black to continue by10 ... B–N2, on account of 11 Q–Q2, BxB; 12 RxB, Q–Q1; 13 Q–R6, winning a Pawn and attacking the Black position from the side. Note how 10 R–B1 retains a measure of initiative for White by *indirectly* threatening Black's Queen.

10 ...   P–Q3

Making room for the Queen and preventing an eventual break by P–Q6.

11 N–B3

There is no direct way of taking advantage of the exposed position of the Black Queen and of other weaknesses of the hostile position. So White can do no better than complete his development and bring fresh forces into the struggle in order to exploit the advantage already attained.

11 ...   P–KR3?

Black feared 12 N–N5, which could have led to complications, and for that reason made this weakening move. The curse of evil is that it always creates new evil. The text move prevents 12 N–N5, but it was not absolutely necessary to prevent it. There were other and more important things to be done on the Q side.

When you have a bad game, as Black has here, it is generally impossible to parry all threats, and it is therefore a good psychological device to give the opponent a choice that will make him lose time and energy. Here, for instance, instead of making a move that White can answer without effort, it would be better for Black to make a move that would force White to lose time and energy analyzing. After 11 ... N–R3 or 11 ... N–Q2, White would have had to choose between the normal continuation of development 12 B–N2 and the aggressive move 12 N–N5, and whichever is better can be determined only by exact analysis.

12 B–N2   N–R3

One might wonder why in positions like this the Knight should go to R3, away from the center, instead of to Q2, in the center. If the Knight is moved to Q2, it will require another move to get it to KB3, and it cannot very well stay on Q2, partly because it blocks the development of Black's QB and partly because the Knight itself is not very effective on Q2.

Is the Knight better on KB3, where it would take two moves to put it, than on QR3, where it can go in one move? Perhaps, but it is not certain.

From QR3 the Knight can go to QB4, but at present it can remain on QR3. It could have gone to its QB4 from its Q2 as well, but it would have had to do so soon, so as not to hamper the development of the QB.

13 O–O   P–KN4

Black wishes to play ... B–B4, but first desires to prevent White from playing N–R4. The remedy is worse than the disease, for this Pawn advance allows White to penetrate into the hostile position.

14 Q–Q3!

In the same move White prevents ... B–B4 and takes a position on the diagonal that will allow him to penetrate Black's weakened K side. White threatens 15 B–N7!, taking advantage of the indirect attack of White's QR against the Black Queen; e.g., 15 B–N7, Q–Q2; 16 BxB, RxB; 17 Q–R7, winning an important Pawn

and pressing on the Black position from the side.

14 ...   Q–Q2?
15 N–Q4

The beginning of the last stage —the exploitation of White's advantage. Black's handicap lies in the insecure position of his King. To exploit this insecurity of the King, White must advance his pieces and open up the position along the KB file. Both things will happen soon.

The text prevents ... Q–B4 and prepares 16 P–B4!

15 ...   B–N2

White threatened 16 Q–R7, R–N3; 17 N–K6! and 15 ... N–B4 would not have stopped it on account of 16 Q–R7, R–N3; 17 P–QN4, N–R5; 18 N–K6, etc.

16 Q–R7   K–B1

This was one of the purposes of Black's last move. The Black King has a place after all—but what a place! Notice that it is in a direct line with White's KR, even though there are two intervening Pawns.

17 P–B4!

The deciding advance. White threatens to open up the position and to win immediately by 18 PxP, PxP; 19 N–K6 ch.

17 ...   P–N5

Forced, as 17 ... R–R1 will not do: 18 N–K6 ch!, PxN; 19 QxB ch, etc.

18 P–B5

Again threatening 19 N–K6 ch.

18 ...   Q–Q1?

The only way of putting up any resistance whatever was by 18 ... BxN ch; 19 BxB, although after the exchange of the fianchettoed Bishop, Black is bound to lose at least his RP at once and more later.

19 N–K6 ch

An easy combination, since Black's moves are practically forced.

19 ...   BxN

Or 19 ... PxN; 20 BPxP dis ch, B–B3; 21 Q–B7 mate.

20 BxB ch

An in-between move that forces Black's reply. Notice the impor-

tance of the order of the moves in this combination.

20 ...   RxB
21 Q–R8 ch   R–N1
22 QxP ch   R–N2

Also hopeless for Black is 22 ... K–K1, for after 23 BPxB,
(a) 23 ... P–B3; 24 Q–R5 ch, followed by mate;
(b) 23 ... R–B1; 24 RxP, RxR; 25 Q–R8 ch, R–B1; 26 Q–R5 ch, followed by mate;
(c) 23 ... PxP; 24 PxP, Q–N3 ch; 25 K–R1, and there is no defense against 26 Q–R7.

23 BPxB   P–B3
24 R–KB5

The advantage of the text is that from KB5 the Rook can go either to KN5 (as will be seen from the conclusion of the game, ... PxR does not work because of R–B1 ch) or to KR5 with various threats.

Notice that 24 R–KB4 would not be adequate here, for (a) after 24 ... K–N1 there is no convincing continuation; (b) after 24 ... Q–N3 ch; 25 K–R1, QxP; 26 QR–B1, K–N1, there is no direct win, either.

After 24 R–KB5, on the other hand, (a) 24 ... K–N1; 25 R–R5, threatening mate, and if 25 ... K–B1, 26 R–N5, as in the game; (b) 24 ... Q–N3 ch; 25 K–R1, (1)1) 0ll QR B1, and now there is no defense against 27 R–N5.

24 ...   N–B2

Hoping to bring his Knight to the defense.

25 R–N5!   Resigns

For the text threatens an early mate, and if 25 ... RxR; 26 Q–R8 ch, R–N1; 27 R B1 ch, K–K1; 28 QxR mate

Sometimes games go wrong from the very beginning. At times this also holds true for masters, but by force for the amateur. One wrong idea, and the whole position is spoiled. In such cases it is difficult to attain anything at all, and in this game the amateur did not succeed.

Game 21

There are often positions on the chessboard in which a concession is made by one of the players in order to get some corresponding advantage in exchange. This might be termed an exchange of positional values, as contrasted with the exchange of Pawns and pieces in the material sphere. It is very difficult to weigh a positional advantage against a disadvantage. In this realm there is no scale such as exists in the realm of pieces and Pawns. Everything depends on special circumstances. Does White's possession of the Two Bishops, for instance, compensate for the weakening of his Pawn position? Or is the *hole* in White's Pawn position compensated for by the *hole* on Black's K side? The latter case permits a more general answer, for weaknesses related to the King's position are generally more serious than those that are not.

In this game positional values play an important role. On his 10th move White advances his KP, giving the Black Knight the opportunity of occupying a strong square. In exchange White gets the chance to bring one of his attacking Knights to the *hole* very near the Black King. A skirmish follows and apparently nothing special is happening, but when the smoke of the battle has disappeared, we see that the result of the skirmish is that the position of the Black King is weakened in that he now has only two Pawns on his 3rd rank, instead of the original three

Pawns on his 2nd rank. This double weakness—one Pawn missing and the remaining Pawns advanced one square—gives White the opportunity to storm against the Black position with all his forces and to decide the struggle with a sharp sacrifice.

King's Indian Defense: Semi-Grünfeld

Master	Expert
White	*Black*

1 P–Q4	N–KB3
2 P–QB4	P–KN3
3 P–KN3	B–N2

Instead of trying to build up a defensive Pawn wall to oppose the action of White's fianchettoed Bishop, as Black did in Game 20, here Black fianchettoes his own Bishop.

4 B–N2

The fianchettoed White Bishop will exert pressure along the diagonal, which will give White a considerable control of the center.

4 ...   P–Q4

Black plays ... P–Q4 as in the Grünfeld Defense, but here White's situation is considerably different from the analogous position in the Grünfeld, for in this game, if 5 PxP, NxP, White can now drive away the Black Knight by 6 P–K4 without Black's having the favorable exchange 6 ... NxN. Compare with Game 9.

5 PxP

White exchanges at this point in order to exploit the pressure of the White KB in the most efficient way. After 5 KN–B3 or 5 QN–B3,

Black could reply 5 ... P–B3, which would hamper the activity of White's fianchettoed Bishop. Black would then have achieved the position for which he was striving in Game 20. Also satisfactory for Black would have been in that case 5 ... PxP.

5 ...   NxP
6 P–K4

White immediately takes advantage of this opportunity to seize the center. We have seen this advance in several other games, and with varying degrees of success. In order to evaluate this type of center, we must consider the following factors:

(a) the degree of mobility of the pieces in comparison with that of the opponent's pieces;

(b) the possibilities of action to follow from this greater mobility;

(c) the vulnerability of the center.

The possession of the center puts a responsibility on the player who has it. If he does not succeed in taking advantage of factors (a) and (b), he will have to suffer the consequences of (c).

Since an attack against the King does not present itself, White has to work in that direction, and his task will not be easy.

6 ...   N–N3

Black is forced to move his Knight. Where shall he move it? Should he simply look for the safest spot, or should he try to find a place where the Knight could annoy his opponent and force him into less advantageous moves?

In this position, the reply 6 ... N–N3 is tame, because it forces nothing. But looking around, we find the move 6 ... N–N5, which is bound to disturb White's position and his control of the center. It practically forces 7 P–Q5, which would be followed by 7 ... P–B3.

Let us consider the reply 6 ... N–N5. White has various possibilities:

(a) 7 N–K2?, BxP, followed by (1) 8 NxB, QxN; 9 QxQ, N–B7 ch; 10 K–Q1, NxQ, winning a Pawn, or (2) 8 QxB?, N–B7 ch;

(b) 7 Q–R4 ch, QN–B3; 8 P–Q5, and Black seems to be on the point of losing a piece, but 8 ... P–QN4!; 9 QxNP, and 9 ... N–B7 ch turns the tide: 10 K–Q1, B–Q2, and White cannot take either Knight: 11

PxN?, BxP dis ch, or 11 KxN?, N–Q5 ch;

(c) 7 P–QR3, KN–B3; 8 P–Q5, N–Q5; 9 N–K2, B–N5; 10 QN–B3, with good chances for Black;

(d) 7 P–Q5 (best) 7 ... P–QB3; 8 N–K2, PxP; 9 PxP, and White's QP can be both strong and weak, strong because it is on an outpost, that is, beyond the middle row, and weak because it is isolated.

Thus, 6 ... N–N5 is better than the text, because it does not leave White in the uncontested possession of his beautiful center.

7 N–K2

The Knight is developed to K2 because of the system chosen (a) to protect the QP in such a way that the defending Knight cannot be pinned (after 7 N–KB3, B–N5, and White's QP is already *en prise*); (b) to keep the diagonal of the fianchettoed Bishop free.

7 ...   O–O
8 O–O   P–K3

By exerting control over his Q4, Black prepares for the advance ... P–QB4. The text has the drawback of creating a hole in Black's K-side position and of weakening Black's KB3 square. We'll soon see what this means.

Black could also have played the advance of his QBP at once without any other preparations: 8 ... P–QB4; 9 P–Q5, P–K3 or 9 ... N–R3, and Black has some counterchances on the Q side. Smyslov

has often played this line. It leads
to a different type of play; e.g.,
Euwe-Smyslov (Candidates' 1950)
8 ... P-QB4; 9 P-Q5, P-K3; 10
P-QR4, N-R3; 11 N-R3, PxP; 12
PxP, B-B4; 13 N-B3, N-N5; 14
R-K3, and White got a good game.
Black need not fear 9 PxP after
8 ... P-QB4, for he wins back the
sacrificed Pawn by 9 ... QxQ; 10
RxQ, N-R5, and stands very well.

9 QN-B3   N-B3

It was impossible to carry out
the planned 9 ... P-QB4 on account of the simple 10 PxP. Compare the same 9 ... P-QB4 in a
position where White has not developed his QN to B3; e.g., 9 P-
KR3, P-QB4; 10 PxP, QxQ; 11
RxQ, N-R5. The point is that after
White's 9 QN-B3, the Black
Knight no longer has its QR5 square
at its disposal.

10 P-K5!

This is the key move. The Black
King has castled, and the White
pieces are sufficiently developed
and ready for action. White prepares
to control his KB6 by means of 11
N-K4 and 12 B-N5, as will be

seen in the game. In other words,
White will try to exploit the weakness of the hole at KB3 in Black's
K-side position. It is true that White
has the same hole, but there is
not a single Black piece in the
vicinity to take advantage of it,
and at least two pieces are needed.

The text move has one drawback—it permits Black to take possession of his Q4 square for his
pieces.

10 ...   N-N5

Black plays thus to control his
Q4 square and to prevent the weak-
ening of his Pawn formation by
White's BxN(B6).

11 N-K4

White now threatens to gain
control of and even occupy Black's
KB3 square by 12 B-N5, Q-Q2;
13 N-B6 ch, BxN; 14 BxB, followed by 15 Q-Q2 and 16 Q-R6,
threatening to mate.

11 ...   P-KR3

Practically forced, unless Black
is willing to allow the aforemen-
tioned invasion by B-N5 and N-
KB6 ch.

12 N-B6 ch!

At this point, White must have
considered 12 ... BxN; 13 PxB,
QxBP; 14 BxRP, R-K1 (14 ...
R-Q1?; 15 Q-Q2, Q-K2; 16 B-
N5, P-KB3; 17 BxBP, etc.); 15
Q-Q2, and White is better devel-
oped and has the Two Bishops,
whereas Black's King is not safe.

12 ...   K-R1

White's Knight is marvelously posted on its KB6 and constitutes a permanent threat to the Black King, but the question is how to make the best use of this favorable position. There are, in general, two big problems in such attacks: how to get a piece to a strong post, and then how to take advantage of the presence of that piece at the strong post. The latter problem requires in most cases the bringing of the pieces to support the strong piece and to cooperate with it.

13 P–KR4

The text can serve as a preparation for P–R5 or (and this is shown by the continuation of the game) for N–N4, and after ... P–KR4, for B–N5, since the KRP now protects this Bishop.

13 ...   P–B4

Black's only counterchance. His indicated strategy is to break White's center position, exchange Queens (which reduces any attack on the enemy King to only five percent of its former vigor) and create possibilities for his QN on its QB7 or Q6.

If White, instead of continuing his own indicated strategy as described under White's 13th move, should try to meet Black's strategy, the whole picture would be changed; e.g., 14 PxP?, QxQ; 15 RxQ, N–N5, with all kinds of threats and strong counterplay for Black.

14 N–N4

White continues to carry out his own plan. This is an interesting example of action and counteraction on opposite wings. Both players are in a hurry in such cases.

14 ...   P–KR4

Alternatives are also favorable for White:
(a) 14 ... PxP; 15 BxKRP,
  (1) 15 ... BxB; 16 NxB, P–Q6; 17 N–B3, K–N2; 18 N–N4, and although there is no direct decision, White's superiority is unquestionable, for (a) White has complete control over the hole on Black's KB3; (b) Black's K side is weakened; (c) Black's QP may become weak; (d) the White KB has great activity.
  (2) 15 ... P–Q6; 16 Q–Q2, PxN; 17 BxB ch, KxB; 18 Q–R6 ch, etc.
(b) 14 ... K–R2; 15 Q–Q2, P–KR4 (forced); 16 N–B6 ch, BxN; 17 PxB, QxBP; 18 PxP, N(N3)–Q4; 19 P–R3, N–QB3; 20 BxN, winning a Pawn, since 20 ... R–Q1 is refuted by 21 Q–R6 ch.

15 B–N5

According to plan—White takes control of his KB6.

15 ...   Q–B2
16 N–B6

The logical continuation of White's strategy.

16 ...   PxP

Black must also continue his strategy.

17 N–B4

And White his. Black now has no defense against N(4)xRP.

17 ...   QxP

What else can he do?

18 N(4)xRP

If now 18 ... PxN; 19 QxP ch followed by mate.

Thus Black cannot accept the sacrifice, and White is able to exchange his N(R5) for Black's KB and then try to attack via the weakened Black squares of the K side, playing Q–Q2 followed by B–R6.

If 18 ... KN (or QN)–Q4, White continues 19 R–K1, Q–Q3; 20 NxB, KxN (as in the game); 21 QxP. This Pawn is protected in the game, but not in this variation.

18 ...   N–Q2

Black must try to undermine the White stronghold at Black's KB3.

White can now win the exchange in several ways; e.g., by (a) 19 NxN, RxN; 20 NxB, KxN; 21 B–K7, N–B3 (or 21 ... N–Q4); 22 BxR ch, RxB, etc.; or (b) 19 N–N1, Q–Q3; 20 NxB, KxN; 21 B–R6 ch, K–N1; 22 BxR, NxR. Neither of these continuations would have eased White's task, as Black's passed Pawn on his Q5 will prove to be a real obstacle. For this reason, White chooses a continuation by which he first eliminates Black's QP. He begins:

19 R–K1

A convenient in-between move.

19 ...   Q–Q3
20 NxB

This was White's intention all the time, for the Bishop must be eliminated in order to make Black's K position still more vulnerable.

20 ...   KxN
21 NxN

If instead 21 Q–B3, then 21 ... P–K4, which would prevent the 22 NxN followed by 23 Q–B6 ch.

21 ...   BxN

Forced, for if 21 ... QxN; 22 Q–Q2!, winning the Black Knight or the exchange (23 B–R6 ch followed by 24 BxR). It is true that one might think this would lead to positions similar to those mentioned as possibilities for White's 19th move. But the great difference is that in this variation White can win the Black QP (which is the dangerous passed Pawn in the former variation) in the bargain, as will become clear from 22 ... N–B3; 23 B–R6 ch, K–N1; 24 BxR, KxB; 25 QR–Q1, followed by 26 BxN and 27 QxP.

22 B–B4

Note how after the disappearance of Black's fianchettoed Bishop the Black squares in his territory become weak.

The alternate 22 Q–Q2 leads to nothing. Black answers 22 ... R–R1.

22 ...   Q–N3

Forced. If 22 ... Q–K2; 23 QxP ch, followed by 24 B–Q6! If 22 ... Q–B4; 23 R–QB1. The text move protects the QP for a while.

23 B–K5 ch   P–B3
24 BxQP

What is the result of all these complicated maneuvers? Material is even, but White has two positional advantages: (a) the Two

Bishops; (b) Black's weakened K side.

24 ...   Q–B2

Black cannot move his Queen indifferently. If 24 ... Q–Q1; 25 B–B5, winning the exchange; and if 24 ... Q–Q3; 25 BxP ch, winning the Queen.

25 R–QB1   N–B3
26 P–R5!

Without any loss of time, White has recovered his sacrificed Pawn and now continues his attack. He will systematically demolish the new line of protection of the Black King.

26 ...   P–K4

If 26 ... P–KN4; 27 Q–Q3 wins at least a Pawn after 27 ... B–K1; 28 RxP.

27 B–B5   R–R1
28 B–Q6

Notice how all White's moves are made with tempo.

28 ...   Q–B1

Black maintains the protection of his Bishop.

29 PxP

White has now attained his goal
of the further weakening of the
K-side position to the point that
he is ready for the decisive blow.

29   B B4

The move 29 ... R-R6 entails
the same consequences as those in
the game, namely 30 BxN and 31
RxP.

Why doesn't Black capture the
White Pawn immediately? The
point is that Black's King position
is ripe for an all-out attack. After
29 ... KxP, we get, as in the game
itself, the sweeping away of the
rest of Black's Pawn bulwark by
White: 30 BxP, PxB; 31 Q-Q6 ch,
K-N2; 32 RxP, and White's attack is irresistible.

With the text, Black tries to
build up a new defensive front
with the help of his Bishop, but
to no avail.

30 BxN   PxB
31 KRxP!

With the Black pieces separated
from their King, White can afford
considerable sacrifice to bring his
own pieces into the immediate
attack.

The consequences of the accept-

ance of the sacrifice should be
studied carefully. It shows the
helplessness of a King without
Pawn protection and assaulted by
hostile pieces. 31 ... PxB; 32
BxP ch,

(a) 32 ... K-B1?; 33 P-N7 ch,
etc.

(b) 32 .., K-N1; 33 BxR,
(1) 33 ... KxB; 34 Q-R5 ch,
K-N2; 35 Q-R7 ch, K-B3; 36
Q-B7 ch, K-N4; 37 R-B5!
(binds almost all the Black
pieces), R-N1; 38 P-N7, and
there is no defense against 39
P-N8[Q] ch and 40 QxB ch or
40 RxB ch.
(2) 33 ... BxP, and White has
two plus Pawns, not to speak
of his attacking chances; e.g.,
34 Q-Q4, Q-B2; 35 RxP!, Q-
B2; 36 Q-KN4.

(c) 32 ... KxP; 33 BxR, QxB;
34 RxP ch,
(1) 34 ... K-N4; 35 P-B4 mate.
(2) 34 ... K-B2; 35 Q-Q5 ch,
winning the Bishop and more.
(3) 34 ... K-N2; 35 Q-Q4 ch,
K-R2; 36 Q-R4 ch, K-N1; 37
Q-N5 ch, winning back the
Bishop.

(d) 32 ... K-R3; 33 Q-Q2 ch,
K-R4 (33 ... KxP; 34 BxR
leads to (c) above); 34 B-B6,
threatening mate on N5.

Faced with this analysis, Black
decides not to accept the sacrifice
and plays

31 ...   KxP

The resistance would have been
lengthened by 31 ... BxP; 32 R-
K7 ch, B-B2.

32 R–K7   R–KR6

Black played this move hoping to be able to continue by 33 ... Q–R1. But nothing helps. If, for instance, 32 ... R–R2; 33 RxR, KxR; 34 Q–R5 ch, K–N2; 35 R–K1, B–K3; 36 B–B4! wins, for the White Queen penetrates. If 33 ... R–K1; 34 R–QB7 wins a second Pawn.

33 R–B4   Resigns

White threatens 34 P–KN4, B–K3; 35 Q–B2 ch. If Black plays 33 ... Q–R1, the game is decided by 34 R–N4 ch, BxR; 35 QxB ch, K–R3; 36 B–B4 mate.

A game very well played on the part of the master, equally well on the part of the expert. The cause of the loss of the game by the expert must be looked for as the consequence of the line he followed in the opening. At the time the game was played, theory had not yet stated: "8 ... P–K3 is not recommendable because the hole on Black's KB3 can become awkward, as shown in games such as Euwe-Lupi (London 1946)." So the expert could not know this, and it is too much to ask that he should foresee (even a master could not) the possible ensuing complications and be able to weigh the pros and cons. The expert really does the impossible without attaining anything. At a proper moment he takes counteraction in the center, breaks through, and by indirect means prevents a debacle on his K side. He discovers the right defensive moves at various points, and he cannot help it that he eventually finds himself faced with unsolvable problems. Here, just as in Games 5 and 17, the loser, notwithstanding his defeat, can in no way be distinguished from a master player.

Game 22

The theory of the White P–KN3 in the King's Indian Defense

The theory of KN play by White in the King's Indian Defense

Pawn-chain technique

Tension

Restricting the mobility of the opponent

Failure to simplify at the critical moment

Danger of mechanical thematic moves

Building up pressure along an open file

The sham sacrifice

One of the merits of the master is that he knows what he is aiming for and that he always keeps an objective view of what is taking place on the board. The amateur lacks this overall picture and is often too optimistic, because he does not have a comprehensive insight into the whole situation, and because the fact that things are developing favorably on one part of the board makes him look with too much confidence to the future.

The amateur can drift into a dangerous situation at the time when his initiative is in the process of slowing down. Despite a change in tempo, he is apt to continue dreaming of success. True, success is not in sight at this point, but the amateur tends to consider this as quite accidental and confidently expects his stock to go up again soon. He does not even take a new look at the shifting position, first of all because he might not be able to make a correct and detailed analysis of it, and secondly because he suspects that he might discover that things are not as promising as he had hoped they would be; his attitude exemplifies a typical human weakness—the desire to keep away from bad news.

When the initiative has tapered off in critical cases and the master realizes that by playing for a draw immediately he can save a game that would otherwise be lost, he generally chooses the appropriate continuation and is satisfied with a draw. But the amateur often hopes for the impossible—that somehow the initiative will reappear out of nowhere and lead him to a win.

This psychological chess motif is found in the game at hand. The amateur has played rather strong chess during the early part of the game, has seized the initiative and tried to break through his opponent's front line. That line, however, was too strong, and the master was able to maintain equality. When the amateur, not realizing that a draw is the most he could hope for, persists in making enterprising moves, the master takes advantage of his opponent's unmotivated plays and seizes the initiative himself. The final phase of the game is characterized by attractive tactical turns, but despite the stubborn defense of the amateur, the latter cannot, in the long run, withstand the powerful blows of the master.

Remarkable are the various sham sacrifices that appear both in the game itself and in variations growing out of the play in the game.

King's Indian Defense:
Main Variation with Fianchetto of White's KB

Expert	Master
White	*Black*
1 P–Q4	N–KB3
2 P–QB4	P–KN3
3 N–QB3	B–N2
4 P–K4	P–Q3

We have already seen this opening and discussed the theory of these moves in Game 19.

5 P–KN3

We have seen this White K-side fianchetto in connection with QP openings in Games 20 and 21.

White could equally well have played first 4 P–KN3 and then 5 P–K4. He could also have played only P–K4, as in Game 19, or only P–KN3, as in Game 20, and much later or never, P–K4.

The purpose of playing both P–K4 and P–KN3 at an early stage of the game is to reserve the possibility of playing KN–K2, a move that certainly deserves consideration, for at its K2 the Knight does not hamper the KB and, what is more important, allows P–KB4.

Black has trumps against this type of development—an early . . . P–K4 (since White's KN is not developed to its KB3) and a strengthening of the pressure by . . . N–QB3 (after . . . P–K4). The QN can then withdraw to its K2 after White has played P–Q5. All this happens in this game.

5 . . .	O–O
6 B–N2	P–K4

Black's basic idea in the K-side fianchetto is to exploit the activity of the KB. One of the means of doing so consists of playing . . . P–QB4, another . . . P–K4, thus

strengthening the pressure of Black's KB against the center. Black could precede ... P–K4 by
- (a) 6 ... QN–Q?, but this does not give him the opportunity to get his QN to his K2, as in the game, and why ... QN–K2 is so strong will become clear later; or by
- (b) 6 ... N–B3, which might induce White to play P–Q5 immediately; e.g., 7 P–Q5, N–K4; 8 Q–K2, and after 9 P–KR3 (to prevent ... B–N5) the Black Knight will be driven back by 10 P–KB4.

7 N–B3

White plays his Knight to B3 in order to exercise pressure on his K5 and Q4 squares.

Possible and also quite good was 7 KN–K2, with the advantages indicated under White's 5th move. Other than 7 KN–K2, White had to consider the following alternatives:
- (a) 7 PxP, PxP; 8 QxQ, RxQ, and Black has command of the Q file, whereas White's KB is behind a closed diagonal. Also, Black's Q5 square could be-

come strong for him, since no White Pawn is situated where it could drive back a Black Knight posted there.
- (b) 7 P–Q5, which is rather good, but then Black could immediately play 7 ... N–K1, followed by 8 ... P–KB4, which is the proper strategy to use against the Pawn chain (compare Game 19). With this variation, Black's pressure on White's QP has forced White to close the game and has allowed Black to start the struggle around the Pawn chain, which is not bad for Black at any time and certainly not under the present circumstances, where Black is ahead in development.
- (c) 7 B–K3, which is not very good because of 7 ... N–N5. Here 7 B–N5 would doubtless be bad, for after 7 ... P–KR3, White must either exchange his Bishop for Black's Knight, which in general does not occur in the opening, or retreat with a loss of tempo.

7 ...   N–B3

A move that develops a piece and exerts pressure on White's QP. Black might also have played 7 ... QN–Q2. This type of move has already been commented on under Black's 6th move.

He might have played 7 ... PxP, which leads to quite another type of game, which is not bad even though Black has surrendered the center, since Black obtains possibilities along his KN2–QN7 long diagonal. One example: 8 NxP, R–K1; 9 O–O, QN–Q2; 10 P–N3? (White's chain of Pawns now becomes vulnerable to the Black attack beginning ... P–QR5; preferable is 10 P–KR3 followed by 11 B–K3), P–B3; 11 B–N2, Q–N3; 12 Q–Q2, N–B4; 13 KR–K1, P–QR4; 14 QR–N1, P–R5; 15 B–QR1, PxP; 16 PxP, N–N5!; 17 P–R3, RxB!; 18 RxR, NxBP, and Black wins, for in both cases he regains all the material sacrificed, plus extra Pawns: 19 QxN, N–Q6 or 19 KxN, NxNP (Zita-Bronstein, Budapest 1946).

8 P–Q5

Since tension should be maintained in the center as long as possible, White deferred this thematic move until now. Other possibilities:

(a) 8 O–O, PxP; 9 NxP, and Black can make the sham sacrifice 9 ... NxP!; 10 NxQN, NxN; 11 NxQ, NxQ; 12 NxNP, followed by (1) 12 ... BxN; 13 BxB, QR–N1; 14 RxN, RxB, and Black is certainly not badly off; or (2) Black can even win a Pawn with 12 ... NxNP (instead of 12 ... BxN), but things are a bit complicated. One example: 13 NxQP, PxN; 14 BxR, NxP; 15 R–N1, B–B4; 16 R–N4, RxB; 17 RxN, B–Q6. This shows how far ahead a player sometimes has to think, and it also shows the force of an indirect attack (9 ... NxP!) when one's own

piece interrupts the line of attack.

(b) 8 PxP, PxP, and the same situation exists as after 7 PxP—no advantage to White, and his Q4 square weak.

(c) 8 B–K3 could be played at this point (even though 7 B–K3 is practically refuted by 7 ... N–N5), for after 8 ... N–KN5; 9 B–N5; P–B3; 10 B–B1. It is true that White's Bishop has lost a few moves, but on the other hand: (1) ... P–B3 hampers Black's KB; (2) a later ... P–B4 is much more effective as a reaction against White's P–Q5 (Pawn-chain struggle), for under the altered circumstances White may prefer not to play P–Q5, so that Black's ... P–B4 would not be an effective move; (3) Black's KN will be driven back with tempo by P–KR3.

8 ...   N–K2

The Knight goes to K2 in order to exercise pressure on Black's KB4 and to participate in the chain struggle that will soon begin.

9 O–O

At this point, both sides have the same number of pieces developed, and both sides still have the QB undeveloped. This is the point at which each side must begin his Pawn-chain strategy. This Pawn-chain strategy is explained in detail in Game 19 under Black's 8th move.

9 ...   N–K1

In general, it is not desirable to move a piece backward and thus "undevelop" it, so to speak, but Black is justified in doing so here in order to be able to attack White's KP, the base of White's Pawn chain.

Also to be considered here is 9 ... N–Q2, which has the advantage of permitting the Knight to go to its QB4, but the disadvantage of blocking Black's QB. At K1 the Knight also protects the Black QP, which could be important if this Pawn should be attacked by P–QB5.

The move 9 ... N–R4 to prepare the same strategy has the disadvantage of not threatening ... P–KB4 or anything else, since 10 ... P–KB4; 11 PxP, PxP? (11 ... BxP is not in accordance with Pawn-chain strategy, since White's K4 square could become a strong square for White); 12 NxP would lose a Pawn for Black on account of the now unprotected state of the Black Knight on its KR4.

White is now faced with the problem of whether to do something about Black's Pawn-chain strategy or not.

If White were to follow the primary goal by playing 10 P–QN1, preparing 11 P–B5, he would get into trouble. After 10 P–QN1 Black answers 10 ... P–QR4, and because White's QR is unprotected, White cannot answer 11 P–QR3. This means that 10 P–N5 or P–QN3 is forced, and in both cases his chances to realize the attack on the Black base by playing P–B5 are considerably reduced.

Why then does White not play 10 B–K3, protecting the White Rook so that now the advance of White's QNP comes into the picture? Let us analyze a little further: 10 B–K3, P–KB4; 11 P–QN4, followed by

(a) 11 ... P–B5; 12 PxP, PxP; 13 B–Q4, and White is all right—he can continue as planned with P–B5. We note in this position that Black's KN would have been considerably better on Q2 than on K1 (see Black's 9th move where he had the choice between ... N–K1 and ... N–Q2), since from Q2 the Knight could immediately jump to K4, occupying a strong center square and preparing a complete catastrophe for the White King position by advancing his K-side Pawns.

(b) 11 ... P–KR3 (more prudent and therefore stronger—Black prepares the advance of his KNP); 12 P–B5, P–B5 (better here than in (a) above); 13 PxBP, KPxP; 14 B–Q4, P–KN4, and Black is threatening both 14 ... P–KN5 followed by 15 ... P–B6 (driving the fianchettoed Bishop into the corner) and 14 ... N–N3 followed by 15 ... N–K4, occupying the strong center square.

He therefore plays

10 N–KR4

White, instead of working toward the primary goal of Pawn-chain strategy, that is, attacking the base of the chain, works toward the secondary goal of attacking the head of the Pawn chain. By the text move he is preparing P–B4, which is also possible.

The danger of the attack against the head of a Pawn chain is that the opponent may get a strong square after the exchange of Pawns. For instance, in this position: 11 P–KB4 followed by some arbitrary Black move 12 PxP?, BxP would be strong for Black. Or 11 P–KB4, PxP, 12 RxP? is also strong for Black, in both cases because Black then has full power over White's K5 square. The conclusions as to attacking the head of the Pawn chain are, therefore: (a) White will play P–KB4 in general only if he is able to answer ... PxP by PxP, thus controlling his K5 square; (b) in general, the idea behind P–KB4 is to advance further—P–KB5—rather than PxP. Some of these points will be illustrated in the continuation of this game.

10 ...   P–KB4

The strategical move for the Pawn-chain technique. In general, this move should be played only if Black can answer White's PxP with ... PxP. If Black should re-

take with a piece, White might become strong on his K4 square.

11 B–N5!

A good move by the expert, showing that he understands the possibilities of the situation.

This move *restricts* Black's possibilities; e.g., (a) 11 ... P–KR3 is now impossible, for 12 BxN would be followed by 13 NxNP; (b) Black wants to play ... PxP and ... N–B4 (see later when the importance of this move becomes clear), but his Knight is pinned. The ... N–B4 move would seem contrary to the earlier idea of Black retaking with the Pawn on his KB4, but with ... N–B4 there are two possibilities for the White Knight, neither of them too good: (a) NxN, PxN, which is good for Black; (b) N–B3 (loss of tempo) and then later, the Black Knight goes to its Q5 square.

11 ...   N–KB3

In order to unpin the other Knight. Instead,

(a) 11 ... P–B5 would be a fine move after 12 PxP, PxP; 13 Q–Q2, B–K4 (with Black's Bishop on a strong square), but White plays 12 Q–Q2 at once, and after 12 ... PxP; 13 BPxP, White's position is superior because he has more space and more development. The opening of the KB file is advantageous only for the better developed side, in this case White.

(b) 11 ... PxP does not attain anything. There is no hurry to play such a move. White will never voluntarily strengthen the Black position by PxBP, PxP. The situation of White's KP vs. Black's KBP poses a difficult problem. For Black, KPxBP is in general favorable, and for White ... BPxKP, unless Black can follow up with ... N–B4. So there is a kind of balance, of mutual tension.

12 Q–Q2

In order to prevent ... P–KR3 and also an eventual ... P–B5. White can now also play B–R6 whenever he wishes.

12 ...   NxKP

This is the beginning of a plan. Black deliberately gives White the White K4 square in exchange for advantages that will soon become clear. It is difficult for Black to wait longer, since White is in a better position to improve his situation than is Black—he has moves like KR–K1, P–B4, or even P–QN4 and P–QB5. Black has less space to move in.

13 NxN   PxN
14 KR–K1!

Here White shows his progress toward mastership by making things more difficult for Black.

White could have (and the ordinary amateur would have) played 14 BxP here, but then it would have been easier for Black to free his game and to exploit the absence of White's KB for its KN2, since Black could then play ... B–R6 with tempo; e.g., 14 BxP, B–R6; 15 KR–K1, Q–Q2, and now ... N–B4 with all kinds of chances.

After 14 QR–K1, White's KR would be shut in, which could be troublesome.

14 ...   B–B4

In order to continue the development by playing ... Q–Q2, once more unpinning the Knight, followed by ... QR–K1. Black need not fear NxB, since 15 ... PxN would give him a solid protection of his PK5, and White had planned to allow Black this extra Pawn only temporarily.

15 BxP

Bad would be 15 NxB?, for after 15 ... PxN, Black would have a solid center and a plus Pawn.

15 ...   Q–Q2

To unpin the Knight after all. The exchange 15 ... BxB would give White more freedom to maneuver, since White himself will *never* play NxB or BxB.

In general, it is wise to maintain the tension that exists between pieces as long as possible, if it is certain that the opponent will not break the tension because it would be to his disadvantage.

16 P–B4(?)

White attacks the head of the Pawn chain. Enterprising, and perhaps hoping for 16 ... PxP??; 17 BxN, QxB; 18 BxB, winning a piece and trying to open the K file. This move also eliminates the White KBP as a possible object of attack. But it actually opens the KB file where Black is master, and it also opens the White QN2–KN7 diagonal for Black's KB.

This move is the beginning of a wrong attitude on the part of the White player, who persists in maintaining the initiative when he should have been satisfied with a more quiet or even simplifying line such as alternates (a) and (b), which follow. There are several alternates:

(a) The less enterprising move 16 P–B3 must be considered.
(b) Satisfactory and preferable is 16 BxN, QxB; 17 P–B4, B–R3; 18 Q–N2. Sometimes the less energetic move is better.
(c) 16 BxB?, PxB gives Black a very strong Pawn center, as has already been noted.

16 ...   BxB

It was Black's intention all along to play ... BxB in order to follow up with ... N–B4, thus bringing his Knight into the battle. He could not do this earlier, since his Knight was pinned.

17 RxB   N–B4

The plan is finally realized with the following implications: (a) 18 NxN, PxN need not be feared; (b) from its KB4, the Black Knight can jump to its Q5, where it will be strongly posted; (c) Black is threatening 18 ... P–KR3, gaining material.

18 PxP

Best, for it opens an avenue for White's Bishop in case of ... P–KR3. Not recommendable would be 18 NxN, PxN; 19 R–K1 (or R–K2 or R–K3), P–K5.

18 ...   BxP

Poor would be 18 ... PxP, for it would leave Black with an isolated Pawn.

19 NxN

When White plays NxN in this position, there is no advantage for Black to retake with his NP, for there would be no resultant duo. The expert understands the difference between NxN at this point and at earlier points, when retaking with the NP would have given his opponent the duo.

(a) 19 N–N2 would also have been good, but 19 N–B3, bringing the Knight into the direct line of the Black Rook would have been bad because of 19 ... NxP (the sham sacrifice); 20 NxB, NxR; 21 NxQ, NxQ; 22 NxR, N-B6 ch followed by ... NxN, and Black has won a Pawn. In case of an indirect threat, one must always investigate the possibility of sham sacrifices. See the comments under White's 8th move, variation (a).

(b) After 19 QR-K1, NxN and (1) 20 RxN, Q-B4 or (b) 20 BxN, Q-B4, Black comes out a bit better, because as in the game he dominates the KB file, whereas the K file, where White should dominate, is closed.

19 ...   RxN

Here, as has already been pointed out, 19 ... PxN would leave Black with an isolated Pawn, instead of with the desirable duo that Black sometimes gets in similar situations when his KP is still on K4.

20 QR-K1?

The expert's one serious mistake. This serious mistake, plus his questionable 16th move, is enough.

This move is too thematic—to double Rooks without definite aim and to overlook the importance of Black's doubling on the next move is bad chess thinking. There is a Latin proverb that says: "If two people do the same thing, it is not exactly the same." *

Bad would have been 20 QR-KB1, RxR ch; 21 KxR, Q-B4 ch, and if 22 R-B4, QxB, winning the Bishop, and if 23 R-B8 ch, RxR ch!!, and it is not Black but White who loses his Queen.

White should have played 20 B-B4, BxB; 21 RxB, QR-KB1; 22 RxR, QxR; and (a) 23 R-K1, or perhaps simpler (b) 23 Q-K2, followed by 24 R-KB1 and more simplification, both of which would lead to a draw, because too little material is left on the board, and both players have open files.

20 ...   QR-KB1

Black thus commands the open KB file and already threatens to penetrate by 21 ... R-B7; 22 QxR?, RxQ; 23 KxR, Q-B4 ch.

Bad would be 20 ... BxQNP; 21 QxB, RxB; 22 R-K7!

21 R(4)-K2

This parries the threat, but it should be noted that White is already on the defensive. Yet, the expert does find the right move here and later.

At this point 21 B-B4 would weaken the position: 21 ... BxB; (a) 22 RxB?, RxR; 23 PxR, Q-N5 ch, and Black wins a Pawn; or

---

* Duo cum faciunt idem, non est idem.—TERENCE

(b) 22 PxB, R(4)–B2, to prevent 23 R–K7 and to open the diagonal for the Black Queen to go to its KB4, KN5 or KR6, and White's Pawn will get lost in the long run.

21 ...   Q–B2

Now the master begins to build up pressure. He is threatening 22 ... R–B8 ch; 23 K–N2 (23 RxR?, QxR mate), Q–B6 ch; 24 K–R3, R–B4, and White's situation is precarious, for Black threatens both 25 ... P–KR3 and 25 ... Q–R4 ch, winning a piece in either case. The move 25 ... P–KR3 wins a piece, because the Bishop cannot withdraw on account of mate.

22 K–N2!

Good defense by the expert to prevent the above threat from being carried out.

If, for instance, to prevent ... Q–B6, White plays 22 Q–K3?, R–B6!; 23 Q–K4, R–B8 ch, and wins: 24 K–N2, RxR; 25 RxR, Q–B7 ch; 26 K–R3, followed by either 26 ... QxNP, winning a Pawn, or by 26 ... R–B4 with pressure.

22 ...   R–B8

He moves down anyway in order to renew the threat ... Q–B6.

23 Q–K3

White parries the threat and plans an eventual P–B5 in order to undermine the position of the Black Bishop, since under the circumstances Black would not answer ... PxP.

23 ...   Q–B4

If 23 ... R–B6 immediately, 24 Q–Q2 is good, and even 24 Q–K4 is possible: 24 ... R–B7 ch; 25 K–R3; but after 23 ... Q–B4, Black threatens 24 ... R–B6; 25 Q–K4, QxQ (or first 25 ... R–B7 ch); 26 RxQ, R–B7 ch, winning a Pawn under favorable circumstances.

24 B–R6!

Again, a very good defense that creates possibilities for the near future.

This move drives the Black Rook from the first rank so that from now on Black must take into account the check at his K1 after he has moved his Bishop.

24 ...   R–B2
25 P–QN4

The expert not only finds the best defense, but also looks for counterchances.

This move does not change the position too much, but it does bring the QNP out of the line of Black's Bishop and strengthens a later P–B5. It leaves the choice to Black.

However, 25 P–B5 would also have deserved consideration: 25 ... R–B6; 26 Q–N5, and now the apparently strong 26 ... R–B7 ch does not work at all (27 RxR, QxR ch; 28 K–R3!—one sees the importance of White's 24 B–R6, which makes a mating threat possible). Black must play 26 ... QxQ; 27 BxQ, R–Q6, and he will soon win a Pawn.

25 ...   R–B6
26 Q–Q2

The reply 26 Q–K4 loses at least a Pawn after 26 ... QxQ; 27 RxQ, R–B7 ch, but with 26 Q–N5 White could have reached an ending in which he could have put up great resistance: 26 ... QxQ (26 ... R–B7 ch?—see remarks on same move immediately above); 27 BxQ, K–N2 (or 27 ... R–B6). Sooner or later, White has to lose a Pawn. Black's position is more solid, and there cannot be any doubt as to the final result. With the text, White prefers to die in the open field.

26 ...　　　　　　　R–B3

Black prevents 27 P–B5 in a complicated way: 27 P–B5, R–Q6; 28 Q–N5 (look at the importance of the Rook on its B3—now there is no threat of Q–Q8 ch), Q–B6 ch; 29 K–R3!, RxP; 30 PxP, BxQP!; 31 R–K8 ch, B–B1, which leads to a loss for White. Without this strong move, White could perhaps have held the game.

(a) Not 26 ... B–B6?? because of 27 R–K8 ch, etc. (see White's 24th move);

(b) Nor 26 ... R–Q6; 27 Q–N5, and Black has nothing: 27 ... Q–B6 ch; 28 K–R3, and White is again threatening Q–Q8 ch;

(c) Nor 26 ... R–B6; 27 QxR!, BxQ; 28 R–K8 ch, R–B1; 29 BxR (much better than 29 RxR ch), BxR; 30 R–B6 dis ch, K–B2; 31 R–R8 ch, K–K1 31 RxQ, PxR, and White is a little better off because Black has two isolated Pawns.

27 B–K3

Relatively best. Black has no special threats, but every White move weakens the position. Keep in mind that 27 B–N5 loses after 27 ... R–Q6; 28 Q–B2, Q–B6 ch; 29 K–R3, R–B4, and (a) if White moves his Bishop on the QB1–KR6 diagonal, 30 ... R–R4 mates; (b) if White plays 30 B–K7, Black mates in three, beginning 30 ... R–R4 ch; 31 B–R4, RxB ch, etc.; (c) after 30 B–R4, 30 ... P–KN4 either wins a piece or mates; (d) 30 Q–B1 releases the pressure against Black's R(Q6) so that the Queen can move freely: 30 ... Q–R4 ch; 31 B–R4, P–KN4. It is noteworthy in this variation that 29 ... BxP, which looks good, leads to complications after 30 R–K8 ch.

27 ...　　　　　　　Q–K5

Black threatens mate on the move by the double discovered check 28 ... RxP dbl ch!

28 K–N1

If now 28 ... RxB?; 29 RxR, B–Q5; 30 Q–KB2!!, a most remarkable unpinning, giving up the Queen, and Black gets only a draw. This is a fine resource for the expert. But Black does not fall into the trap. He plays the simple

28 ...   QxBP
29 R–QB1

If 29 B–B2, RxB; 30 RxR, B–Q5. Notice this sham sacrifice that always exists on B2 or K3. However, it would not work in the variation under White's 28th move, as has already been shown.

29 ...   Q–N5

(a) Protecting his QB1 square, which is important in the variation that follows. If now 30 RxP, R–B8 ch; 31 K–N2, BxP; 32 PxB, Q–B6 ch; 33 K–R3, R–R8 ch; 34 R–R2, Q–R4 ch, etc.

(b) Threatening the sham sacrifice ... RxB and ... B–Q5.

(c) Threatening a possible ... BxP.

30 R–KB2   RxB!

The sham sacrifice again.

31 Resigns

For if 31 RxR, BxR; 32 QxR, B–Q5; or 31 QxR, RxR; 32 KxR (or 32 QxR), B–Q5.

The sham-sacrifice theme has dominated the entire last phase of the game.

Game 23

The theory of the 4 ... Q–K2 variation of the Giuoco Piano

Holding the center

Avoiding exchange:
  (a) when the opponent is in a cramped position
  (b) to conserve the Two Bishops
  (c) to keep a piece for attack

Exchanging to prevent an opponent's piece from becoming too powerful

Giving up the center

Finding the right plan

Accumulation of force along file and diagonal

It sometimes happens that an amateur wins from a master, and even from a grandmaster. When this occurs, it may be assumed first of all that the amateur plays excellent chess and is well on his way to becoming a master himself, second that the defeated master has made some sort of misjudgment that has cost him the game.

But a master's error is usually different from an amateur's error, so that a game lost by a master to an amateur is instructive in a different way than is a game lost by an amateur to a master.

In the game that follows, it is a question of maintaining the center. Maintaining the center is one of the big problems in chess. Possession of the center generally constitutes a considerable advantage, and this is especially true for the group of classical KP openings, because in these openings possession of the center usually involves the possibility of initiating a K-side attack. Therefore, one finds in Ruy Lopez, Giuoco Piano, and other KP openings certain lines that are primarily directed toward maintaining the center on the part of the Black player. This does not mean that there are no alternatives. A player should be on the constant lookout for possibilities of giving up the center in a favorable way. However, if one is playing a line in which the chief objective is to maintain the center, one must be perfectly sure of adequate compensation in some other direction before giving up the center. Whether to maintain or to surrender the center is a question of evaluation. On surrendering the center, the tension will be broken, and from it will result a new situation in which the opponent's superiority in the center must be compensated for by some positional counteradvantage. One must be quite sure of the correctness of one's evaluation before making such a decision.

In the game that follows, the master gives up the center without sufficient compensation. His evaluation is faulty, and he pays the penalty. However, he cannot be criticized too severely, since he has been caught in a situation that poses both technical and psychological problems.

As soon as the moves in a tense position begin to give out, the defender may become afraid that he has maintained the tension too long. He may then try to find a somewhat acceptable variation by giving up the center. But being emotionally concerned with his evaluation, he is less likely to be able to make an objective judgment, which explains why even a master can go wrong under such difficult circumstances.

There is still another psychological factor in a master-vs.-amateur game, namely, the obligation for the master to win from the amateur. This may induce the master not to be satisfied with a passive attitude, but rather to take risks in order to win. Under such circumstances, it is a wise policy for the amateur to play simple and solid moves, allowing his opponent to hang himself in his eagerness to seize the initiative.

Giuoco Piano: Closed Variation (4 ... Q–K2)

Expert	Master
White	*Black*
1 P–K4	P–K4
2 N–KB3	N–QB3
3 B–B4	B–B4
4 P–B3	

The classical line of the Giuoco Piano. White plans to attack Black's center and to emerge with a superior Pawn formation.

4 ...   Q–K2

Instead of the more usual 4 ... N–B3, Black defends his center with his Queen, planning to main-

tain his Pawn on K4 instead of exchanging it.

Together with 4 ... N–KB3, 4 ... Q–K2 is the best defense in the Giuoco Piano. The text is less enterprising than 4 ... N–KB3, inasmuch as Black fails to attack and therefore has a more passive game. Still, with 4 ... Q–K2—and only with this move—Black succeeds in maintaining the center; that is, after White has played P–Q4, he cannot force Black to play ... PxP.

5 P–Q4

White plans to force the exchange of center Pawns, as in the 4 ... N–KB3 variation, with the difference that in the 4 ... Q–K2 variation, Black is not forced to play 5 ... PxP.

If instead 5 O–O, Black continues his development by 5 ... P–Q3, and the position will eventually be the same as in the game.

5 ...   B–N3

Black withdraws his Bishop in accordance with the general strategy of this variation—the maintenance of the Black Pawn at its K4.

Against the principle of this variation of the opening would be the surrender of the center by 5 ... PxP. White would answer 6 O–O! (after 6 PxP, White loses a Pawn under less favorable circumstances; e.g., 6 ... QxP ch; 7 B–K3, B–N5 ch; 8 N–B3, P–Q4!; and Black does not have much to fear), and then Black would have the choice between:

(a) 6 ... P–Q3 or 6 ... N–B3, both followed by 7 PxP, and Black would have given up the center for nothing; his Queen on K2 stands bad in this case because it is exposed to a possible attack (N–Q5).

(b) accepting the gambit by 6 ... PxP; 7 NxP, and White has a considerable advance in development. One example: 7 ... P–Q3; 8 N–Q5, Q–Q1; 9 P–QN4!, BxP; 10 NxB, NxN; 11 Q–N3, N–QB3; 12 BxP ch, with a strong attack for only one Pawn.

(c) 6 ... N–K4; 7 NxN, QxN; 8 P–B4!, PxP dis ch; 9 K–R1, PxP (better 9 ... Q–Q5, but after 10 Q–N3, N–R3; 11 NxP, White again has sufficient compensation); 10 PxQ, PxR[Q]; 11 Q–Q5, and wins: 11 ... P–QB3 (to avoid mate after following moves); 12 QxKBP ch, K–Q1; 13 B–N5 ch, K–B2; 14 QxNP, etc.

(d) 6 ... P–Q6—a solid but not quite sufficient continuation—solid because by returning the Pawn in this way, Black forces White to take in such a manner that he both loses some time and has a Pawn position that is not conducive to swift development: 7 P–K5!, P–Q3; 8 B–KN5, P–B3; 9 PxBP, NxP; 10 QN–Q2 (10 R–K1, N–K4), B–KN5; 11 P–N4, B–N3; 12 P–QR4, P–QR4; 13 P–KR3, and White is a little better off because he has castled, because he can regain the sacrificed Pawn at any time (whereas Black's King is exposed, and for the moment he cannot castle K-side), and because his Queen is situated on the K file along with his King.

6 O–O

An important alternative is 6 P–Q5, N–N1 (or 6 ... N–Q1); 7 P–

Q6, QxP; 8 QxQ, PxQ, and Black has a cramped game. However, if 6 ... N–Q1, it appears that Black can hold his own with a later ... N–K3 and he has a sound plus Pawn.

If 6 PxP, NxP; 7 NxN, QxN (compare the second comment under White's 7th move).

6 ...   N–B3
7 R–K1

It would be useless to pin Black's KN by 7 B–KN5, for White has castled, and Black has not. In such a case, Black could unpin by ... P–KR3 and ... P–KN4 and at the same time build up an attacking position.

One might ask, however, whether 7 PxP would not in effect force Black to give up the center. When White exchanges, the position is less advantageous for him than if Black exchanges. After 7 ... NxP, White would have only *one* center Pawn, whereas if Black had played ... PxP and White had replied PxP, White would have *two* center Pawns, the ideal center. But after 7 PxP, NxP; 8 NxN, QxN; 9 K–R1 (to prepare for P–B4), P–Q3; 10 P–B4, Q–K2, Black is better off, for his BN3 is very powerful. White has only a little superiority in the center, whereas Black's pieces are very active. Black threatens both 11 ... NxP and 11 ... N–N5, and it will be impossible for White to avoid a decisive disadvantage; e.g., 11 B–Q3, N–N5; 12 Q–B3, NxP!; 13 KxN, Q–R5 ch. After 11 P–K5, either 11 ... N–N5 or 11

... N–K5 is good and even 11 ... PxP; 12 PxP, QxP; 13 R–K1, N–K5, for if 14 Q–K2, B–KB4; 15 N–Q2, O–O–O, etc.

7 ...   P–Q3

Equally good was 7 ... O–O.

8 P–KR3

To prevent Black from pinning White's KN. It is important to prevent such a pin, for the pin would strengthen Black's pressure against White's QP and might induce White to play P–Q5, which relieves the center pressure and is satisfactory for Black in view of a later ... P–KB4.

To a certain extent, 8 P–KR3 is weakening. The Rellstab-Sämisch game (Kiel 1949) continued: 8 ... P–KR3 (to take advantage of White's weakening); 9 N–R3, P–N4; 10 N–B2, P–N5; 11 N–R4, PxP; 12 P–KN3, R–KN1, and Black has the better of it. Preferable, however, was 11 PxP, BxNP; 12 N–K3, and White is not badly off.

Bad is 8 B–KN5 for the same reason as was 7 B–KN5 (see comment under White's 7th move).

If 8 B–K3, B–N5 with pressure against White's QP, as has already been mentioned. Less good after 8 B–K3 is 8 ... N–N5; 9 B–KN5, P–B3; 10 B–QB1, followed by 11 P–KR3, and Black's Knight is not so well off.

8 ...   O–O
9 N–R3!

Although the Knight is developed to the side of the board against the rule, there is a reason. Up to now, we have seen mainly masters break rules for some reason. Here the expert shows progress in violating a rule because of a good reason.

This is a tricky move. The main plan is N–B2–KR–Q5, possibly in connection with B–KN5. A minor plan could be: B–Q3 (or B–B1) followed by N–B4. This sequence does not seem promising, but look at 9 ... N–Q1 (to prepare ... P–QB3, which protects Black's Q4 square and allows the Bishop to retreat); 10 B–B1, N–K1? (to strengthen PK4 by ... P–B3); 11 N–B4, P–KB3; 12 P–QR4, P–B3; 13 NxB, PxN; 14 Q–N3 ch, and White wins a Pawn. A most surprising tactical turn in a seemingly quiet position!

Either 9 B–KN5 or 9 B–K3 would not have been bad at this point, but the text is sharper.

9 ...   K–R1

Black must maintain his center—as soon as he gives up the center, his Queen is very poorly placed, and threats like P–K5 come into the picture. The text helps maintain the center, for after this move Black can play ... N–KN1 or ... N–K1, followed by ... P–B3.

A by-product of the text move is that from now on White has to take into account the variation ... PxP; PxP, NxKP, because after the Black King has been moved out of the field of White's KB, Black is able to support the Knight on K5 by ... P–KB4. In this variation,

Black gives up the center, but by giving it up, he wins a Pawn.

10 N–B2

At this point 10 B–B1, which was so successful in the variation cited under White's 9th move, would lose a Pawn: 10 ... PxP; 11 PxP, NxKP. The point is that Black need not fear the self-pin of the Knight, as he has the move ... P–KB4. A self-pin is a situation where Black would put his Knight on its K5 when there was a White Rook on its K1 and a Black Queen on its K2.

After 10 B–Q3, White would lose his QP.

10 ...   N–Q1

In order to be able to play his QB to K3 and after BxB retake the White Bishop with the Knight, or to force White to play P–Q5. Also to make possible ... P–B3, preventing a later N–Q5 on the part of White. It should be noted that 10 ... PxP; 11 PxP, NxKP (as suggested in the previous comment) does not work, on account of 12 N–N5, P–B4; 13 NxP, KxN; 14 Q–R5 mate.

11 P–QN3

Opening the possibility of 12 B–R3, which might be disagreeable for Black.

11 ...   B–K3

In this position Black seeks to neutralize White's power by an exchange of Bishops or to force White to play P–Q5.

If 11 ... N–N1 (in order to protect PK4 by ... P–KB3, in accordance with the dominating strategy of the game); 12 N–K3!, P–QB3; 13 B–R3 or 12 N–K3!, P–KB3; 13 N–Q5, Q–Q2; 14 P–QR4, P–B3; 15 NxB, PxN; 16 B–R3, threatening 17 PxP, and White is better off, since he has the Two Bishops and pressure against his Q6 square, whereas Black's pieces are displaced.

12 B–B1

White wished to avoid the exchange of his Bishop, since every exchange favors the side that has a cramped game.

If 12 PxP, PxP; 13 NxP, BxRP; 14 NxP ch (a *desperado* move; that is, one in which a piece has to be lost anyway, so the player gets the most out of losing it—in this case, meaning that White must lose his Knight in order to gain the Black QB, therefore he makes the most advantageous move possible in losing his Knight), NxN; 15 PxB (wins a Pawn but loses the game), N–K4! (giving a terrific attack):

(a) 16 B–R3, BxP ch!
  (1) 17 KxB, NxP dis ch, and White is so restricted in squares

and in such an open position that mate is inevitable;
  (2) 17 K–R1, P–B4; 18 R–K2, KN–N5, all of which is terrible for White;
(b) 16 B–K3, NxP; 17 BxB, N–B6 ch; 18 K–N2 (18 K–R1, Q–K4; 19 K–N2, Q–R7 ch; 20 K–B1, N–N6 ch and mate on the next move), Q–N4 ch; 19 K–B1, N–R7 ch; 20 K–K2, NxP ch.
(c) 16 N–K3, NxP, with two powerful threats: 17 ... N–B6 ch and 17 ... NxKBP;
(d) 16 B–B1, BxP ch; 17 KxB, NxP dis ch
  (1) 18 K–N2, R–B7 ch
  (2) 18 K–N1, N–B6 ch
  (3) 18 K–K2, R–B7 ch; 19 K–K3, Q–N4 ch; 20 KxN, Q–B4 ch; 21 K–K3, N–B5 ch; 22 PxN, R–K1 ch, etc.
  (4) 18 K–K3, N–B7, followed by a killing discovered check.

All this shows how careful one should be in making a combination to win a Pawn without calculating the final position exactly, weighing the factors that have changed during the combination.

12 ...   N–N1

The key move of the whole system. As soon as Black has played the move ... P–KB3, his center is safe against PxP, which he can then answer by ... BPxP, opening the KB file, in which case he can strive for higher goals. In brief, the theme of the entire opening is: first consolidate, then look for initiative.

13 N–K3

In order to play the Knight to
Q5, followed perhaps by P–QR4,
and to threaten P–R5 as outlined
under White's 9th move.

The move 13 PxP would certainly not lead to more than equality after 13 ... PxP; 14 NxP,
BxRP; 15 PxB, QxN, and Black is
better off, for White's K wing is
mutilated.

13 ...   P–KB3

This is the end of a well-known
theoretical variation. Black has
consolidated his center and now
has a solid if undynamic position.
The variation is very logical in that
one can follow the struggle for the
center. Should White have succeeded in forcing ... PxP, then
White would be very well off. But
Black has prevented this and has
almost an equal game (White has
some preponderance in space).

The struggle here centers around
White's pressure against his K5
square and Black's defense of the
point. Let us now appraise the situation. White controls more territory, has more mobility, but he
cannot yet start an attack against
Black's K side, since he controls no
important squares. On the other
hand, as soon as White plays P Q5,
Black can use the Pawn-chain strategy and can attack by a Pawn
advance on the K side.

For the moment, White can
move more freely, but everywhere
Black's pieces and Pawns are bringing some pressure to bear on the
White camp. White must always
be on his guard.

The classical variation of the
Giuoco Piano (4 ... N–B3) leads
to an open game with good attacking lines for White, although it
may be at the price of one or two
Pawns. If Black does not like this
sort of game, he should choose the
4 ... Q–K2 variation.

14 N–Q5

White now brings a piece into
hostile territory. He need not fear
the exchange, which would leave
him with the Two Bishops. Of
course, White could now get the
Two Bishops anyway by NxB, but
then ... RPxN would give Black
compensation in the open file.

14 ...   Q–B2

Threatening to win a Pawn by
... BxN.

15 P–B4

White defends his Knight a second time, at the expense of slightly
weakening his QP.

To be considered here is 15 P–
QR4. Then (a) 15 ... BxN is not
satisfactory because of 16 PxB,
QxP?; 17 B–QB4, Q–B3; 18 P–R5!
The reason for 15 P–QR4 is to

force Black to play (b) 15 . . . P–B3, after which 16 NxB, PxN, which leaves Black with a somewhat weakened position. However, it does not necessarily work out that way, for after 15 P–QR4, P–B3; 16 NxB, Black need not retake at once, but could first play 16 . . . BxNP, thus winning a sound Pawn.

15 . . .   B–R4

To avoid the exchange of the Bishop for the Knight, and Black also hopes for 16 B–Q2, BxB, easing his position. Moreover, Black wishes to remobilize his QN to QB3, bringing pressure against White's QP, but this he cannot do as long as his Bishop is on QN3, for 15 . . . N–B3??; 16 NxB, followed by 17 P–Q5.

16 R–K2   N–B3

In order to bring additional pressure on White's QP. White has greater mobility, and Black tries to compensate by additional pressure. All Black can do in his type of position is to apply pressure and hope for some simplification in this tug-of-war.

An alternate line of play was 16 . . . P–B3; 17 N–K3, P–QB4, forcing White to a declaration of intentions. After the exchange of center Pawns, White could again establish a Knight on Black's Q5, but if this were done, then Black could do the same, N–B3–Q5. This would lead to a mutual passivity, since exchanging the Knight on Q5

for either side would give the other side a protected passed Pawn, and a new type of tug-of-war would have arisen, but in this case White would no longer have a preponderance of terrain. The game would probably result in a draw, and the master does not wish to draw.

17 B–N2

This move (a) protects the QP once more; (b) clears the first rank for the development of the QR; (c) prevents Black from playing . . . B–B6 after . . . BxN.

White now threatens 18 P–R3, in order to win a piece by 19 P–QN4 and 20 P–B5. This would force Black to exchange on his Q5 one move later, under about the same circumstances, which is neither particularly good nor bad.

Since White has a threat, Black cannot wait, cannot now make moves like . . . QR–Q1 and . . . KN–K2.

It looks as if Black, by playing 16 . . . N–B3, has missed the possibility of getting a drawish game with 16 . . . P–B3 and . . . P–B4, so that it might appear that 16 . . . N–B3 should be considered as a mistake. However, the position still contains one logical continuation: 17 ... QN–K2! This prepares for 18 ... P–B3 under better circumstances, e.g., 18 QR–D1, R–D0, 19 N–K3, N–N3 followed by 20 N–B5 and 21 ... P–KN4. Black thus gets the attack he is aiming for and which is often the result of the 4 ... Q–K2 variation of the Giuoco Piano. This variation justifies 16 ... N–B3.

It should be noted that in the above variation 18 P–QN4 would lose a Pawn after 18 ... BxN.

17 ...   PxP?

Up to this point, chances were about equal. Now Black, the master, in order to have more possibilities, gives up the center. After 17 ... PxP, White emerges with more terrain and more freedom, but Black exchanges in order to facilitate his game and to make it easier to maneuver.

This is one of the points of decision of the game. White's preponderance of space has increased. He now controls four ranks to Black's three. Black, however, hopes for counterplay. But his evaluation of the situation was wrong. He should have played either 17 ... QN–K2 or, one move earlier, 16 ... P–B3.

In general, the stronger player tries to maintain the tension, giving the opponent the opportunity to make mistakes. As we have seen at the 16th move, Black did not want the struggle of each Knight on its Q5, since the counterplay for White would have been too

easy, and therefore the drawing chances would have been too great.

18 NxQP   NxN
19 BxN   Q–Q?

To prepare ... N–K2 and to prevent White from playing P–N3. The position is very subtle. Black would like to play 19 ... N–K2 at once, but he fears 20 P–QN4, BxN; 21 BPxB, BxP; 22 R–N2, B–R4; 23 RxP, and now 23 ... B–N3 does not work because of 24 BxB.

Favorable for White is 19 ... BxN (or ... BxN at any time). It leaves him with the Two Bishops, and, after 20 BPxB, gives him a half-open QB file along which to play.

20 Q–B2

This permits White to develop his QR to his Q1 and also prepares for a later P–B5.

If 20 P–QN4, BxN; 21 BPxB, BxP; 22 R–N2 (better is 22 Q–N3) would not be good here (compare previous remark). 22 ... B–R4; 23 RxP, B–N3, and the Rook is indeed caught, because Black's QBP is protected.

20 ...   N–K2

To bring the Knight into the game via B3 or N3, followed by N–K4 or N–B5.

Not 20 ... P–B3, which would weaken Black's QP, since that Pawn is on an open file and cannot easily advance because Black's Q4 square is controlled by two White Pawns. As a matter of fact, after White moves such as N–K3, Q–Q3, R–Q1, B–N2, B–R3, the Black QP seems untenable.

21 NxN

White exchanges to prevent Black's Knight from becoming powerful. Otherwise, Black can continue ... N–B3–K4 or ... N–N3–K4 (or –B5).

If 21 N–B4, B–B2 with no special significance.

21 ...   QxN

White could now play 22 P–B5, after which 22 ... KR–Q1; 23 P–B6, PxP; 24 QxP, B–N3. But White, the weaker player, does not want to take the initiative. He wants to tire the stronger player out, to make him take chances, to give him the opportunity to make a mistake. So he plays

22 P–N3

Since the Black Queen has been forced off the diagonal, White's fianchetto has now become possible. At KN2, the White Bishop presses against Black's Q wing. White consolidates his position. The expert uses good psychology against the strong player.

The position is now somewhat favorable for White, but it will be difficult for him to force a win, since his superiority is so small. In such situations, a master, knowing that he is a superior player, sometimes deliberately takes a chance in order to start an attack, notwithstanding the fact that he is somewhat behind. If he succeeds, he wins; if he fails, he loses. If he had not taken this chance, he might have gotten a draw with a great deal of effort. But it is always discouraging to struggle hard, knowing that your maximum reward will be no more than a draw. That is what makes the master say at this point, "It's everything or nothing," and the expert was clever enough to provoke the atmosphere that led to this sort of decision by the master.

22 ...   B–N3

This prevents P–B5, and now the Bishop is not in danger of being exchanged for a Knight.

23 B–QN2

White wants to keep his Bishop
for the attack. In general, one does
not exchange if one controls more
space. On the other hand, Black
now controls one long diagonal with
his Bishop.

23 ...   Q–Q2?

In order to play ... P–KB4, but
this was the wrong plan. Correct
was 24 ... Q–B2, followed by
either ... P–QR4–5 or ... P–B3
and ... P–Q4. On the other hand,
White will never allow Black to
advance ... P–Q4 after ... P–B3.
This is one of the purposes of
White's 22 P–KN3, to be followed
by the fianchetto on KN2.

The text is a master error. Notice that a master error is based
on a wrong plan, or on the consequence of a wrong evaluation,
whereas an amateur error is often
based on an oversight or on nothing at all.

24 K–R2   P–KB4?

Loss of patience. Black asks too
much of the position. Now he comes
into difficulty, because his K file
is more important than his KB file.
Moreover, Black opens two diagonals for his opponent's Bishops.

Black had hoped for pressure
against White's KB2, but the simple move 28 P–B4 ends all hope,
and then Black remains only with
the bad consequences of his super-
ficial move.

He should have played 24 ...
P–QR4 followed by ... Q–B2.
The purpose of 24 ... P–QR4 is
to continue by ... P–QR5, thus

opening the QR file or (after P–
QN4) push ... P–QR6, with all
sorts of counterchances.

25 PxP   BxP
26 Q–B3

26 ...   R–B2?

The only chance of holding the
position was to exchange on the K
file, as, for instance, 26 ... QR–
K1; 27 RxR, RxR, followed by ...
P–B3, ... B–Q1, and ... B–B3.
True, the position would have remained difficult, but perhaps was
not yet lost.

But White now has a decisive
advantage.

From now on, the game becomes
a real master-expert game, but here
it is the expert who is the master.
He makes excellent use of the advantages acquired.

27 QR–K1

White now gets control of his
K file, and he is in complete possession of his QR1–KR8 diagonal.
Look at the combined possibilities
of these two open lines!

27 ...   QR–KB1
28 P–B4!

Making all counteraction impossible. Black now gets nothing further out of the KB file, whereas White has complete control of the K file.

Black cannot eliminate the pressure along White's QR1–KR8 diagonal. This pressure ties up Black on different fronts and promotes combinations by White. First of all, White threatens P–KN4, winning a piece by . . . B–N3, P–KB5; e.g., the threat is 29 P–KN4, B–N3; 30 P–KB5, P–KR3 (to make room for the Bishop in case White decides not to exchange Bishops); 31 PxB, RxB; 32 RxR, RxR; 33 QxP ch!, followed by mate. If Black makes room for his Bishop by playing 28 . . . P–KR3; 29 P–KN4, B–R2, White successfully continues his attack by 30 R–K6 (or 30 P–B5 —safety first!), K–N1; 31 P–KB5, and Black is not able to parry the threat 32 RxRP (32 . . . PxR; 33 Q–R8 mate)—it is always the pressure along the long diagonal that comes into play.

> 28 . . .   Q–Q1

To open a retreat for the QB.

> 29 B–N2

Now he develops his other Bishop and brings pressure along the other long diagonal.

> 29 . . .   P–B3

Black weakens his QP, but only under pressure (compare Black's 20th move).

> 30 B–B3!

Killing! White does not play to take advantage of this new weakness, but continues his attack! He threatens 31 B–R5. The Rook is attacked and cannot move (31 . . . R–B2; 32 R–K8). So Black is forced to allow the doubling of his Pawns after 31 . . . B–N3; 32 BxB, PxB. There are positions in which a double Pawn does not cause much damage, but here the defense is considerably weakened, and White has all sorts of trumps: an open K file, an open KR file, and the diagonal. We give a few variations to show how White could make use of this weakening: 33 R–K6, P–N4 (or 33 . . . R–B3; 34 Q–B3, attacking the Rook and forcing the exchange 34 . . . RxR; 35 RxR, P–N4; 36 Q–R5 ch, K–N1; 37 R–R6 —the old trick); 34 Q–B3, and now

(a) the threat (e.g., after 34 . . . P–Q4) 35 Q–R5 ch, K–N1; 36 R–R6—the old trick again.

(b) 34 . . . PxP; 35 Q–R5 ch, K–N1; 36 P–KN4 (now the old trick 36 R–R6 would fail against 36 . . . PxP ch, and the Black Rooks come to life, but after the text the trick threatens), Q–Q2 (parries the trick because of 37 R–R6, PxR; 38

Q–N6 ch, R–N2); 37 P–N5, and there is no defense against 38 P–N6.

We have seen how strong the threat 31 B–R5 is. But how can Black parry it? Suppose Black plays 30 ... K–N1; 31 B–R5, R–N6, 32 BxB, PxB, and Black plays the above variation with one more tempo. Apart from the question as to whether this would be sufficient to hold the game (and we do not think it would), White has the stronger 32 B–N4 (instead of 32 BxB), and White threatens both 33 B–K6 (winning the exchange) and 33 P–B5 (winning a piece).

30 ...   P–Q4

Despair. Yet, White cannot now carry out his threat. If 31 B–R5, P–Q5!, closing the diagonal.

31 P–B5   B–R4

Still hoping for counterplay.

31 ... B–B2 would be followed by 32 B–R5, B–N3 (forced); 33 BxB, PxB; 34 R–K6, P–KN4, and the position is similar to the one developed under White's 30th move, but not identical. White can win here, for example, as follows: 35 R–R6 ch, K–N1; 36 Q–Q3, R–B4 (the only move); 37 R–N6, and (a) 37 ... R(1)–B2; 38 RxP ch, RxR; 39 QxR, and the position is hopeless for Black; (b) 37 ... R(4)–B2; 38 RxP(5).

32 P–QN4   P–Q5
33 Q–B4!

Bad would be 33 QxP?, QxQ; 34 BxQ, BxNP.

33 ...   P–QN4

If 33 ... B–B2; 34 BxQP, and White's victory is certain, since he is a Pawn up and has all the trumps.

34 QxR!

A sham sacrifice of the Queen to free White's 8th rank, after which White immediately wins back the Queen under favorable circumstances. Without this surprising move, things could have been difficult: 34 PxP e.p., BxP, and Black's QP was in the way, for it closes the diagonal QR1–KR8, which is so important in most variations. But the expert plays like a master—exploits the opportunity to make a sham sacrifice, has his eye open for tactical possibilities.

A further merit of the combination is that if White should win only a Pawn, he would have given up his overwhelming position too cheaply. But the expert has evaluated the final position at the end of the combination not only materially (the plus Pawn), but also positionally (superior mobility of all his pieces, and further weaknesses on Black's Q side).

34 . . .	RxQ
35 R–K8 ch	R–B1
36 RxQ	BxR
37 BxQP	B–Q2

To protect his QBP. It seems as if Black has saved himself, not without scars, but nonetheless, the pressure is off. White's plus Pawn certainly must decide in the long run, but one would not expect a quick finish. Still, Black's position is riddled with weaknesses. His pieces cannot move freely, for they have to protect Pawns, or to prevent penetration. Moreover, they are in each other's way. Look at the Black Rook, which is at the mercy of White's Two Bishops. And Black's King needs constant care!

38 B–K5

Opens the Q file and prepares the way for R–Q1.

38 . . .   R–B2

Protects Black's B(Q2) in anticipation of White's attack, but does not improve the Black position. The difficulty is that Black is still fighting against restriction of movement!

If instead 38 . . . B–B3; 39 BxB, PxB; 40 R–K7, R–Q1; 41 P–KN4, and Black is in a hopeless position with a Pawn down and with White in control of his 7th rank, threatening B–K4; or 38 . . . B–B3; 39 BxB, RxB; 40 R–K7; or 38 . . . B–K2; 39 BxP ch; or if 38 . . . B–K1; 39 R–Q1, B–K2; 40 B–Q6, and wins at least a second Pawn.

39 R–Q1   K–N1

If 39 . . . B–B3, then 40 BxB, PxB; 40 R–Q6 wins "only" a second Pawn.

40 B–N4   Resigns

For White wins a piece. Black can no longer hold both Bishops.

In this game the expert has shown: (a) good positional judgment—his play is solid, making his position difficult to be approached —has no weaknesses; (b) good combinative power—the maneuver B(KN2)–B3–R5 is a killer after all; (c) good psychology (which his opponent certainly did not show)— no hurry—let my opponent come on first—my position will stand up to him. Black, the master, being impatient: (a) avoided the draw on the 16th move; (b) made a bad choice—an error of evaluation—between 17 . . . PxP? and 17 . . . QN–K2!; (c) tried to get more out of a position than the position warranted; (d) made bad judgments on his 24th and 26th moves.

Game 24

The theory of certain variations of the Queen's Indian Defense

Putting the question to the White QB early

Exerting pressure along the long diagonal

Material vs. position

Pawn-snatching

Incorrect judgment of a position due to psychological factors

Exploitation of weaknesses along the file

Attack against a weakened Q-side castling

Attacking force of connected passed Pawns in the endgame

It is important to look ahead in chess, but one should not look so far ahead that one neglects the immediate problems. Chess is so complicated, and there are so many variations, that in trying to visualize distant possibilities, one runs the risk of overlooking nearby dangers.

As soon as he has won a Pawn in this game, the master begins to consider how he can exploit this material advantage in a still-distant endgame. To advance his long-range plan, he makes several moves that would have been excellent, if there had been no opponent and no immediate problems. But there was an opponent who was quite ready to take advantage of weaknesses resulting from Black's one-sided strategy.

This type of play can be found in many master games, and especially in those where one of the players is stronger than the other and thereby feels obligated to demonstrate his superiority by winning the game. Here again the psychological aspect emerges.

If the master had won a Pawn from an opponent of equal strength, he might have been inclined to study the situation carefully and to appraise judiciously the counteradvantages his opponent had gained in return for the Pawn he gave up. But winning the Pawn from a weaker opponent, he felt bound to exploit his material advantage and failed to take into account certain weaknesses in his own position.

234

The expert deserves credit for bringing the master into such an ambivalent position and, still more, commendation for being able to take advantage of the faulty strategy followed by the master. In this game the expert excels both technically and psychologically.

Queen's Indian Defense

Expert	Master
White	*Black*

1 P–Q4	N–KB3
2 N–KB3	

The more common move is 2 P–QB4.

The text is neither superior nor inferior to 2 P–QB4, but it does (a) exclude the possibility of Black's playing the Budapest (2 P–QB4, P–K4); (b) exclude the possibility of a later . . . B–QN5, as long as White postpones his P–QB4 (. . . P–K3 and . . . B–N5 ch would be answered by P–B3); and (c) exclude the possibility of White's playing KN–K2 and P–KB3, which can be important under special circumstances.

2 . . .	P–QN3

Amateurs often wonder why Black fianchettoes on the Q side after an early White N–KB3, but not after an early White N–QB3. The point is that the purpose of Black's Q-side fianchetto is the control of his K5 square by both his QB and his KN. As long as White has not yet developed his KN to B3, he has the possibility of meeting Black's Q-side fianchetto by P–KB3, followed by P–K4, after which White keeps control of his K4 and

Black's Q-side fianchetto is pointless.

Black could equally well answer 2 N–KB3 by 2 . . . P–Q4, which would lead to the normal QP game, probably an eventual Queen's Gambit, or by 2 . . . P–KN3, which would lead to the King's Indian.

3 P–QB4	B–N2
4 N–B3	

Notice that White is now bringing one piece to bear on his K4 square, whereas Black is bringing two pieces to bear on it.

White could also play 4 P–KN3 here. He need not fear 4 . . . BxN; 5 PxB, since this sequence would (a) strengthen the White center, as his PKB4 would then control his K5 square; (b) leave him with the Two Bishops.

4 . . .	P–K3

This move develops Black's position. Now he can play . . . B–N5, bringing indirect pressure on his K5 square.

(a) 4 . . . P–Q4 is not bad, but it is not in accordance with the theme of bringing ever increasing pressure against Black's K5 square, for after 5 PxP, NxP, the pressure is relieved, or at least lessened—since after 6 . . . NxN, Black controls his K5 square with only the

Bishop and White can obtain prior control of that square by 6 Q–B2.

(b) 4 ... P–KN3 would be answered by 5 Q–B2, and Black cannot prevent 6 P–K4. Still the move is not bad.

5 B–N5

Indirect pressure, for it momentarily negates the pressure Black was exerting on White's K4 square.

The text is as good as but not better than 5 Q–B2 or 5 P–KN3 —simply another system.

5 ...   P–KR3

Black puts the question to the White Bishop immediately: exchange or withdraw. It is wise for him to put the question immediately, for if he puts it off until later, he gives White more information as to the advantages or disadvantages of the exchange, as, for instance, if he had first played 5 ... B–K2. Black is now also ready for the push ... P–KN4, possibly followed by ... P–KN5.

6 B–R4

(a) After 6 BxN, QxB; 7 P–K4, White has the center, but Black has the Two Bishops, one about as strong as the other, since the position is not open. Were it open, then the Two Bishops would be stronger.

(b) 6 B–B4 represents the loss of a half-tempo, that is, one must ask oneself: "Since 5 ... P–KR3 represents no weakness here, why not 5 B–B4 instead of 5 B–N5?" Also,

the KB4 square is not as effective a place to post the QB for an attack as in certain other variations, for if White later plays N QN5 in order to attack Black's QBP, Black answers with ... P–Q3.

6 ...   B–K2

Equally good is 6 ... B–N5, which accomplishes the same thing, namely, the equalizing of pressure on White's K4 square.

7 P–K3

The best move for rapid development. Also a logical move is 7 N–Q2, for it gives White the same amount of pressure as Black on the White K4 square. In this variation, the square is so important that it is worth the loss of a tempo to be able to control it. Perhaps Black would answer 7 ... P–Q4, to prevent 8 P–K4, or 7 ... P–B4 to undermine the center. Note that the variation 1 P–Q4, N–KB3; 2 N–KB3 has an element of disadvantage to White because of the reply 2 ... P–QN3 and the control by Black of White's K4 square, since 2 N–KB3 decreases the possibility of control of the White K4 square by eliminating the possibility of White's playing P–KB3. However, 2 N–KB3 has the advantage of controlling White's K5, and P–KB3 is not always advantageous.

7 ...   P–Q3

A preparation for ... QN–Q2, followed by ... P–K4.

The text creates a hole at Black's QB3, but this is not a weakness as long as Black's Bishop stands on its QN2.

Black's center formation PQ3–PK3 can lead to (a) ... P–K4, which is best, or (b) ... P–Q4, which has the disadvantage of hampering the action of Black's QB on the long diagonal.

Black could have played 7 ... O–O here, but instead he plans to play ... P–KN4, which he will want to do only if he has not castled.

8 B–Q3(?)

Dubious because it removes protection on White's KNP and permits Black to win a Pawn. Better was 8 Q–B2, or 8 N–Q2 followed by 9 P–B3.

Black's strategy now is: (a) to increase pressure on White's K4 square; (b) to exploit the long diagonal.

8 ...   P–KN4

The follow-up shows how this is part of the strategy to exploit the long diagonal. Note the cooperation between the fianchettoed

Bishop and the Pawns on the other wing.

9 B–N3   P–N5

This is a rather bold move, but it wins a Pawn, and besides, Black need not fear the weakening of his K-side Pawns too much, because he plans to castle on the other side.

Should White now save his Pawn with 10 N–KR4 and displace his Knight? Or should he give up the Pawn and strive for counterplay on a solid strategic basis? Naturally, White has to ask himself which is more important, the Knight well posted for action, or maintaining equality in Pawns. He decides to keep his Knight active and plays

10 N–Q2

In the choice between the loss of a Pawn and a bad Knight position, the expert shows progress by making the choice of a master.

Should Black now take the Pawn? After the weakening move 9 ... P–N5, Black *should* be consistent and take. But Black could ask himself this question *before* playing 9 ... P–N5. He should ask himself whether White will get a sufficient compensation for the loss of the Pawn. White will always get an advantage in time, but sometimes also a preponderance in space and a better center. In this specific position, White gets just a little compensation in all these areas, but certainly not overmuch.

Whether or not Black takes the Pawn, White now has a preponderance in space and a better center.

This is no case of Pawn-snatching, as it sometimes is when a player takes a Pawn at a time when his whole position is hazardous. Therefore, Black plays

    10 ...   BxP
    11 R KN1

Black now has an extra Pawn, but White has greater mobility and more possibilities as a compensation.

    11 ...   B–N2

How will White now make the most of his possibilities? Part of his compensation is that he now has control of his K4 square. He therefore occupies it by

    12 P K4!

The expert again shows progress by not losing his head at the loss of a Pawn, but continuing confidently, and by a move based on solid strategical considerations.

White now has possession of the center, in that he occupies his Q4 and K4 squares, but that is not absolute, for Black also has a hold on the center, in that he controls his Q4 and K4 squares with his 3rd rank Pawns, and by playing ... P–K4 he soon gets a satisfactory center as well.

    12 ...   P–K4

Black will not permit White to play an eventual P–K5. Moreover, he has now built up his center in the way that was his first choice after his 7th move (see comment).

If 12 ... P–Q4; 13 BPxP, PxP; 14 P–K5, now looks good for White.

Also deserving of consideration is 12 ... N–B3, for 13 N–N3, P–K4, 14 P–Q5, N–N5; 15 B–K2, P–KR4; 16 P–QR3, N–R3, and Black's QN is rather active on the Q side. It is not better than the text, however.

Black could have prepared ... P–K4 by 12 ... QN–Q2. But if possible, ... P–K4 should be played directly and without preliminary preparation, for thus it gives Black more choice of whether to develop his QN, depending on White's reaction. The text has the advantage of forcing White to a declaration (either PxP or P–Q5), and it prevents White from playing a later P–K5. It is quite logical that Black will strive for the PQ3-PK4 center as soon as he can.

It is possible for Black to play 12 ... P–K4, even though the Black KP is now protected once and attacked twice, because after White exchanged on Black's K4, White's Bishop on his Q3 would be *en prise,* and while White is withdrawing that Bishop to save it, Black has time to protect his PK4 once more. Moreover, if 13 PxP, PxP; 14 B–B2, QN–B3, and White would have a bad hole at his Q4.

    13 P–Q5

White now has more space, but Black has a plus Pawn. Black's strategy must be to exploit this plus Pawn as soon as possible, and the way to do so is by trying to push his KBP to B4. This is not an easy task, especially since in the coming moves White finds the right strategy to prevent Black from attaining his goal.

13 ...   QN–Q2

An immediate 13 ... P–QB4 in an attempt to lock the whole position might be a good idea, because it immediately presents White with a difficult choice. Should White take *en passant*, the Black QN would retake and, if possible, jump to Q5, and if White does not take, his chances to get such a tremendous attack against the hostile King as in the game would be considerably reduced.

14 P–B3!

By exchanging his KBP, White opens his KB file, and this means strategically that the carrying out of Black's plan of playing ... P–KB4 becomes impossible for a long time. In other words, after 14 ... PxP; 15 QxP, Black's Pawn-plus will be devaluated, since it becomes the backward KBP on an open file. White, the expert, shows initiative and positional feeling.

But Black will not play 14 ... PxP, because this is just what White wanted. Instead, he protects his KNP by

14 ...   P–KR4

But White now forces Black to exchange and thus devaluate his plus Pawn as follows:

15 B–K2!

By forcing this exchange, the expert again shows progress toward mastership. He reduces the value of the plus Pawn considerably.

15 ...   PxP

Another possibility would have been 15 ... R–KN1, after which White continues 16 Q–B2 and 17 O–O–O.

16 BxBP

Also deserving of consideration is 16 NxP, planning eventually to bring this Knight to KB5 via KR4.

16 ...   N–B1

Making room for the Queen in his preparation for castling long.

Also to be considered here was 16 ... N–B4, but this Knight has no future on its QB4 square, for White plays 17 Q–K2 and possibly later P–QN4.

After the text, what should White's plan be? He could play 17 N–B1, planning N–K3–B5. Instead, he prepares to castle on the Q side, so he plays

17 Q–K2

Strong for Black would have been 17 B–R4, N–N3; 18 BxN, BxB; 19 BxP, B–R5 ch; 20 K–B1, N–B5, and White has regained his Pawn, but his King stands hopelessly bad

17 . . .   N–N3

Black is maneuvering to seize his KB5 square. This is an important part of his strategy, since in bringing his QN to KB5 he closes the KB file, which might enable him to realize the move . . . P–KB4 behind his N(B5).

18 O–O–O

As usual, White castles for two reasons: to bring one of his Rooks into the game, and to bring his King to a safer position. The fact that the QBP is advanced should not be considered as a weakening of the King's position in this case. White has only to move his King to N1 to put it into a completely safe position. However, in the present situation this is absolutely unnecessary, because none of the Black pieces on the Q wing can constitute a threat to the White King.

18 . . .   B–QB1??

Thus far the master has dictated the course of affairs. He has won a Pawn, and his only drawback is that he is a bit cramped in the center and on the Q side.

But now Black asks too much of the position. He is already concerned as to how to make the most of his plus Pawn. So he prepares to bring his QB to the K wing, which is the correct wing for that Bishop, but he underrates the extent to which the move will weaken the Q side, where the Black King must find a safe spot.

The fact that a master is always playing for a win, looking into the future, seeking too much initiative at times when the initiative and the win are not in the position, is sometimes a handicap to him.

Correct was 18 . . . Q–Q2, followed by 19 . . . O–O–O. Black would have kept his plus Pawn, but in view of the circumstances he would have had only small chances for a win, since Black's plus Pawn is backward and on an open file.

19 N–B1

This Knight will be brought to K3 to control the KB5 square.

19 . . .   P–R5

Black hopes to exert some additional pressure on the K side. He will continue by bringing his Knight and Bishop into the hostile position. But these maneuvers are of minor importance, since the chief struggle will take place on his Q wing after Black has incorrectly castled long.

20 B–K1

White moves here, rather than 20 B–B2, where Black could attack the Bishop by ... N–B5–R6.

20 ... N–B5

Black's pressure increases here and on the next move.

21 Q–QB2

Since the Queen had to move, it moved to the square nearest the main battlefield of the chessboard. Black now wishes to castle long. In order to do so, he must have his Q2 square for his Queen, and he therefore moves his QB to the only possible square by playing

21 ... B–R6
22 N–K3!

The crucial square in the endgame is White's KB5.

22 ... Q–Q2
23 B–B2

To connect the White Rooks and to direct the Bishop against the Black King when it is castled on the Q side.

23 ... O–O–O

This is an important point in the game. After Black has castled, a tremendous attack will start against his Q side. To consider, however, that this castling is a serious mistake is going too far. On the one hand, castling is desirable in order to bring the QR into the game.

This means that Black has a choice only between two evils. If Black refrains from castling, he will never succeed in winning the game, because he cannot open the position, for his King is unsafely situated in the middle of the board. That Black now decides to castle in spite of the following attack against the position must be seen as a kind of overconfidence that he will somehow be able to withstand the storm.

24 P–R4

The beginning of the attack against Black's weakened Q side. In this position it is rather arbitrary whether the QRP or the QNP should be moved first.

A Pawn advance against the hostile King position is justified by (a) a weakened Pawn protection of the opponent's King (here Black's PQN3, which is weaker when the fianchettoed Bishop is missing); (b) well-directed attacking pieces; (c) control of more ranks than one's opponent (here White controls five ranks, Black three ranks).

The expert's progress toward mastership is exemplified by his awareness of the proper strategy to use here.

24 ... K–N2
25 P–N4! P–B4

Waiting would also be very dangerous. Consider the impact of White moves such as P–N5, N–R2–N4–B6. And Black did not have much choice, for after 25 ... P–R4; 26 PxP, PxP; 27 P–B5, PxP;

28 N–B4 is almost killing. To be considered is 25 ... R–R1, in which case White best continues with 26 P–R5, since 26 P–N5 could be answered by 26 ... P–R4, preventing the maneuver N–R2–N4–B6. Black therefore decides to be brave. He goes directly into the line of fire and hopes to be able to meet the consequences.

26 PxP e.p. ch

Of course, White seizes this opportunity to open the position. The text frees the diagonal for the White QB at B2, and it frees the strong square at White's Q5 for occupation by one of the White Knights, which will allow him to attack the strong Black Knight at Black's KB5 in such a way that Black is practically forced to exchange. The exchange will entail serious consequences, for White's KP will then go to his Q5, making White's Bishop on KB3 stronger and more effective.

26 ...	QxP
27 N(K3)–Q5!	N(3)xN
28 NxN	NxN
29 KPxN	Q–B1

Supporting his Bishop so that it can come to B4. Black makes the most active move possible.

Notice that Black's problem of the backward KBP is now completely solved, since it can now go to B4 at will. Black even has two passed Pawns. The expert seems to have taken all this into consideration and to have weighed the alternatives accurately. He has compared the value of Black's two passed Pawns to the force of his attack on Black's King. Comparing is one of the most difficult problems in chess, and in this respect also the expert has shown considerable progress. He is well aware that his attack will succeed, and that therefore Black's positional advantage will not enter into the picture.

30 P–B5!

White accurately judges the strength of his Bishop on KB2 in combination with his BP and NP. The expert shows not only positional sense, but also fine attacking sense.

30 ...　　　　　QR–N1

Trying to reduce the opponent's power and to make one more square available to his fleeing King.

About as good was 30 ... B–B4; 31 P–B6 ch.

If 30 ... NPxP?, then 31 PxP would bare the Q side still more by opening the QB file and the long diagonal, and a further 31 ... PxP?? is naturally out of the question on account of 32 P–Q6 ch.

31 P–B6 ch

White thus obtains a powerful passed Pawn and maintains the possibility of opening the position at will by P–R5—preceded, if necessary, by P–N5. Besides, there were no good alternatives, for 31 PxQP or 31 PxNP would lead to an exchange of heavy pieces, which would dissipate or destroy White's attack.

31 ...   K–B2
32 P–R5

Further attacking Black's Q-side Pawn structure and making room for his Queen at R4 with all kinds of threats.

32 ...   PxP?

Black hopes for 33 PxP, Q–R3, but White answers 33 Q–R4!

Better is 32 ... Q–B4, but after 33 Q–R4 the game does not seem tenable either, for 33 ... QxB?; 34 PxP ch wins; or 33 ... P–N4(!); 34 QxP, R–N1; 35 Q–Q3 (or even 35 Q–R6, which is still more complicated: 35 ... QxB; 36 QxRP ch, K–B1; 37 R–Q2, and the situation is difficult, but probably a win for White), Q–B5 ch;

36 R–Q2, which leads to a very complicated position that is difficult to judge. Everything depends on accidental details. In view of the enormous force of White's QBP, his chances have to be considered best. This force is lasting and always reappears as soon as Black's counterattack has come to a stop. Two possible continuations are: (a) 36 ... QxNP; 37 R–R2, P–B4; 38 R–N7, P–K5; 39 RxB ch, K–Q1; 40 R–Q7 ch, K–K1; 41 Q–B2, PxB; 42 R–R4, Q–N6; 43 R–K4 ch and wins; (b) 36 ... B–N4; 37 RxB, QxR; 38 BxP, RxP; 39 B–N6 ch, RxB (39 ... K–N1; 40 Q–R6); 40 PxR ch, KxP; 41 Q–N3 ch, and wins.

33 Q–R4!

Again the expert shows progress by his precise handling of this part of the attack.

33 ...   K–N1

If 33 ... PxP?; 34 Q–R5 ch, K–N1; 35 QxP mate.

34 QxP   Q–B2
35 QxQ ch

To obtain two passed Pawns. If White avoids the exchange by 35 Q–N5 ch, K–R1, Black still has his plus Pawn, and the position becomes tenable for him.

35 ...   KxQ

Now that the Queens are off the board, we will see an example of the expert's increased skill in handling an endgame precisely.

36 BxQRP

Both sides now have a pair of passed Pawns, but White's Pawns are more advanced. He now threatens P–N5–N6.

36 ...   B–N4 ch

Better was 36 ... R–R1; 37 B–K3, KR–QN1; and either (a) 38 R–Q?, protecting the QNP, thus maintaining two connected passed Pawns and threatening 39 R–N7, or (b) 38 R–N7, at once. White must still win.

37 RxB!

Pushing the passed Pawns speedily is worth more than the exchange.

The expert is ready for the sacrifice—characteristic of master play.

37 ...   RxR
38 P–N5   B–N5

If 38 ... R–QN1; 39 BxR ch, KxB; 40 P–N6 wins.

39 BxB   RxB
40 P–N6 ch   K–B1

If White should now play 41 P–N7 ch, it would not mean much; the game would continue: 41 ... K–B2; 42 P–N8[Q], RxQ; 43 BxR, KxB. But as soon as the White Rook can intervene, the game is decided. Therefore:

41 R–B1   R–N2

Or if (a) 41 ... R–B1; 42 P–N7 ch, K–B2; 43 RxP ch!!, or (b) 41 ... R–B5—a very instructive line: 42 RxR, PxR; 43 P–N7 ch, K–B2; 44 P–N8[Q] ch, RxQ; 45 BxR ch, KxB; 46 K–Q2; at this point, White's protected passed BP is unassailable, and in the bargain, it limits the Black King to a narrow area, so that the White King can now gobble up all the Black Pawns it meets!

42 R–B6   KR–N1

If 42 ... R–Q1; 43 RxQP!, RxR; 44 P–N7 ch, followed by 45 P–N8[Q] ch.

43 RxQP

White now threatens 44 P–N7 ch and 45 R–Q7 mate.

43 ...	P–B4
44 R–B6	

Threatening P–Q6, etc.

44 ...	R–N8 ch
45 K–B2	R(8)–N7 ch
46 K–B3	RxP

Hoping for a perpetual check to begin after ... R–N6 ch, but White's attack is already overwhelming.

47 P–N7 ch	K–B2
48 R–B7 ch	K–Q3
49 R–Q7 mate.	

Game 25

In many chess games the battle is fought out on one part of the board only, but in a few games there are many fronts. Games in which all parts of the board are involved are more interesting, but also more difficult to handle. The fact that a player can make only one move at a time means that even if there are several fronts, he can improve his position on only one front at a time. If there is danger on more than one front, he has to choose where to strengthen first. By the same token, if he has chances on several parts of the board, he has to judge where his chances will count most. In such games, the handling of the position consists in a continuous comparison of the relative importance of momentary possibilities on various fronts and arriving at a valid conclusion as to where to act. Games with many fronts require the maximum skill on the part of a player.

Sometimes an amateur wins from a master because of just one good inspiration, or by a fortunate combination, or by a lucky grip on the position. But if an amateur succeeds in controlling a struggle over the whole board without losing command of the various parts, it may be considered without exaggeration that this, indeed, is a master performance. In games with many fronts, only amateurs of master strength can succeed in finding their way through the labyrinth of moves without losing the thread.

This last game of the series shows the expert who has attained full mastership in his many areas: in his positional inventiveness without putting too much emphasis on this quality alone, in his combinational skill, in his accurate calculation of the exact consequences of a sacrifice, in his ability to defend when his opponent, by sacrificing a couple of Pawns, is exerting strong counterpressure, and finally in his endgame technique.

Pseudo-Reti Opening

Expert	Master
White	*Black*

1 P–QB4

For the ideas behind this move, see Game 3.

1 ...   P–K3

A move that rules out the King's Indian and the English continuations, but makes for flexibility inasmuch as it could lead to a number of other openings. After 2 P–Q4, P–Q4, it could lead to the Queen's Gambit Declined; after 2 P–Q4, P–KB4 to the Dutch Defense; and after 2 P–Q4, N–KB3 to the Nimzo-Indian Defense.

More usual here is 1 ... N–KB3, leading to one of the Indian openings, or 1 ... P–K4, the English Opening, in which White plays the Sicilian in reverse.

2 P–KN3

A system in which White will fianchetto his KB in order to control the center by pressure brought to bear along the diagonal by the Bishop. This is in contrast to the older methods of controlling the center by occupying it with Pawns or pieces. This system is different from the Reti Opening in that in the latter, the White KN goes to its B3, whereas in this game it does not go there at all. But the system is similar to the Reti Opening in that there is the K-side fianchetto, moves like P–QN4, and so we speak of it as the Pseudo-Reti Opening.

2 ...   P–Q4

Black strives for center control by occupying the center. It is the logical continuation of 1 ... P–K3, for by playing 1 ... P–K3, Black has renounced the idea of controlling the center from afar. For instance, after 2 ... P–KN3, Black would have created holes at his KB3 and KR3, and a master almost never accepts such holes.

If White now or at some time within the next few moves should play P–Q4, we would have a Catalan Opening.

Instead of 2 ... P–Q4, Black could reply 2 ... P–KB4, leading to the Dutch Defense, or 2 ... N–KB3, leading to a variation of the

Nimzo-Indian or Queen's Indian, but sooner or later Black would have to continue by ... P–Q4, and problems similar to those in the game would arise.

3 B–N2

By completing the fianchetto, White brings additional pressure to bear on the center, and in particular on his Q5 square.

Note that although White's QBP is *en prise*, after 3 ... PxP, he could win it back immediately by 4 Q–R4 ch. On the other hand, the routine 3 P–QN3? would lose White a Pawn after 3 ... PxP; 4 PxP, Q–Q5.

White could have played 3 PxP, but he would have gained no advantage in taking, and in so doing he would have opened the diagonal for the Black QB. As a rule of thumb, when two Pawns of opposite colors are standing in what Kmoch calls the *lever* position so that they could take each other, except for a very special reason, one should not play PxP as long as one does not fear ... PxP.

In this position, if Black plays 3 ... PxP, he gives up the center.

He could play 3 ... N–KB3, which is relatively good, after which he would have a perfectly playable game, although slightly cramped, just as in the classical variation of the Queen's Gambit Declined or in the French Defense. The same would be true after 3 ... P–QB3.

In order to avoid giving up the center or remaining with a cramped game, Black continues

3 ...   P–Q5

This gives Black some advantage in space, but on the other hand, it gives White a target. If the outpost PQ5 should be liquidated, it might turn out that the maneuver had taken too much time. The move is not outstandingly good, but neither is it definitely bad.

We sometimes find this move in the sequence 1 N–KB3, P–Q4; 2 P–B4, P–Q5, in which case 3 P–QN4 is a strong reply. In the text position, P–QN4 is prevented, and this may be the reason that Black chose the advance.

4 P–K3

White attacks Black's spearhead Pawn at once. This he can do safely, for if (a) 4 ... PxP; 5 BPxP, and White gets an excellent center with P–Q4 plus the open KB file, and he need not fear (b) 4 ... P–Q6, for Black's advanced Pawn does not hamper White's development; White can play his Knight to QB3, and perhaps his QB to QN2. Apart from that, the Black QP must get weak later, and untenable in the long run, for much later White has at his disposition moves such as B–KB1, N–K1, and Q–N3.

White could also play 4 N–KB3 or 4 P–Q3, but in general, if one decides to attack a hostile outpost, one does well to attack it at once. However, if the White player unnecessarily fears ... P–Q6, he should first play 4 P–Q3.

4 ...   P–QB4(?)

The text has one drawback, which will be seen from the continuation.

Why did the master make this somewhat questionable move? He might have deliberately been a bit careless, knowing that he could recover later. It is now generally conceded that one moderate mistake is not sufficient to lose a game. It is the second mistake that loses. There are players who deliberately make a first mistake for psychological reasons. Their opponents, who do not succeed in gaining an advantage because there is no second error, get discouraged and then become careless themselves. Other possibilities are:

(a) 4 ... PxP (see note under White's 4th move).

(b) 4 ... N–QB3 to discourage White from playing PxP. But on QB3 the Black Knight restricts the development of Black's QBP. The game might continue: 5 N–K2, P–K4, followed by Pawn-chain strategy with 6 P–Q3 and 7 P–K4.

(c) 4 ... P–K4 (best), which has the advantage of maintaining an advance in space but the disadvantage of costing a tempo.

5 PxP

White takes at this point, in order to obtain a Q-side majority. As soon as Black plays ... N–QB3, taking is less attractive, because after PxP, NxP, there is no Q-side majority.

The alternatives 5 N–KB3, 5 N–K2, 5 P–N3 are all playable, but they are simply routine developing moves with no particular purpose. More to the point is 5 PxP, because it has the strategic purpose of obtaining a Q-side majority for White.

5 ...   PxP

Obvious is 5 ... QxP, because then White gets a backward QP, but only temporarily, because the Black Queen cannot maintain itself on its Q5 after 6 P–Q3 followed by 7 B–K3 or 7 N–KB3. After the Queen has been driven away, there follows P–Q4, and then after ... PxP, White also has a Q-side majority, but without the pressure of Black's QP on its Q4 square, as in the game.

6 P–Q3

White now has the Q-side majority with the pressure of his KB along the long diagonal to support it, which is ideal. Black, on the other hand, has the center majority.

6 ...   B–N5 ch (?)

Perhaps a little thoughtless. Black had hoped for 7 B–Q2, BxB ch, thus exchanging his KB, which was more or less hampered by his QP. Although Black's KB was not "too bad," its movements were somewhat curtailed by his Pawn on Q3.

Slightly better here was 6 ... N–QB3 or 6 ... N–KB3.

7 K–B1!!

The master awakens in the amateur! This is a most original way to prepare the advance of the Q-side Pawns, the first step in taking advantage of a Q-side majority. This shows good positional judgment in the amateur. Surprising is the way in which he mobilizes his Q-side majority. White now threatens (a) strategically, P–QR3 followed by P–QN4; (b) tactically, Q–R4 ch, winning a piece.

The tactical threat must be parried in any case, but the strategical threat is difficult to meet. Generally in such positions, with the Black Bishop on K2 or B1, White's P–QR3 is met by ... P–QR4. If possible, Black does *not* allow P–QN4. But here 7 ... B–K2 does not work, for White will play 8 P–QN4! The only try is the unnatural 7 ... P–QR4, but then after 8 Q–N4 Black gets into difficulties—he must weaken his K wing by ... P–KN3; e.g., 7 ... P–QR4; 8 Q–N4, and now

(a) 8 ... P–N3 (a weakened K wing);

(b) 8 ... Q–B3; 9 N–K2,

(1) 9 ... N–B3; 10 BxN ch, winning a Pawn;

(2) 9 ... B–B4; 10 B–N5, Q–B1 (10 ... Q–N3; 11 N–R4 makes things worse), 11 QxQ, RxQ, and White has active pieces and Black an isolated Pawn and a set of doubled Pawns.

These variations seem to indicate why the master does not make a forceful attempt to stop White's Q-side advance.

Notice that after 7 B–Q2 (instead of 7 K–B1), White could not have advanced his majority, for 7 ... P–QR4 and, e.g., 8 P–QR3, BxB ch, followed by 9 ... P–R5; or 8 Q–R4 ch, B–Q2; 9 Q–N3, B–B3. Therefore, the move 7 K–B1 is strategically indicated.

7 ...   N–K2

Parries the threat of 8 Q–R4 ch, which can now be met by 8 ... QN–B3.

8 P–QR3

The beginning of the realization of the advance of the Q-side majority.

8 ...   B–Q3
9 P–QN4

The proud advance! White has established his majority.

9 ...   O–O

The reader, remembering how Black, the master, broke up White's similar advance in Game 2, might ask: "Why not 9 ... P–QR4 here?" After 9 ... P–QR4, White continues 10 P–B5, B–B2; 11 P–N5, and White's majority will be no less dangerous. This situation will arise later in the game. The critical difference between the situations in the two games is this: If White can attain the formation PQN5–PQB5 without losing a Pawn, he is safe, since the Black countermove ... P–QN3 can be met by P–QB6. On the other hand, the formation PQN5–PQB4 is bad for White, since it gives Black his QB4 square, and PQN4–PQB5 is not satisfactory for White either, after ... P–QN3; BPxNP, QxNP! and White's PQN4 will be isolated after ... RPxP.

10 N–K2

Attacks Black's QP and keeps the diagonal of the KB free, thus tying down Black's QB to the defense of his QNP.

10 ...   B–B2

Notice that Black is almost forced to move this developed piece in order to protect his QP.

With his KB at QB2, Black's outlook is better. He does not always have to consider the possibility of White's playing P–B5, and

he could now himself play ... P–QR4.

Also possible at this point would be 10 ... P–K4, which is played on the next move. By 10 ... QN–B3, Black would lose a Pawn after 11 P–N5—the advanced position of White's Q-side Pawns is already telling.

11 B–N2   P–K4

Protects and at the same time strengthens the center.

12 N–Q2

For the moment, a simple developing move which, however, offers White multiple possibilities: (a) It enables the White Knight to guard the center against a possible ... P–K5. (b) The White Knight could go to N3 to support the Q-side attack. (c) It could go to QB4 after P–QB5. (d) It could go to KB3–KN5, as actually happens in the game.

12 ...   P–B4

To get counterweight in the center, and with the hope of eventually playing ... P–K5 or even ... P–B5. However, this move weakens Black's KP and the White diagonal QR2–KN8, which will prove almost fatal ten moves later. Commentators used to term such moves decisive mistakes, which is nonsense. This is only an aspect of the position that accidentally comes to the front ten moves later.

Black could have played 12 ... P–QR4, after which White would leave things as they are. He need not fear ... PxP.

13 P–QR4

The advance. With the exception of his KR, all White's pieces are posted usefully, and now he plans to make use of his Q-side majority.

13 ...   P–QR4

This does not stop the advance, but breaks it. In other words, White will now be practically forced to play 14 P–N5, after which he has a 2–1 majority (White: QNP + QBP–against Black: QNP). The 2–1 majority is not as easily realized as the 3–2 majority, because after a later push of the QBP (P–B5–B6), ... PxP, PxP, from a 2–1 majority an isolated Pawn easily results.

Moreover, the text move will create in the White phalanx a hole on White's QB5. Theoretically speaking, it also creates one on White's QN4, but this is of little importance, since no Black Knight is likely to occupy White's QN4 square.

14 P–N5

Strategically forced, for the alternative 14 PxP, BxP leads to inactivity and almost paralysis on the wing.

14 ...   N–QB

If Black now had one more move (... N–B4), he would have an overwhelming position, one in which he would have blocked and annihilated White's majority and would have been ready to realize his own center majority.

15 B–QR3

Prevents 15 ... N–B4. If now 15 ... B–N3, then 16 N–N3, and White maintains control over his QB5. Notice that 15 ... P–QN3, which would refute the whole White strategy, is not possible, and that 15 ... R–N1 (or ... R–R2) to prepare ... P–QN3, is answered by P–B5, threatening P–N6. It is important to realize how cramped Black is on the Q side because of White's majority and without White's even having used that majority.

15 ...   R–K1

Unpins the Black KN.

16 Q–N3

This phase of the game is extremely important. White does not play P–B5, only threatens to play it, thus preventing Black from taking measures to occupy his QB4 and by so doing hold back White's wing advance and make White's majority useless. The advance of White's QBP would have the disadvantage of giving Black his Q4 square; e.g., 16 P–B5, N–KB3; 17 Q–N3 ch, N(2)–Q4, followed by 18 ... B–K3, and White's Q–side attack is blocked and his KB shut off on the diagonal, whereas Black is ready for counterplay in the center.

16 ...   K–R1

Giving the opponent the opportunity to play the bad move 17 P–B5.

Black could have played 16 ... N–KB3 here, but then White would have played *not* 17 P–B5 dis ch (on account of 17 ... N(2)–Q4, as explained in the previous remark), but a move such as, for example, 17 R–K1, preventing ... B–K3 because of N–KB4 (17 R–K1, B–K3; 18 N–B4, PxN; 19 RxB, PxP; 20 RPxP, and the picture is completely changed—White has the Two Bishops, an open R file, pressure against his QN7, etc.). After 16 ... N–KB3; 17 R–K1, the move ... K–R1 would then have followed at some time or other, because moves such as ... R–QN1 would be impossible as long as the Black King was on its KN1 (... R–QN1; P–N6 or P–B5, winning a piece). The character of the game would thus not have changed much after 16 ... N–KB3 instead of the text, 16 ... K–R1.

17 N–KB3

Threatening 18 N–N5 and 19 N–B7 ch. Under some circumstances, a later P–B5 could become

very powerful because of combinations such as N–B7 ch and discovered check.

But at this point, the immediate 17 P–B5, N–KB3 gives Black the advantage in that he has more counterplay than has White. The fact that the expert does not play an immediate 17 P–B5 shows how he has grown. He not only knows what the Q-side majority means, but he also knows how to use it and, still more important, that there are circumstances under which you must postpone the execution. As Tarrasch put it: "The threat is often more serious than the execution."

Notice that as soon as White runs out of active moves, the unsafe position of White's King may also count.

17 ...   P–R3

Countering White's threat of 18 N–N5.

18 P–R4!

A fine move, which again threatens N–N5 and shows sharp calculation on the part of the expert. For instance, 18 ... N–KB3; 19 N–N5, and

(a) 19 ... PxN; 20 PxP dis ch, N–R2; 21 BxN, followed by 22 P–N6;

(b) 19 ... N–B1; 20 P D3, and (1) 20 ... N(3)–Q1, 21 P–N6, winning the exchange, for the Rook must protect its KD2, e.g., 21 ... B–Q3; 22 BxN, BxB; 23 N–B7 ch;

(2) 20 ... N(3)–Q4; 21 P–N6 (this would also have been possible in the previous variation), B–N1; 22 P–B6!, etc., and if 22 ... PxP; 23 P–N7;

(3) 20 ... PxN; 21 PxP dis ch, N–R2; 22 P–B6!, PxP; 23 BxN, QxB; 24 P–KN6, B–K3; 25 RxN ch, K–N1; 26 Q–B2, B–Q4; 27 BxB ch, PxB; 28 K–N2, threatening 28 ... R–B3; 29 QR–R1, RxP; 30 R–R8 ch, winning the QR.

18 ...   N–B1

This stops the sacrifice N–N5 and thus the attack. If now 19 N–N5?, PxN; 20 PxP dis ch, K–N1; 21 P–B5 ch, B–K3. In view of this, the expert might play 19 P–B5? again threatening 20 N–N5, but after 19 ... B–K3, he would have nothing but a bad game.

In this position, Black has a fixed way of strengthening his position, namely by playing ... B–K3 and then trying to take possession of his QB4 square.

How does White prevent this? One of the characteristics of master play is to ask not only: "What is my strongest move?" but also to ask: "How can I prevent my opponent from making his strongest move?" Think of Tarrasch's "Immobilize your opponent's pieces." In other words, White has no positive threat, but all his forces are at hand in such a way that almost any move by Black hurts himself.

19 R–K1!

Full mastership for the expert! White becomes active on three fronts—both sides and the center. Nothing he does here will bring immediate results, but every small change in the position could enable one of the now latent lines to become a successful reality. Let us examine a few of the possibilities, keeping in mind that lines in (a) are very favorable for White because of his Q-side majority, which is ready to advance but does so only when such an advance brings a clear advantage.

(a) 19 ... R–N1 (in order to continue ... P–QN3, winning the strategical struggle by controlling his QB4 square); 20 P–N6! (taking advantage of the fact that Black's QN square is now occupied, for without the Rook on its QN1, the advance would mean only a weakening of White's Pawn structure), BxP; 21 NxKP wins after (1) 21 ... K–R2; 22 N–B7, Q–B2 (the Bishop on QN3 must be protected); 23 B–Q6, etc., or (2) 21 ... B–K3; 22 N–B4 (White threatens 23 NxB and 24 N–B7 ch) and (2a) 22 ... K–N1; 23 NxB, NxN; 24 P–B5, etc., or (2b) 22 ... K–R2; 23 NxB, NxN; 24 N–B7, etc., winning a piece because the Black Queen cannot defend the Bishop and Knight at the same time.

(b) 19 ... R–R2; 20 P–N6 leads to the same type of play.

(c) 19 ... B–K3; 20 N(2)–N1! wins a Pawn after 20 ... N–Q2; 21 NxQP, or 20 ... N(2)–N3; 21 P–R5. Note how useful White's wing forces are.

(d) 19 ... N–K3; 20 N–B1 (or 20 N(2)–N1), and Black's KP fall.

19 ...   B–Q3

To entice the advance of White's QBP and then bring his QB to K3, where it attacks the White Queen. One now sees how clever White was to postpone this advance. At this point he wins two moves with the advance.

20 P–B5   B–K3

Not simply 20 ... B–B2, because of 21 N–N5 (action on both sides of the board), PxN (forced); 22 PxP dis ch, N–R2, and the game is decided by 23 Q–B7, followed by 24 Q–R5.

21 Q–N2   B–QB2
22 N(2)–N1

This is a sharp calculation on the part of the expert.

Notice that there are objections to 22 N–B1: 22 ... B–Q4; 23 NxKP (now or never), BxB ch; 24 KxB, Q–Q4 ch; 25 N–B3, QR–Q1 (to protect the QP) and the relative situation of NB3 + KN2 is much worse than after 22 N(2)–N1, where the NB3 is protected a second time. (See the position after 25 N(N1)–B3 in the analysis that follows.)

How does Black continue after the text? Now 22 ... B–Q4 leads to nothing. One example: 23 NxP, BxB ch; 24 KxB, Q–Q4 ch; 25 N(1)–B3 (pinning his Knight—but note how useful the Knight is on N1 rather than on QB1), and (a) 25 ... N–N1; 26 N–B4, N–K3; 27 N–N6!, BxN; 28 PxB, and the threat of 29 R–K5 followed by 30 KR–K1, possibly triplicating 31 Q–K2, that is, having Rooks at K5 and K1 and a Queen at K2, forces Black to give up another Pawn, either his PQ5 or PKB4; (b) 25 ... QR–Q1; 26 R–K2, N–N1; 27 KR–K1, N–B3; 28 N–B4, RxR; 29 RxR, N–K5 (a fine resource); 30 N–N6, BxN; 31 PxB, N–B6; 32 R–K5, Q–Q2; 33 Q–N3, and White rules the waves.

These are "master variations" to show that Black cannot profit from the powerful pin ... Q–Q4; N–B3, K–N2. This is because he must always take care of his QP, thus losing time, which White uses to carry out the manuever N–B4–N6, exchanging it for Black's KB in order to free his K5 square and obtain control over the K file. Black therefore plays

22 ...   P–K5

One of the latent possibilities of the Black position. This was the master's resource. After 23 PxP, B–B5 ch; 24 N–K2, P–Q6 wins. This move would not have been possible without the advance P–K5 and the driving back of the White Queen. Note how the unsafe position of White's King finally plays a role.

23 NxP

He makes this move despite Black's dangerous threat ... B–K4.

23 ...   B–Q4

The alternate 23 ... B–K4; 24 NxB, BxQ; 25 NxQ, BxB; 26 NxP would mean a certain loss for Black. But with the text 24 ... B–K4 is a terrible threat.

In this position there are two dangers for White: (a) the N(Q4) may be pinned, because it is on the same diagonal as the White Queen; (b) the immobility of the White King, a result of N–N1, which had advantages but, as it appears, now also has disadvantages.

24 PxP   B–B5 ch
25 N(4)–K2

In this way White eliminates the possible pin of the N(Q4). On the other hand, the whole block—KB1, RK1, NK2, NN1, BN2, and PKB2 —is inactive and vulnerable.

The move 25 N(1)–K2 loses after 25 ... B–K4.

25 ...   PxP
26 BxP

Thus the Bishop comes into the field of fire of Black's KR, but White must try to hold out. The text has one good side—it makes room for the King and prepares the possibility of planning something like K–N2, N(2)–B3, and N(1)–B3. In three moves White could have an excellent game, and moreover, he is two Pawns up.

26 ...   N–Q4

To bring all possible pieces against the White bulwark. The move has one disadvantage— Black's B(B5) is in the air.

27 Q–Q4

If now 27 ... B–N6; 28 Q–Q3, and the Bishop would have to make up its mind. And 28 ... BxP would fail against 29 BxN.

27 ...   Q–B3!!

If ever a master had a way out, Black had one. Now after 28 QxQ, PxQ, White's position would be very much compromised despite his two extra Pawns, for the idea is: Black has superiority in forces available. White has little available. Most important is his Queen. Black exchanges this powerful Queen and notwithstanding the natural reduction of possibilities without Queens, Black's superiority with the remaining pieces would still be overwhelming. For instance, if 29 B–B2, BxKNP; or 29 BxN, BxB; 30 P–B3, R–K3; 31 K–B2, QR–K1.

28 K–N2!

At last the King is out of the pin. This is one of the three freeing moves previously mentioned. The expert has kept his head at the time of the counterattack and found an excellent defense.

Not 28 QxB?, because of 28 ... N–K6 mate.

28 ...   QxQ

White threatened QxB. By QxQ Black hopes to exploit the pin on the K file.

29 NxQ

White is still in trouble, for his KB is pinned. All the moves now revolve around this pin.

29 ...   N–B3

Black also had another possibility: 29 ... B–Q6. Analysis will show that the text is best, because White could sacrifice the exchange; e.g., 29 ... B–Q6; 30 BxN, RxR; 31 BxP, and White's passed Pawns decide.

30 P–B3

The only move.

30 ...   NxB

If 30 ... B–Q4 (attacking the pinned piece once more); 31 P–N6!, and White has the advantage, for he has driven the Bishop to a bad square (on its K4 it unpins and White plays BxB, on QN1 or Q1 it breaks communication between Rooks). After 31 ... B–Q1, White could even play 32 BxB, RxR; 33 BxP, R–N1; 34 B–R6, and White's connected Pawns are irresistible. Or if Black simplifies on his K5: 31 ... NxB; 32 PxB, N–B6; 33 N–R3, NxP; 34 N–QN5, and White is well-off, with all his pieces in play and an advanced passed Pawn to the good.

31 PxN

If 31 RxN, RxR; 32 PxR, B–Q6; 33 K–B3, N–N3, and things are perhaps a bit more difficult.

31 ...   B–Q6
32 N(1)–B3

White now has to give back one of his extra Pawns, but hopes to do something with the other one. If 32 K–B3, QR–Q1, and White remains in trouble.

32 ...   BxKP

Prevents the doubling of the Rooks; e.g., 33 R–K3, BxN ch, and (a) 34 KxB, RxR ch, followed by 35 ... BxP; (b) 34 RxB, R–K5, and Black has the file.

With 32 ... RxKP; 33 RxR, BxR; 34 R–K1, and White gets the open file and has the same pos-

sibilities as in the game, that is,
P–N6 followed by N–QN5.

33 P–N6!

This is an unusual positional move
in that it blocks its own Bishop
and immobilizes the majority to a
certain extent. But it forces the
Black KB to a bad place.

33 ...   B–Q1

34 N–QN5

White now threatens to make
the strong move N–Q6, attacking
his K4, K8, and QN7 squares, and
has the possibility of going to his
QB4 and KB7 squares.

34 ...   B–KB3

To connect Rooks and to meet
the threat of N–Q6 as well as is
possible.

35 N–Q6	BxN ch
36 KxB	RxR
37 RxR	R–N1

The only move—it protects the
QNP.

38 R–K8	RxR
39 NxR	N–Q2
40 NxP	

It is to White's advantage to
exchange the greatest number of
pieces possible, since he knows that
the resulting Pawn position will be
in his favor.

40 ...   PxN

White now sacrifices a Pawn in
order to break through—and he can
well afford to do so.

41 P–B6!   PxP

Or 41 ... NxP; 42 P–B7, followed by 43 B–B5, and Black can
no longer prevent White from
queening.

42 P–N7	K–N2
43 B–Q6	K–B2
44 P–N8[Q]	NxQ
45 BxN	P–QB4
46 B–B7	Resigns

The Black King can stop White's
QRP from queening only by hurry-
ing to the Q side of the board, and
in the meanwhile, the White King
can win Black's remaining Pawns
on the K side and queen his own
K-side Pawns.

Index of Openings

All references are to pages

Index of Techniques

Index of Topics

References are to pages (ex. 54), to pages and moves (ex. 68, W30; 91, B25), and to introductory pages (ex. xxiii)

Threat (*cont.*)
  importance of, 138, W17; 177,
    B23; 195, W10; 196, W14
  indirect, 9-10, B18; 55-56, W25;
    180; 183, W7; 195, W10
Triple Pawn, 28, W7
Two Bishops
  vs. doubled Pawn, 177, W20
  vs. initiative, 1-2; 5, B5
  play with, 88, B18; 89, B20
  when strongest, 2
  worth giving up for a doubled
    isolated Pawn, 95, W12

Waiting move, 135, W11
Weaknesses
  basis of strategy, xviii; 68, W30;
    114, B11
  exploitation of, 29, B9; 86, W12,
    B13; 151, B16; 187, B16; 196,
    W15
  hole, 202, W10
  inducing in opponent's position,
    7, W11
  insecure King position, 196,
    W15
  justification for attack, xxiii

  lack of control of squares, 34; 37,
    W10; 205, W22
  listed, 65, W15; 68, W29; 86,
    W12, B13; 202, W10; 205,
    W24
  Pawn, 9, W15; 68, W28; 97,
    W18; 117-118, B21
  position riddled with, 233, B37
  Q-side Pawn formation, 16-17,
    W7–12; 29, B9–W11
  result of Black's premature initia-
    tive, 192
  strengthening position before ex-
    ploiting, 87, B14
  two, 64, W15; 86, B13; 150-151,
    B14; 151, B16; 187, B16
  weak squares, 34; 37, W10
  weakened King position, 38, B12
  when to exploit, 87, B14
Win
  finding shortest, 109, B30
  playing for one when there is
    none, 215, W16; 240, B18
  sometimes not far from draw,
    142, W44

Zugzwang on full board, 128, W24